The
Nazi
Revolution

PROBLEMS IN
EUROPEAN CIVILIZATION

Under the editorial direction of
John Ratté
Amherst College

The Nazi Revolution

Hitler's Dictatorship and the German Nation

Edited by the late John L. Snell
Revised and with a. introduction by

Allan Mitchell
University of California, San Diego

D. C. HEATH AND COMPANY
Lexington, Massachusetts   Toronto   London

CONTENTS

INTRODUCTION   vii

I THE NAZI MOVEMENT AND GERMAN HISTORY   1

A. J. P. Taylor
THE IMMEDIATE CIRCUMSTANCES   3

Edmond Vermeil
THE INTELLECTUAL BACKGROUND   16

Gerhard Ritter
THE EUROPEAN CONTEXT   22

Eugene N. Anderson
THE NATIONAL ASPIRATIONS   34

II THE PERSONALITY OF THE LEADER   41

Karl Dietrich Bracher
FANTASY AND FACT   43

Alan Bullock
DECEPTION AND CALCULATION   56

Ernst Nolte
INFANTILISM, MONOMANIA, MEDIUMISM   69

Robert G. L. Waite
GUILT FEELINGS AND PERVERTED SEXUALITY   78

Peter Loewenberg
THE APPEAL TO YOUTH   93

III POLITICS, INDUSTRY, AND THE ARMY

117

Franz Neumann
DEMOCRACY AND MONOPOLY 119

Wolfgang Sauer
CAPITALISM AND MODERNITY 123

George W. F. Hallgarten
THE COLLUSION OF CAPITALISM 131

Henry Ashby Turner, Jr.
THE LEGEND OF CAPITALIST SUPPORT 143

Gordon A. Craig
MANIPULATION BY THE MILITARY 155

Gerhard Ritter
MILITARISM AND NAZISM 164

IV THE SOCIAL IMPACT OF NAZISM

171

Robert H. Lowie
THE COMPLEXITY OF GERMAN SOCIETY 173

William Sheridan Allen
THE NAZIFICATION OF A TOWN 179

Gerard Braunthal
THE GERMAN LABOR MOVEMENT 186

Guenter Lewy
THE ROMAN CATHOLIC CHURCH 198

David Schoenbaum
THE ELEGY OF A SOCIETY 208

SUGGESTIONS FOR ADDITIONAL READING 220

INTRODUCTION

The title of this anthology announces one of the most extraordinary subjects in all of history. In a sense German National Socialism was only an episode, lasting in Europe as it did for barely a decade; but in another it was both a final legacy of the entire nineteenth century and a terrifying symptom of the twentieth. No phenomenon in recorded experience ultimately occupied the energies of so many humans or ended in such extensive devastation. Short of a complete atomic holocaust, our world is unlikely to witness anything comparable ever again.

Although Nazism can thus be perceived as a universal event, or as the most strident example of a fascist epidemic which has infested all of Western civilization, the focus here is deliberately confined to the national context of Germany following the First World War. After all, there is only limited value in speculating about some totalitarian typology until specific instances have been understood as the product of a certain time and place. The chronological distance between our own time and the Nazi years is now sufficient for such comprehension to be possible.

Lamentation is not explanation. Only a few souls wandering somewhere on the sunlit uplands of idiocy could suppose that Nazism was other than an outrage. Yet to denounce Nazism is simply to express a kind of elementary morality; it is not to engage in historical criticism. If we are to begin to penetrate the historical reality we must ask, and attempt to answer, a number of complex and disturbing questions for which a moral standard provides no absolute guide. We are obligated to regard Nazism with a certain scholarly detachment—which need not be equated with moral indifference—in order to take a more searching look beneath the polemics of years past.

This volume is intended to raise such questions and to provide a basis for formulating some of the answers.

All of history is contemporary in the obvious sense that we can only view the past from our own vantage. In the initial decades after 1945 the most pressing issue seemed to be: Could it happen again? So far as Germany was concerned, this preoccupation was kindled by the appearance there of a "neo-Nazi" movement which was alarmingly successful in several local elections and which even made an ominous debut on the national scene. But the collapse of that movement as an autonomous political force and, more recently, the rapprochement of the present West German republic with its eastern neighbors has made the question of a revived German fascism largely rhetorical. So it would seem for the time being. If there is justice in this, then students of history are free to investigate Nazi Germany in much the same spirit as they treat the Fall of Rome, the Age of Louis XIV, or the impact of the industrial revolution.

Already we can locate at least four perceptible tendencies toward a change of attitudes and interpretations among professional historians.

1. They are inclined to concentrate less on the collective guilt of an entire people and more on structural explanations for the advent of Nazism in Germany. Interest has shifted away from a search for the general intellectual origins of National Socialism to a closer study of the mechanics of the Nazi seizure and exercise of power.
2. At the same time, a deeper research has begun into the individual and collective psychology of those who participated in or were directly responsive to the Nazi movement in Germany. New techniques of psychobiography and psychohistory have raised different problems about the motivation of Nazi leaders and their followers.
3. Greater attention has been devoted to the social thrust of Nazism. Both the immediate and enduring effects of dictatorship on German society have increasingly come under scrutiny in an effort to evaluate more precisely the elements of continuity and change.
4. A subtle but significant alteration has occurred in analysis of the force with which Nazism overcame the possibilities of resistance within the German nation: the leading question has become not so much "was it inevitable?" as "was it avoid-

able?" That is, historians have come to adopt a less metaphysical and, as a rule, a less ideological approach toward the problem of National Socialism.

The articles and excerpts collected in this book should illustrate these trends in historiography. They have been selected with this aim in view, and not simply to create an artificial juxtaposition of issues which must be debated in terms of stark either/or alternatives. Dialectical formulations can seldom be resolved categorically in one direction or the other. There is no valid history without nuance, only partisanship. Yet neither can the reader hope to escape responsibility for personal judgment by retreating into a bland objectivity. Some opinions are better than others; and all conclusions have been more or less well conceived. In this regard it is appropriate to reiterate an admonition of the late John L. Snell from the introduction to the original edition of this volume: "Realization that the ideal of absolutely 'objective' truth cannot be achieved should lead neither to opportunism nor to despair, but to a more critical, wiser, and therefore more realistic striving to achieve it. It should lead to the study of as many serious approaches to truth as can be found in varying historical interpretations of important events."

History does not speak for itself. It is articulated only by individual historians and their critics.

I THE NAZI MOVEMENT AND GERMAN HISTORY

We begin with an international forum of historians who, in order of appearance, are British, French, German, and American. Their differences in national origin are perhaps less significant, however, than the various terms in which they choose to analyze the historical antecedents of Nazi Germany.

A. J. P. Taylor plunges the reader at once into the circumstances of the crisis years from 1930 to 1933; and he immediately poses some of the hard questions. What was "normal" in the course of German history up to that time? Did Nazism represent an aberration from the previous pattern of German development? Or was it, rather, an all too appropriate culmination of Germany's past? Taylor dismisses the view that the Weimar Republic was undone primarily by the economic crisis and calls attention to other factors: the structural weakness of the constitutional system; the manipulation by such men as Brüning, Papen, and Schleicher; the vested interests of the military organization (Reichswehr); the internecine rivalry of leftist parties; and the sheer dynamism of the National Socialists. In all of this he finds the Nazi accession to power largely inevitable and wonders only that it required so long to accomplish.

Edmond Vermeil offers a more sweeping perspective of Germany's cultural, religious, and intellectual heritage. He points to a strong undertow of irrationalism and racism, which unsuccessfully converged with modern Germany's science and technology. This misalliance, he concurs with Taylor, led inexorably to Nazism and made its appearance less than fortuitous.

Gerhard Ritter draws attention away from the strictly German circumstances and traditions in order to emphasize the European arena in which fascism was everywhere a threat to parliamentary democracy. He lists the developments which crippled liberalism and strengthened the tendency to dictatorship, especially, but not exclusively, in Germany. Ritter's argument obviously rests on the assumption that leaders like Hitler and Mussolini represented a rupture with the mainstream of their national traditions, not

1

a continuation. In his view Nazism emerged at a time when an impasse had been reached among competing elements of the old order; these were then swept aside in what Ritter implicitly describes as a moment of aberration.

Eugene N. Anderson constructs a subtle and complex case. He grants that Nazism arose in unbroken succession from a nationalistic tradition; but he agrees with Ritter that this was not a distinctively German phenomenon. Every European country strove to attain its cultural ideals and national goals. Only Germany adopted such radical means to do so. Anderson rejects any notion of inevitability and denies that National Socialism, despite the obedience of the majority of Germans to it, was other than a corruption of their legitimate aspirations.

These four essays should make it possible to distinguish many of the distant and proximate reasons for the establishment of a Nazi regime in 1933. They should also help to define some of the issues concerning the relationship between the history of the German people and the character of the political movement that presumed to rule in their name.

A. J. P. Taylor
THE IMMEDIATE CIRCUMSTANCES

The republic created by the Constituent Assembly at Weimar lasted in theory for fourteen years, from 1919 to 1933. Its real life was shorter. Its first four years were consumed in the political and economic confusion which followed the Four Years' War; in its last three years there was a temporary dictatorship, half cloaked in legality, which reduced the republic to a sham long before it was openly overthrown. Only for six years did Germany lead a life ostensibly democratic, ostensibly pacific; but in the eyes of many foreign observers these six years appeared as the normal, the "true" Germany, from which the preceding centuries and the subsequent decade of German history were an aberration. A deeper investigation might have found for these six years other causes than the beauty of the German character. . . .

The appointment of Brüning as chancellor in March 1930 marked the end of the German republic. Germany had slipped back without effort to the days just before defeat when, too, a Roman Catholic chancellor had carried out the orders of Hindenburg. Then it had been the ultimatum from Supreme Headquarters, now it was the "emergency decree," by which Germany was ruled; both were signed by the same hand. The "crisis" of March 1930, which brought Brüning into power, was the deliberate manufacture of the army leaders, and especially of General Schleicher, the army specialist for political intrigue. The decline in world trade, the increase in unemployment, had hardly begun; the only crisis was that even in the years of prosperity the budget had failed to balance. The "national" classes still drew the line at direct taxation; and it was to impose direct taxes that Müller, Social Democratic chancellor of a coalition government, proposed to use emergency decrees. But Schleicher and his associates would not put Hindenburg's prestige behind a democratic government; for while the Social Democrats did not impede German rearmament they would not actively promote it. On the other hand, the "national" party leaders were too wild: if called

From *The Course of German History: A Survey of the Development of Germany since 1815,* by A. J. P. Taylor. Copyright 1946 by A. J. P. Taylor. Reprinted by permission of Coward, McCann & Geoghegan, Inc. and Hamish Hamilton Ltd.

to office, they would at once denounce the Young Plan and overthrow the shell of the constitution. The Reichswehr leaders were not driven on by a demagogic demand: quite the reverse, their action provoked the demagogic demand. When Brüning became chancellor there were only 12 National Socialists in the Reichstag; it was owing to his policy that in the general election of September 1930, 108 National Socialists were returned. The National Socialist victory, abhorrent to Brüning, unwelcome to the Reichswehr, was the inevitable outcome of Brüning's dictatorship.

The "crisis" of March 1930 was provoked by the Reichswehr, and Brüning chosen as chancellor, for the sole purpose of speeding up German rearmament. The economic crisis was an afterthought, an accident, which took the Reichswehr by surprise. The Reichswehr leaders stood behind Brüning, gave him assurance against disorder, enabled him to disregard, as imperial chancellors had done, defeat in the Reichstag. Brüning, in return, pushed on rearmament, redoubled the campaign against the remnants of Versailles, yet, being a member of the Center, served as window dressing both to Germans of the Left and to the Allies, who, forgetting his activities during the Four Years' War, failed to see in the pious Roman Catholic the spokesman of German militarism. Yet Brüning's position was sincere enough: wishing to serve Germany, he could serve only the army. Moreover in promoting rearmament he was pursuing a policy in which he himself believed: thus being in a superior position to all other Center politicians, whether under the empire or of the republic, who were indifferent to the policies which they excluded. The army was the sole "authority": that was the key to Brüning's position. The republic had failed to develop a "governing class." The middle classes, themselves in awe of authority, had never forgiven the republic for the defeat of 1918; the working classes, with no social revolution to inspire them, were loyal, devoted, but ineffective. The economic crisis of 1929–1933 did not give the deathblow to the republic; at most it drew attention to the fact that the republic was dead. Any system can stand in fair weather; it is tested when the storm begins to blow. This test the German republic could not pass: with few supporters and no roots, it fell at the first rumble of thunder.

In 1930 parliamentary rule ceased in Germany. There followed, first, temporary dictatorship, then permanent dictatorship. Technically the Reichstag remained sovereign (as it does to the present day);

actually Germany was ruled by emergency decrees, which the democratic parties tolerated as the "lesser evil"—the greater evil being to provoke a civil conflict in defence of democracy. Unemployment, the result of the economic crisis, sapped the spirit of the skilled workers, who were the only reliable republicans. Their skill had been the one secure possession to survive the inflation; unemployment made it as worthless as the paper savings of the middle classes. Therefore, though still loyal to the republic, they became half-hearted, indifferent to events, feeling that they stood for a cause which was already lost, ready to respond, though with shame, to a "national" appeal. The depression, too, completed the demoralization of the respectable middle class. The brief period of prosperity had stimulated a tendency, or its beginning, to postpone "revenge" to a distant future—just as French pacifism after 1871 began as a very temporary affair. Of course Versailles had to be destroyed, but not while profits were mounting, not while salaries were good, not while more and more bureaucratic posts were being created; the German bourgeoisie felt that their generation had done enough for Germany. But in 1930, with the ending of prosperity, the distant future of "revenge" arrived: the crisis seemed almost a punishment for the wickedness of neglecting the restoration of German honor and power. As for the great capitalists, they welcomed the depression, for it enabled them to carry still further the process of rationalization, which had been its cause. As one of them exclaimed: "This is the crisis we need!" They could shake off both the remnants of Allied control and the weak ineffective brake of the republic, could make their monopolies still bigger, could compel even the Allies to welcome German rearmament as the only alternative to social revolution.

The republic had been an empty shell; still its open supersession in 1930 created a revolutionary atmosphere, in which projects of universal upheaval could flourish. Now, if ever, was the time of the Communists, who saw their prophecies of capitalist collapse come true. But the Communists made nothing of their opportunity; they still regarded the Social Democrats as their chief enemy, still strove to increase confusion and disorder in the belief that a revolutionary situation would carry them automatically into power. The German Communists, with their pseudorevolutionary jargon, were silly enough to evolve this theory themselves; but they were prompted on their way by the orders of the Comintern, which was still obsessed with the fear of a capitalist intervention against the Soviet Union and so desired above everything else to break the democratic link between Germany and Western Europe. The Soviet leaders, with their old-fashioned Marxist outlook, thought that the German army leaders were still drawn exclusively from the Prussian Junkers and therefore counted confidently on a renewal of the old Russo-Prussian friendship. In 1930 German democracy was probably too far gone to have been saved by any change of policy; still the Communist line prevented the united front of Communist and Social Democratic workers which was the last hope of the republic. The Communists were not very effective; so far as they had an effect at all it was to add to the political demoralization, to act as the pioneers for violence and dishonesty, to prepare the way for a party which had in very truth freed itself from the shackles of "bourgeois morality," even from the morality devised by the German bourgeois thinker, Karl Marx.

To talk of a "party," however, is to echo the misunderstandings of those lamentable years. The National Socialists were not a party in any political sense, but a movement: they were action without thought, the union of all those who had lost their bearings and asked only a change of circumstances no matter what. At the heart of the National Socialists were the Free Corps, the wild mercenaries of the postwar years, whose "patriotism" had taken the form of shooting German workers. The Munich rising in November 1923 had been the last splutter of their Free Corps days. Since then they had been taught discipline by a ruthless gangster leader, Hitler, a man bent on destruction, "the unknown soldier of the last war," but unfortunately not buried, expressing in every turn of his personality the bitter disillusionment of the trenches; and a greater master of hysteric oratory than either Friedrich Wilhelm IV or Wilhelm II. The National Socialists had no program, still less a defined class interest; they stood simply for destruction and action, not contradictory but complementary. They united in their ranks the disillusioned of every class: the army officer who had failed to find a place in civil life; the ruined capitalist; the unemployed worker; but, most of all, the "white collar" worker of the lower middle class, on whom the greatest burden of the postwar years had fallen. The unemployed clerk; the university student who had failed in his examinations; the incompetent lawyer and the blundering doctor: all these could exchange their shabby threadbare suits for the smart uniforms of the National Socialist army and could find in Hitler's promise of action new hope for themselves. In England they would have been shipped off to the colonies as remittance men: their presence in Germany was the high price which the victors of 1918 paid for the worthless tracts of German colonial territory.

The failure of the Munich rising in 1923 had taught Hitler a bitter lesson: he must not run head on against the army and the possessing classes. From that moment until September 1933 he used the method of intrigue, of terror and persuasion, not the method of open assault. Just as the Communists had tried to outbid the "national" parties in whipping up nationalist passion, so now Hitler outbid the Communists, but with the added attraction, for the upper classes, that this nationalist passion would be turned against the German working classes as well. He was at once everyone's enemy and everyone's friend: his program of contradictory principles could succeed only in a community which had already lost all unity and self-confidence. To the workers he offered employment; to the lower middle classes a new self-respect and importance; to the capitalists vaster profits and freedom from trade union restraints; to the army leaders a great army; to all Germans German supremacy; to all the world peace. In reality it mattered little what he offered: to a Germany still bewildered by defeat he offered action, success, undefined achievement, all the sensations of a revolution without the pains. In September 1930, when the economic crisis had hardly begun, but when the French had evacuated the Rhineland, the National Socialists were already hot on the heels of the Social Democrats as the largest party in the Reichstag; the "national" card was irresistible.

This moral was drawn too by Brüning, who, in his hatred of National Socialist paganism, adopted in succession almost every item of the National Socialist creed. Called in to save German capitalism and to promote German rearmament, Brüning went further on the path already marked out by Stresemann. Stresemann had tried to make the republic popular by winning concessions in foreign affairs. Brüning demanded concessions in foreign affairs in order to win support for his system of presidential dictatorship. If Germany was allowed to rearm, the Germans might not notice the reductions in their wages. More than that, if Germans were brought together in a campaign of hatred against Poland, the disparities between rich and poor would be overlooked. Where Stresemann had tried to conciliate the Allies, Brüning blackmailed them: if they did not make concessions to him, they would have to deal with Hitler and the National Socialists. Brüning knew that the economic crisis was due to deflation, the decline of prices and wages; still, far from attempting to arrest or even alleviate this deflation, he drove it on—forced wages and, less effectively, prices, still lower—perhaps to get the crisis over all the sooner, perhaps to threaten the Allies with the prospect of German ruin. For the Brüning cabinet was primarily a cabinet of "front-line fighters," officers of the Four Years' War, who were dominated by the resolve to reverse the verdict of 1918. Stresemann too had desired to liquidate Versailles, but he had cared also for democracy; Brüning was for the undoing of Versailles pure and simple, hoping, no doubt, to win popularity with the German people, satisfying still more his own deepest feelings. For him, as much as for the great capitalists, the crisis was welcome, the crisis he needed. His most ambitious effort was the customs union with Austria in March 1931, ostensibly a measure against the depression, though it is difficult to see the use of a customs union between two countries both suffering from unemployment and impoverishment. In reality the purpose of the customs union was not economic, but demagogic, an evocation oт the program of Greater Germany, and, so far as it nad any sense, a move of economic war against Czechoslovakia, exposed outpost of the system of Versailles. France and her Central European allies protested and, almost for the last time, got their way: the separation of Austria from Germany was the only remaining guarantee against an overwhelming German power, and this last fragment of victory was shored up for a few more years.

The Brüning policy of combating evil by taking homeopathic doses of the same medicine, far from checking the National Socialists, aided their advance. If the Allies trembled before Brüning's blackmail, they would collapse altogether before the blackmail of Hitler. Brüning made everyone in Germany talk once more of rearmament, of union with Austria, of the injustice of the eastern frontier; and every sentence of their talk made them turn, not to Brüning, but to the movement of radical revision. Above all, Brüning had overlooked the lesson of the Four Years' War which Ludendorff had learned too late—that a program of German power must rest on a demagogic basis. Austria, Poland, Bohemia could not be conquered, and Versailles defied, by a chancellor supported only by a section of the Center party; for that, a united German will was needed. Captain Brüning was half way between General Ludendorff and Corporal Hitler, with the weaknesses of both, the advantages of neither. Brüning, the defender of the Roman Catholic Church, shared the error of Stresemann, the defender of the republic: both thought to draw the sting of nationalism by going with it, to silence demagogy by trying to capture its tone. Neither grasped that his every step strengthened his enemy; neither understood that the only security for German democracy, or for German Christian civilization, lay in a full and sincere acceptance of the Treaty of Versailles. Only if Germany made reparation; only if Germany remained disarmed; only if the German frontiers were final; only, above all, if the Germans accepted the Slav peoples as their equals, was there any chance of a stable, peaceful, civilized Germany. No man did more than Brüning to make this Germany impossible.

The decay, disappearance indeed, of peaceful Germany was openly revealed in 1932 when the time came to elect a new president. The candidate of upheaval and violence was Hitler; the candidate of the peaceful constitutional Left was Hindenburg, hero of the Four Years' War and candidate in 1925 of the "national" parties. The "left" had moved immeasurably to the "right" in the last seven years: what was then a defeat would now rank as a dazzling victory —for it could not be supposed that a senile soldier of over eighty and never mentally flexible had changed his outlook since 1925, or for that matter since 1918. The German people had accepted militarism: the only dispute was between the orderly militarism of a field marshal and the unrestrained militarism of a hysterical corporal. Hindenburg carried the day, evidence that the Germans still craved to reconcile decency and power, militarism and the rule of law. Yet Hindenburg's victory, strangely enough, was the prelude to National Socialist success. Brüning drew from the presidential election the moral that his government must win greater popularity by some demagogic stroke; and, as a stroke in foreign policy was delayed, he sought for achievement in home affairs. His solution was his undoing. He planned to satisfy Social Democratic workers and Roman Catholic peasants by an attack on the great estates of eastern Germany, breaking them up for the benefit of ex-servicemen; and as a first step he began to investigate the affairs of the *Osthilfe*, the scheme of agrarian relief inaugurated in 1927 by which tens of

FIGURE 1. The Bearing of a Leader. Even as a young politician, here before a party rally in 1929, Hitler knew how to assume a pose of authority. (*Library of Congress*)

millions of pounds had been lavished on the Junker landowners. This was a program of social revolution, and it could be carried out only with the backing of enthusiastic and united democratic parties. But Brüning's solution of Germany's ills was the restoration of the monarchy, and he would not condescend to democracy by a single gesture; he relied solely on Hindenburg, and this reliance was his undoing. For Hindenburg, once himself the patron of land settlement for ex-servicemen, had been long won over by the Junker landowners, who in 1927 had launched a plan for presenting Hindenburg with an estate at Neudeck, once a Hindenburg property, but long alienated. It was characteristic of the Junkers that even for their own cause they would not pay: all the estate owners of eastern Germany only subscribed 60,000 marks, the rest of the required million was provided by the capitalists of the Ruhr—principally by Duisberg, manufacturer of paints and cosmetics. But thereafter Hindenburg counted himself a Junker landowner; and he turned against Brüning the moment that he was persuaded that Brüning's plans threatened the great estates. On May 29, 1932, Brüning was summarily dismissed.

With the dismissal of Brüning there began eight months of intrigue and confusion, in which the old order in Germany, which had now come into its own, struggled to escape from the conclusion that, to achieve its ends, it must strike a bargain with the gangsters of National Socialism. Fragments of past policies were resurrected haphazard, as a dying man recalls chance echoes of his life. First device was the Roman Catholic cavalry officer, Papen, and his "Cabinet of Barons," a collection of antiquarian conservatism unparalleled since the days of Friedrich Wilhelm IV, the sort of government which might have existed for a day if a few romantic officers had refused to acknowledge the abdication of Wilhelm II in 1918. Papen's great achievement in the eyes of the Prussian landowners was to end constitutional government in Prussia: the Socialist ministers were turned out without a murmur. It was both curious and appropriate that Prussian constitutionalism, which had originated in the Junkers' selfish interest in the *Ostbahn,* should owe its death to the Junkers' selfish interest in the *Osthilfe.* Papen, in his daring, blundering way, continued, too, Brüning's undoing of Versailles, and accomplished the two decisive steps: reparations were scrapped in September 1932; German equality of armaments recognized in

December. But it was impossible for a government of frivolous aristocrats, which would have been hard put to it to survive in 1858, to
keep Germany going in 1932. Even the Center, with its readiness to
support any government, dared not offend its members by supporting Papen and expelled him from the party. The Germans, divided
in all else, were united against the "Cabinet of Barons."

The army was forced to the last expedient of all: it took over the
government itself. In December, Papen in his turn was ordered out
of office and succeeded by General Schleicher, forced into office
by his own intrigues. Schleicher, too, intended to do without the
National Socialists, though he had often flirted with them in the past.
He was the first professional soldier to rule Germany without an
intermediary since Caprivi. Like Caprivi he was a "social general,"
intelligent enough to see the advantages of an alliance between the
army and the Left, not intelligent enough to see its impossibility. To
win over the Social Democrats, he revived the proposal for agrarian
reform in eastern Germany and proposed to publish the report of
the Reichstag committee on the *Osthilfe* at the end of January; in
return he asked the trade union leaders to stand by him in his quarrel
with the National Socialists. The prospect of the publication of the
Osthilfe report made the Junkers around Hindenburg abandon all
caution. The agent of reconciliation between the conservatives of
the old order and the demagogic National Socialists was none other
than Papen, who now hoped somehow to maneuver himself into the
key position of power. Papen not only swung the Junkers behind
Hitler. Early in January 1933 he negotiated an alliance between
Hitler and the great industrialists of the Ruhr: Hitler was to be made
chancellor; the debts of the National Socialists were to be paid; and
in return Hitler promised not to do anything of which Papen or the
Ruhr capitalists disapproved. Papen's sublime self-confidence had
already landed him in many disasters; but even he never made a
more fantastic mistake than to suppose that Hitler's treachery and
dishonesty, immutable as the laws of God, would be specially suspended for Franz von Papen. Against this combination Schleicher
was helpless. He could not even count on the support of the Reichswehr; for though the army leaders had often acted independently
of the Junkers and sometimes gone against them in great issues of
foreign policy, they were not prepared to become the agents of
agrarian revolution. They returned to the union of generals and

landowners from which Bismarck had started. The *Osthilfe* report was to be published on January 29. On January 28 Schleicher was dismissed and publication held up; and on January 30 Hindenburg, a field marshal and a Prussian landowner, made Hitler chancellor.

It was a symbolic act. The privileged classes of old Germany—the landowners, the generals, the great industrialists—made their peace with demagogy: unable themselves to give "authority" a popular color, they hoped to turn to their own purposes the man of the people. In January 1933 the "man from the gutter" grasped the "crown from the gutter" which Friedrich Wilhelm IV had refused in April 1849. The great weakness of the Bismarckian order, the weakness which caused its final liquidation in January 1933, was that the interests of the "national" classes could never correspond to the deepest wishes of the German people. It was the Center and the Social Democrats, not the Conservatives and still less the National Liberals, who had gained mass support. There was no need for a new party or a new leader to carry out the wishes of the landowners and the industrialists; but there was need for a new party and a new leader who would capture the mass enthusiasm, formerly possessed by the Center and the Social Democrats, for the "national" program. This was Hitler's achievement, which made him indispensable to the "national" classes, and so ultimately their master. He stole the thunder of the two parties which even Bismarck had never been able to master. The sham Socialism of his program captured the disillusioned followers of the Social Democrats; the real paganism of his program rotted the religious basis of the Center.

There was nothing mysterious in Hitler's victory; the mystery is rather that it had been so long delayed. The delay was caused by the tragic incompatibility of German wishes. The rootless and irresponsible, the young and the violent embraced the opportunity of licensed gangsterdom on a heroic scale; but most Germans wanted the recovery of German power, yet disliked the brutality and lawlessness of the National Socialists, by which alone they could attain their wish. Thus Brüning was the nominee of the Reichswehr and the enemy of the republic, the harbinger both of dictatorship and of German rearmament. Yet he hated the paganism and barbarity of the National Socialists and would have done anything against them— except breaking with the generals. Schleicher, in control of the Reichswehr, was obsessed with German military recovery; yet he contemplated an alliance with the trade unions against the National Socialists and, subsequently, paid for his opposition with his life The generals, the judges, the civil servants, the professional classes wanted what only Hitler could offer—German mastery of Europe. But they did not want to pay the price. Hence the delay in the National Socialist rise to power; hence their failure to win a clear majority of votes even at the general election in March 1933. The great majority of German people wanted German domination abroad and the rule of law at home, irreconcilables which they had sought to reconcile ever since 1871, or rather ever since the struggles against Poles, Czechs, and Danes in 1848.

In January 1933 the German upper classes imagined that they had taken Hitler prisoner. They were mistaken. They soon found that they were in the position of a factory owner who employs a gang of roughs to break up a strike: he deplores the violence, is sorry for his work-people who are being beaten up, and intensely dislikes the bad manners of the gangster leader whom he has called in. All the same, he pays the price and discovers, soon enough, that if he does not pay the price (later, even if he does) he will be shot in the back. The gangster chief sits in the managing director's office, smokes his cigars, finally takes over the concern himself. Such was the experience of the owning classes in Germany after 1933. The first act of the new dictators won the game. When the terror of their private armies looked like failing, the National Socialists set fire to the Reichstag, proclaimed the discovery of a Communist plot, and so suspended the rule of law in Germany. The Reichstag fire, burning away the pretentious home of German sham-constitutionalism, was the unexpected push by which the old order in Germany, hesitating on the brink, was induced to take the plunge into gangster rule. The new Reichstag, still, despite the outlawing of the Communists, with no clear National Socialist majority, met under open terror. Hitler asked for an enabling bill, to make him legal dictator. He was supported by the "national" parties, and the Center, faithful to its lack of principles to the last, also voted for Hitler's dictatorship, in the hope of protecting the position of the Roman Catholic Church; impotent to oppose, they deceived themselves with the prospect of a promise from Hitler, which was in fact never given. Only the Social Democrats were loyal to the republic which they had failed to defend and by a final gesture, impotent but noble, voted unitedly against the bill. But even the Social Democrats went on to show the fatal weakness which had destroyed German liberties. When in May 1933 the Reichstag was recalled to approve Hitler's foreign policy, the Social Democrats did not repeat their brave act: some abstained, most voted with the National Socialists. This was an absurdity. If Germany intended to undo the system of Versailles, she must organize for war, and she could organize for war only on a totalitarian basis. Only by renouncing foreign ambitions could Germany become a democracy; and as even the Social Democrats refused to make this renunciation the victory of the National Socialists was inevitable.

This is the explanation of the paradox of the "Third Reich." It was a system founded on terror, unworkable without the secret police and the concentration camp; but it was also a system which represented the deepest wishes of the German people. In fact it was the only system of German government ever created by German initiative. The old empire had been imposed by the arms of Austria and France; the German Confederation by the armies of Austria and Prussia. The Hohenzollern empire was made by the victories of Prussia, the Weimar Republic by the victories of the Allies. But the Third Reich rested solely on German force and German impulse; it owed nothing to alien forces. It was a tyranny imposed upon the German people by themselves. Every class disliked the barbarism or the tension of National Socialism; yet it was essential to the attainment of their ends. This is most obvious in the case of the old "governing classes." The Junker landowners wished to prevent the expropriation of the great estates and the exposure of the scandals of the *Osthilfe;* the army officers wanted a mass army, heavily equipped; the industrialists needed an economic monopoly of all Europe if their great concerns were to survive. Yet many Junkers had an old-fashioned Lutheran respectability; many army officers knew that world conquest was beyond Germany's strength; many industrialists, such as Thyssen, who had financed the National Socialists, were pious and simple in their private lives. But all were prisoners of the inescapable fact that if the expansion of German power were for a moment arrested, their position would be destroyed.

But the National Socialist dictatorship had a deeper foundation. Many, perhaps most, Germans were reluctant to make the sacrifices demanded by rearmament and total war; but they desired the prize which only total war would give. They desired to undo the verdict of

1918; not merely to end reparations or to cancel the "war guilt" clause, but to repudiate the equality with the peoples of Eastern Europe which had then been forced upon them. During the preceding eighty years the Germans had sacrificed to the Reich all their liberties; they demanded as reward the enslavement of others. No German recognized the Czechs or Poles as equals. Therefore every German desired the achievement which only total war could give. By no other means could the Reich be held together. It had been made by conquest and for conquest; if it ever gave up its career of conquest, it would dissolve. Patriotic duty compelled even the best of Germans to support a policy which was leading Germany to disaster. . . .

Edmond Vermeil
THE INTELLECTUAL BACKGROUND

Bismarckian Germany was divided between two great Christian faiths, the Evangelical Lutheran bloc of North Germany opposing the Catholic regions of Bavaria, Rhenish Prussia, Westphalia, and Poland. Between these two were five regions of mixed faith—Hesse, the Palatinate, Baden, Württemberg, and Silesia. In 1890 there were altogether 31 million Lutheran or reformed Protestants in the Reich, and some 18 million Catholics. While the Protestants were spread among various groups or political parties, the Catholics by contrast were gathered into a single party—the Center (Zentrum), which defended the interests of their faith. Indeed, the Center was in a better position to protect its interests than the twenty-eight Protestant churches, which were territorial in character.

Lutheranism directed the political, social, and cultural history of Germany into attitudes of mind and conceptions of collective life which were handed down from generation to generation. A Germany that had remained Catholic or become converted to Calvinism would have had very different destinies; she would have been more distinctly

From Edmond Vermeil, *Germany in the Twentieth Century* (New York, 1956). Reprinted by permission of Praeger Publishers, Inc. and George G. Harrap and Company, Ltd.

Western, for Lutheran religious ideas, which embraced forms of territorialism, generally caused Germans in the various regions to abandon political thought and action for what they called *Obrigkeit,* a sort of monarchism with an authoritarian bent founded upon a mixture of civil and religious power.

If, in addition to the influence of territorial Lutheranism, we take into account the influences of Counter-Reformation Catholicism and Romantic idealism, from which the twentieth-century national ideology stems, we can understand the German social mystique. To Germans this meant the organic state, the new Reich conceived as a planned community, more or less solidly established upon the compromises which Bismarck tried to integrate within his empire— Prussia and the Reich, unitary and federal institutions, monarchy and parliament, agriculture and industry, Lutheranism and Catholicism, capitalism and socialism. Here was the *Volkstum,* the popular totality of Germany.

Henceforth, because of this rapprochement between political thought and the religious spirit, national might came to be treated as an end in itself, justifying every means. It was the true source of imperialism, of power politics, of that singular Machiavellism which seems to reveal itself at every instance in German history. It is the proper meaning of the term "political realism." Collective Machiavellism offered the Germans three prospects. The first was political indifference, an escape from the harsh authority of the state to find refuge in inward piety or in Utopianism, just as classical cosmopolitanism had once done. The second offered itself when the wars of the [French] Revolution and of the empire revealed to Germany her own impotence, and led her no further to separate the private sphere from the state sphere, but individual morality from political Machiavellism. . . .

Why, then, should there be anti-Semitism in a country where the Christian faiths played so important a part of public life? We have noted how Germany had always been a state with a leader at its head, but not a society led by a true elite. For this reason Germany, unlike England and France, did not possess a social element with powers of leadership that could integrate the Jews settled in the country within the national life. Jewry therefore remained an alien body, despite its immense influence. The tragedy of the German Jews came about because they lived like those ill-assorted couples between whom there is perpetual tension owing to a lack of strength and firmness in the two parties. Here, perhaps, lies the most probable explanation of that anti-Semitism which was later to be the leitmotiv of the Hitlerites. Its solid roots, its most profound origins, however, lay in the Bismarckian Empire.

German Jews were emancipated by the law of 1869. They looked upon the new Reich as a kind of *terra nova,* as another New World to conquer, where they would be sure of economic, social, and cultural advantages superior to those in the East, and even in the West. They quickly gained prominence in industrial circles, stimulated political and economic liberalism, and at the same time took an interest in the aspirations of the proletariat. They were, moreover, needed in the world of science, of the press, of literature and art, and in important matters touching international affairs.

However, their situation changed after the financial crisis of 1873, in which they were involved. They were chosen to play the scapegoat so as to absolve the Gentiles from responsibility for the disaster. Pamphlets stressed the antithesis between *German* and *Jew,* accusing the Jew of wishing to dominate the German world and of fostering both large-scale capitalism and Marxism in it.

If the chief aim of the imperial government was to win the confidence of the working class, to turn it away from international Marxism, and so consolidate the social position of the middle classes, who were seeking shelter with the state and the industrialist employers, then the measures adopted by the middle classes between 1919 and 1935 may be said to have originated during the reign of Wilhelm II. The churches directed their claims and their hopes. They did not yet know that there would be anti-Christianity as well as anti-Semitism one day.

From 1881 so-called "Social Christianity" broke loose against the Jews. Pastor Stöcker, chaplain to the imperial court, led the offensive. Bismarck resisted and curbed the anti-Semitic movement, because, realist that he was, he respected the superiority of the Jews in business. No doubt it later became apparent that the social agitation of Pastor Stöcker could be as dangerous as that of the Social Democrats. The young emperor dropped him very quickly, but anti-Semitism, defending a monarchy of divine right and the middle class, had received its impetus, and was soon to penetrate the countryside and the small towns. Under Wilhelm and during the twentieth century it was not slow to combine with racialism. While the two Christian faiths tended to become united as the foreign situation grew more complex, the idea of a "Germanic" Christianity, as formulated by H. S. Chamberlain in his famous *Foundations of the Nineteenth Century,* took hold of people's minds. It was favored by Pan-Germanism and encouraged by the emperor.

Culture in Peril

The problem of the relationship between militarism and culture engaged the attention of numerous writers during the time of Wilhelm II. They asked themselves whether the Germany of Bismarck, dedicated to the rule of bureaucracy, industry, and arms, was destined to create a true civilization, to unite the myrtle and the sword. The question assumed full significance only if the term militarism were given a wide meaning. It was applicable not only to activities directly connected with the army, but also to professional work involving discipline, conscientious labor, constant intensity of energy, and that rigidity of thought and attitude which, in the German, nearly always verges upon the pedantic.

Nietzsche showed why the German state, with its unwieldy armor, its thousands of bureaucrats, engineers, and technicians, ran a strong risk of destroying all higher culture in Germany, and of breaking with the true spiritual traditions of the nation. It was just this radical pessimism that the Pan-Germanists opposed with their crude optimism. They took up again the theme of Latin and Western decadence, vying with each other in celebrating German virtues and affirming that Germany could remain strong by creating the most refined civilization, or, if they preferred, could create it by remaining strong. From 1890 the *Rembrandt Deutsche* of Julius Langbehn proclaimed the union of Christianity and militarism, while in his *Foundations of the Nineteenth Century* H. S. Chamberlain claimed that the Germans alone were capable of purifying the religion and culture of Europe. On the eve of war a certain Friedrich Lange saw in Prussian militarism the purest emanation of culture in Germany. Such theories, and their success among the cultivated elite and the average public, were evidence of the dangers threatening humanism in Wilhelmian Germany. Modern instruction and new teaching methods with a bias towards technical realism, the triumph of irrationalism in philosophy, the crisis in literature, and other symptoms in their turn bore witness to a certain intellectual and moral unbalance, which was not to escape analysis by the historian.

In his youthful writings, and right up to his final works, Nietzsche put German culture as he saw it on the morrow of the Franco-German War on trial. Naturally he adopted a highly superior point of view, casting a saddened eye upon the gymnasiums and the modern schools. In the former classical culture was rapidly degenerating, and, though technical instruction has its legitimate demands, it was none the less true that, more than anywhere else, in Germany instruction and culture were confused. Both science and art suffered from this decline, journalistic style destroyed the taste for a style of expression which conformed to the great traditions of the past. Nobody saw more clearly than Nietzsche the tragic breach which, in the Bismarckian Empire, was opening between ancient classicism and the new tendencies in education.

During the Wilhelmian era German philosophy seemed to be moving in three directions. Some, while sacrificing everything to Nietzsche's relativism, strove nonetheless to justify objective science. Others, extending Nietzschean irrationalism beyond its natural limits, explored the unconscious basis of the human being—those forces and instincts that Nietzsche himself had christened "Dionysian." Finally, it was at this time that the early outlines of existentialism were drawn. . . .

Nietzsche had established a clear distinction between the Dionysian unconscious and the intellect, between a kind of initial barbarism, the sign of powerful vitality, and evolved thinking, the product of refined civilizations. And he wondered if, in contrast to the force of the elementary instincts, there was not a secret threat of degeneracy in societies which had grown old and become separated from their original vitalism.

This irrationalism, which was soon to end in the racialism of the Pan-Germanists and of the Hitlerites, played a determining part in the German thought of this period. Both in the individual and in society it was the manifestation of obscure forces that tended to destroy the refuges provided by thought and by religion to protect human weakness. From Jean-Jacques Rousseau to Schelling, then to Eduard von Hartmann, a tradition was formed which placed unconscious life in the foreground of inquiry. Here Freudianism had its point of departure, and here, too, arose the danger of extreme irrationalism, from which Richard Wagner was not exempt, and which, shortly after 1871, was to pass from Karl Bachofen to the Nietzsche of *Die Geburt der Tragödie.*

Later, in a study of Germany's moral and intellectual situation, Karl Jaspers spoke of the seductive appeal launched by those pretending to substitute the somber, mysterious realities of the unconscious, of the blood, of mystical faith, of the soil, and of the terrestrial Dionysian instinct for the clarities of the consciousness. Such views were found again under the Third Reich in Hitlerite doctrine and in the "German Faith Movement." On the one hand were the philosophers, who restored rationalism and scientific objectivity to their rightful places; on the other hand was the irrationalism, visionary and nocturnal, of the pseudophilosophers, the belief that unconscious life was of greater interest than the clear, conscious activities of its ends.

The link between educative and philosophical conceptions and literature is easily seen. While humanism and science had to defend themselves against both industrial mechanization and excessive taste for the mysteries of the unconscious life, there was a division among the writers—between the novelists and dramatists, who dealt with social problems, and the poets, who raised up the inner shrine.

Thus Wilhelmian Germany oscillated between a fierce, implacable industrial rationalization and this mystical communion which was its counterpart. When war broke out in 1914 precious few thinkers, writers, or artists in Germany could resist the delirium of collective enthusiasm and the freeing of national ambitions. They found themselves defenseless before this inruption (*Durchbruch*) of Germanism in Europe, before the barbarism which had long been simmering under the thin crust of Wilhelmian culture. . . .

In the cultural sense also certain currents bore the nation in similar directions. Mechanized industry and science with a predilection for biology encouraged a mentality which had already been created by the communal mystique of Romanticism. Moreover, it must be admitted that the Nietzschean ideology of the will to power furnished the future Nazis with parts of their doctrine once it had been misinterpreted and distorted, and once its real meaning had been twisted. The Pan-Germanism of the Kaiser's day, when it had been vulgarized and padded out with anti-Semitism, directly inspired National Socialism. . . .

Gerhard Ritter
THE EUROPEAN CONTEXT

The Weimar Republic failed because it did not succeed in winning general confidence, in becoming genuinely popular through successes which could be appreciated from a distance. So the rejection of democratic slogans became one of the essential conditions for the rise of Hitler's party. But to attribute this rejection simply to "the Germans' lack of a sense of liberty" explains nothing; it only disguises with a grand phrase the true historical problem: the reasons why the chances of liberals have much diminished in this century, particularly in Germany after the First World War.

The desire to replace the unsettled parliamentary coalition governments with a strong and lasting authority certainly played a very large part in Hitler's rise to power. In his propaganda for such an authority Hitler never ceased to praise, as an ideal model for the constitution of the state, the army, with its definite orders and clear responsibility derived from above, not from below, from those who lead, and not from those who are led; and this won the approval of many old soldiers of the First World War, just as Mussolini did when with his Blackshirts he appealed to the instincts of the old "front-line soldiers" and "fighting men." These instincts were certainly much more developed in Germany than in Italy. Perhaps, too, the pedantic eagerness to serve with which the subalterns carried out their Führer's orders and plans after the establishment of the dictatorship was greater in Germany.

The great electoral successes of Hitler since 1930, however, cannot be explained by the Germans' wish to find in political life a military discipline, by a desire to be given orders and to be able to obey them. The masses who rallied to him did not at all believe that they were helping a dictator to seize power; they supported a man of the people who had their confidence and from whom they expected the fulfillment of their wishes—of a thousand vast hopes.

The same thing had already occurred in Italy, and its repetition

From Maurice Baumont, John H. E. Fried, Edmond Vermeil et al., *The Third Reich* (New York, 1955). Reprinted by permission of George Weidenfeld and Nicolson Ltd. Footnotes omitted.

after so few years is a striking proof of the fact that ordinary men never learn anything from history. Hitler had clearly copied from Mussolini the technique of setting up, without a coup d'état as such and without violating the constitution, a one-party state.

In any case, the German dictatorship was not the first, but the last to be established in Europe, and it became by far the most dangerous (if the Russian Bolshevist dictatorship is ignored).

The conclusion is, therefore, that in order to examine the historical foundations of National Socialism, one must first of all see what it was in twentieth-century Europe that gave the totalitarian state, composed of one single party, such a good opportunity of taking the place of the constitutional liberal parliamentary state. For the totalitarian state, composed of one single party, is a European, and not solely a German phenomenon.

A great deal could be written about the various causes of the decline of liberal ideas in social and political affairs. I can give only a few brief hints:

1. First, the *changes in social and economic structure* which took place in the nineteenth and twentieth centuries must be borne in mind. Modern industrial society, a mass society of innumerable individuals united by common needs, has taken the place of the former bourgeois society, consisting of a layer of economically independent notables who were the great landowners and bourgeois.

The First World War accelerated and intensified the process of economic and social leveling, by removing differences during wartime, especially in Germany. The whole of society was ground down into a uniform mass, grey as the soldiers; it was subjected to overall state control, to a totalitarian power which deeply affected even private life. It restricted the free expression of opinion, imposed censorship on the press, cut it off from all communication with foreign countries, and made it entirely dependent on the official information office, which accustomed the people to official communiqués which only very rarely divulged the whole truth, and in many cases suppressed, mutilated, or falsified it. More or less compulsory state or war loans swallowed up private incomes, later annihilated by inflation, which practically led to ruin and the end of fiduciary currency. Those possessing real estate (*Sachwertbesitzer*) had a monopoly, all the educated middle classes were impoverished, and large sections of society became solely dependent on state salaries and pensions or on private business; innumerable people who had been independent were so no longer.

As a result of such general changes, the party system on which the liberal state was founded was modified. Under the influence of universal suffrage, the parties were no longer composed of groups of notables, of clubs whose members were men who were socially and financially independent, who knew something about politics and were interested in them. They became mass organizations, directed by the electoral machine formed by a more or less highly organized party bureaucracy. The political agent took the place of the political idealist, and planned propaganda took the place of personal conviction and persuasion.

At the same time, the style and content of publications were changed. Political education, real discussion, individual thought ceased to be important; instead, what was required was mass appeal. In order to interest the masses, they must be attracted by sensationalism. He who is best at sensationalism is also the most popular. The most effective method is always the sermon of hatred, the least effective the voice of peaceable reason, since it makes the reader think, and even requires a certain wish to learn, and some knowledge.

2. Similarly, *political intentions* changed. In the nineteenth century the struggle (particularly in Central Europe) was for national unity and for liberty guaranteed by a constitution—that is to say, for the participation of the governed in state affairs, for an assured, liberal legal system, and for protection against arbitrary acts. These were ideal ends, which had sprung mostly from spiritual impulses. By the end of the century they had been achieved in Italy and in Germany (with two exceptions).

In their place the economic preoccupations of modern industrial society came to the fore. The struggle for a higher standard of living became the main cause of internal political differences; the idea of liberty was eclipsed by the idea of "social justice"; Liberalism was attacked and discarded in favor of Socialism. Political thought became more and more materialistic. Instead of being preoccupied by unity and liberty, it was interested in class conflicts, material interests, and the struggle for daily bread; in foreign policy the questions of the hour were Lebensraum, the great outlets and sources of raw materials, trading profits, and the rate of exchange.

So in general, politics stopped striving towards an ideal, and the prestige of parliaments declined. Since it had now become a matter of the interests of groups of people, the personal integrity of the representatives of these people is doubted. The details of their debates on economic subjects become more abstruse and uninteresting; the great complexity of modern economy partly controlled by the state, and the large number of opposing interests represented in parliament, make definite solutions, understood and approved by all, extremely rare. Therefore there is a great deal of discontent, and discontent breeds the summoning of a "strong man." The great groups of interests take "direct," extraparliamentary action; there are strikes, the big workers' and employers' unions exert pressure on public opinion, there are processions, demonstrations, and mass meetings. The place of real debates is taken by announcements. Political struggles become more violent—he who has armed or semi-military partisans, ready to strike, at his call has the best chance of success.

Here, too, the World War accelerated and exaggerated this evolution. Like all great wars, it left behind it many adventurous spirits who were unable to settle down again to a bourgeois existence. They were nationalists, ready to serve any political adventurer who could use them for his "patriotic" activities. In *Mein Kampf* Hitler severely criticized the indiscipline of these eternal soldiers, without political aims, grouped together in bands (*Freikorps*), secret societies, and armed associations of all kinds, who sometimes supported and sometimes threatened republican governments. To him the fact that these armed bands and *Freikorps* had at times protected the republic from communism showed nothing but unpardonable stupidity. He disapproved strongly of their Vehme murders, too, because they liquidated minor traitors without daring to deal with the "great November criminals."

In fact, however, many of these toughs became members of the *Sturmtruppen,* and the *Führerkorps* was mostly made up of them. There is a close connection between the SA and SS terrorists and these adventurous stragglers from the First World War. The inflation which took place in 1923, as a result of the war, left many people without money and with nothing to lose, so that they were ready to become political agents.

3. *The changes in religious life* produced the same results. Christian teaching scarcely reached the populations of industrial towns; European civilization became more and more secular as a result of the technical progress which took place in this rationalized and "unsupernatural" world. In Germany idealist philosophy, which had been a substitute for religion in bourgeois society for many years, began to be rejected, not in favor of philosophical materialism but of the modern "philosophy of life" which was spreading throughout Europe. This "philosophy of life" influenced large sections of society, and there was much talk of the supremacy of will, of biological explanations of mankind and of society, the glorification of physical strength, and of pure vitality, instead of a higher spirituality; the intellect and the rational were despised, while strong "instincts" (*Triebe*) and the vital impulse (the *élan vital* of H. Bergson) were admired. Nietzsche's doctrine of the superman and of the will to power as the prime force in the world, envisaged at first as an aristocratic ethical system, became in popular literature the deification of brutal mankind, of will to domination, of the eternal struggle for existence, of brute strength—though not without the complicity of that philosopher who unhesitatingly set the most daring aphorisms before the world. Darwinian ideas of the "survival of the fittest," of the eternal struggle for existence of all creatures, influenced all political thought. In all countries, including those of Western Europe, the age of imperialism brought with it books extolling the doctrine of might; with no knowledge of life, wars were no longer thought to be disasters for civilization, but rather creative crises without which there could be no historical evolution.

Marxist theories were even more widespread, although not always recognized as such—the only political reality was the conflict of material interests, and political ideals were only ideological camouflage. (That this was a serious mistake is proved by all history, including that of National Socialism.)

The example of the romanticism of the younger generation at the beginning of the twentieth century, with its scorn of bourgeois security and of reason and its call for "a dangerous life" and for exciting experience (*Erlebnis*), might lead one to believe that European countries were tired of the long period of peacefulness which had brought them their material well-being. Well-being and security were both destroyed by the First World War, which reduced society to a uniformity which could be touched only by mass violence and brutality.

This complete change of the political climate gave a new and troubled reality to the theories of Wilfredo Pareto about the eternal circular movement of activist elites, about the deceit of middle-class morality, and about the propelling force of deep feeling. The same was true of Georges Sorel's theories about "violence" and the "myth" which moves the masses, without the truth of its content having any importance. During their first phase, French syndicalists wished to replace old-style parliamentary groups by the ideal leader's party and militant elite which would pursue the aims of combat rather than the ideals of the bourgeois middle classes, and thus showed the young Mussolini his first and most pressing plan of action. The large-scale destruction of the war showed the way for futurist policies (in the meaning given to them by men like Gentile, Papini, and Marinetti) which refuse all connection with the authorities of the past.

4. *New technical facilities for political propaganda* made the mobilization of the masses much easier than it had been in the age of bourgeoisies; facilities such as loudspeakers, radio, a daily press rapidly printed in thousands of copies, lorries and motor-coaches which made possible the speedy deployment of political shock troops, almost limitless mass transport by railway, road, and air, so that it was possible to go proselytizing from one end of the country to the other and to address a different mammoth meeting each evening. In 1922, forty thousand Blackshirts formed ranks for the march on Rome, and caused a political panic simply on account of their numbers. At each of his national party congresses Hitler assembled and addressed some half a million men.

Thus did it become possible to make a reality of the theory of the sovereignty of the people, in a radical manner that was completely new. The masses could now be activated directly to become the political sovereign, and the roundabout method of the election of people's representatives to parliament was no longer the only one.

It is clear that from the start the direct control of the "will of the people" was fundamental to democratic radicalism, unlike the Anglo-Saxon liberalism. The latter was originally founded not on the political rights of the many, but on the political privileges possessed by the various estates under feudalism, and which were perpetuated in the party groupings in modern parliaments. Groups of important people "represented" the people; in England these groups slowly became parties of the many during the nineteenth century.

The principle of direct sovereignty of the people, on the other hand, was in existence in the primitive democracy of the free American states in the seventeenth and eighteenth centuries. It was manifest in the town meetings of the settlers which constituted the first germs of American democracy; this principle is still in existence today, as shown by the president's position as a man on whom the nation, on whom every voter, but not Congress, can rely; before Congress his position is that of the executor of the will of the people.

Political compromise reached by discussion, the just balancing of the opposing desires and interests of different classes, groups, and individuals, belongs to the liberal parliamentary system. The nation is not regarded as a uniform mass of men, but as a collection of different individuals. The individual is important not only as a comrade of the people (*Volksgenosse*), but also as a person with claims on life and independent action.

Democratic radicalism, on the other hand, with terrible consistency, requires definite decisions instead of compromise. Sovereignty means deciding and not compromising. The best example of this rational principle is the idea, invented by Jean-Jacques Rousseau, of the "general will," an absolute idea which does not recognize any minority rights; if one opposes the general will it is because one has mistaken the general good (*Social Contract,* Book IV, chapter 2). The general will is the sworn enemy of individual intellect, of groups of individuals, because such groups are unaware of, or opposed to, the real public good; the more the individual intellect is overcome, the more probable it is that the real general will, the true interests of the people, will operate (*Social Contract,* Book II, chapter 3). Direct sovereignty of the people is infinitely preferable to any form of parliamentary government, for parliaments are the legacy of feudalism, and therefore the place in which private interests, and not the public good, struggle for supremacy (*Social Contract,* Book III, chapter 15).

Jean-Jacques Rousseau's general will became a myth at the time of the great revolution; aided by groups of individuals, it dominated parliamentary discussion and became increasingly intolerant. The people, now sovereign, is united in a popular political community (this was the most important innovation), a community of which each individual is part, although his particular rights are not protected (as Rousseau required). No appeal to higher authority is possible, because the people is sovereign, and there can be no appeal to ancient rights or privileges of the kind that was possible under the monarchy. Anyone who opposes the will of the people is considered dangerously selfish, and therefore excludes himself from the community (this exclusion may then be made certain by banishment, imprisonment, or the guillotine).

How can the absolute and indivisible will of the people best be expressed? The best and simplest way, as Rousseau saw it, was the convocation of the sovereign people to a citizens' meeting, as in the classical city-state, the Swiss canton, or the American town meeting. But this form of direct democracy is of necessity limited to a very small community.

In large states there is the plebiscite which may be employed to show support for, and to be complementary to, the legislative machinery of parliament; for especially important laws, administrative decisions, and questions of foreign policy there would be a referendum. This system is cumbersome, costly, and difficult to operate, however, and does not really make possible a radical popular government.

A third method may be employed in large countries, however. The will of the people may be transferred to one man in whom confidence is reposed, who thus becomes an embodiment of the people, tangible and visible to all. Such a transference is made directly by the votes of the people, without passing through parliament. . . .

The success of the twentieth-century dictatorships is conceivable only against this broad canvas of history. Of course they should not be considered in any way as the belated result of the French Revolution, or as having been influenced in any way by the works of Jean-Jacques Rousseau—this would be a very false interpretation of these historical remarks. Each of these dictatorships found its opportunity and its particular modern form in an extremely recent past.

Yet the latent possibility of a sudden change from radical democratic liberty to totalitarian tyranny is not modern. It grows where the great, socially disorganized, intellectually uniform masses in the modern city awaken to political consciousness, and where the former public authorities with their roots in the dim past (monarchy or

parliamentary government) are destroyed or discredited. In such circumstances success seems assured if the distrust of a system of
domination, already smouldering, is inflamed and a compact front
is formed with a solid following. The masses are more ready to trust
a living man than an anonymous institution.

Should a leader appear who is able to pass himself off as the
representative of the most pure will of the people and as a real
leader, then he will gain the support of the people, especially if he
has a good few hard-hitting adherents. . . .

It is a very great mistake to believe that the modern function of
leader of the people is in any way the heritage and continuation of
the old, monarchic power of the princes. Neither Frederick the
Great, Bismarck, nor Wilhelm II were the historical precursors of
Adolf Hitler. His precursors were the demagogues and Caesars
of modern history, from Danton to Lenin and Mussolini. It is also
erroneous to see in the fanatical enthusiasm which millions of men
felt for Hitler between 1930 and 1933 a continuation of the traditional
veneration of Germans for their ancient princely houses. Our people's
old attachment to its dynasties was, where it existed, the result of a
traditional feeling; it was primarily caused by respect for a very
ancient custom.

Hitler's party was, on the contrary, composed of numerous up-
rooted individuals whose mentality was revolutionary, who all consciously desired a new order, and who were convinced that their
Führer was superior to any earlier leader. The characteristic of the
Hitlerian movement which most strongly attracted the masses was its
modernity, the fact that it was contemporary (facts which were
brought out by the very far-flung technical apparatus used to gain
support for the party). Hitler's obscure, popular origins added to this
attraction, and seemed an assurance that he could have nothing
in common with the hated right-wing reactionaries—the great Junker
landowners, the officer class, and the great capitalists—even if he
was sometimes obliged by force of circumstances to cooperate with
people like Ludendorff and Hugenberg. Ludendorff himself declared
himself opposed to Junker and capitalist prejudice, and a public-
spirited friend of the people. Hitler and his supporters always con-
tended that the electoral alliance established between the National
Socialists, the Stahlhelm group, and Hugenberg's party—the Harz-

burg Front of 1931—was nothing more than a tactical agreement, for Hitler detested "all reaction." And when he opened negotiations with the big industrialists once more, being short of money and desirous of rapid success, Otto Strasser and the Schwarze Front, the most convinced revolutionary elements in the party, deserted the cause and started an open rebellion. Later he was to seize every opportunity of condemning the "selfishness" of the capitalist class and stating how much his policy favored the workers.

In any case, he did not wish to be a conservative, either socially or politically; he wished to be a revolutionary. But what did this revolution imply? What was the difference between his dictatorship and that of other modern dictators? What was specifically German in it, what could be only explained by specifically German historical events?

If the situation is simplified somewhat, one can answer that Volksführer Hitler's mission in history was to accomplish that which the emperor and his government had been unable to accomplish in the First World War: to weld the nation into a closed, warlike community under the leadership of a really popular Führer, respected by all. . . .

Wilhelm II only once succeeded in getting near the heart of the nation as a whole, on August 4, 1914, when he said to the Reichstag assembled in the Berlin castle: "I know parties no more, I only know Germans." These words had a tremendous effect. The idea of a popular, unified political community struck the people with the same effect that the French had experienced at the festival of the Federation on July 14, 1790. Yet this was an isolated incident; the newfound community broke up in conflicts about the aims of the war and its methods, and the emperor's rule failed so completely that the German monarchy received a deathblow.

The Germans experienced a bitter disappointment when not only was the war lost in spite of tremendous efforts, terrible economic privation, and millions of deaths, but also when the popular community broke up instead of becoming stronger. The Right, bellicose nationalists out for conquest, and the Socialist leaders, who were opposed to imperialism and desirous of peace, no longer saw eye to eye. They attacked one another so violently, supporters of "victorious peace" (*Siegfrieden*) and "peace by agreement" (*Verständi-*

gungsfrieden), the "prolongers of war" (*Kriegsverlängerer*) and 'defeatists," as they described each other, that the nation was split into two halves.

This bitter conflict was the decisive and perhaps fundamental occurrence which led to the rise of National Socialism. In comparison with this, all other considerations seem to me to be of secondary importance. Hitler's party was brought to power primarily by his efforts to overcome the old and fatal conflict between the nationalist bourgeois parties of the Right and the masses of the Left, the working and lower middle classes. It was not called the "German Workers' National Socialist Party" (National-sozialistische deutsche Arbeiterpartei) in vain. The name was a program in itself. . . .

Lacking any kind of critical ability, the masses saw in Hitler a savior and a prophet, as he described in a voice hoarse with passion the violent brutalities committed by the victorious powers on a defenseless Germany, as he promised that the criminals of November 1918 would be punished ("Some tens of thousands," he wrote in *Mein Kampf*, "shall one day expiate this crime against the state"), as he poured ridicule on the bungling of the "Marxist fumblers," as he pilloried the internal corruption of the "system of Weimar," or invoked the satanism of Bolshevism, or the grotesque specter of an international conspiracy of Jews. No one asked how much this deluge of accusations contained of truth, exaggeration, or slander, of wild invention or of lies. We can still remember the horror with which we saw this preaching of boundless hatred echoed in the newspapers of the period, and its effect on a public opinion which was both worried and contaminated.

It is extraordinary that these speeches filled with hatred were interpreted as the preparation for a new and more fundamental popular community (*Volksgemeinschaft*). Yet they were interpreted in this way. Many people were aware of the eccentric side of Hitler's visions of the future and of the fanaticism and furious passion of his movement. His confrères, shadows of demagogy, partly corrupt, partly suspect, and partly plebeian, were much more strongly criticized. It was realized that the minor leaders of the new movement were the men who had created disturbances at public meetings, and were therefore not worthy of confidence; the National Socialist press was unreliable, its intellectual level very low, and its writings peculiar and of miserable quality. Nevertheless, the new popular community, the political and moral regeneration of the whole nation which was extolled in it, was regarded as an imposing doctrine, full of possibilities for the future.

How was such blindness possible? Was it the result of general decadence, of the disappearance of the tenets of religious morality? Did the German people lack moral instinct, and were they therefore unable to sense when a thing came from below? This lack of political and moral flair seems to be the most serious guilt with which the Germans who supported Hitler in these years can be reproached, and this reproach is not diminished by the fact that Germany was certainly not the only country to lack political and moral instinct where Hitler was concerned.

However, three factors must be taken into consideration. In the first place, calumnies, insults, and the moral abasement of the opposition are part of the normal equipment of every political struggle, and the violence with which this deplorable method is used varies only in degree. He who preaches distrust in a tottering government will always have great success in a modern mass democracy (as we have already remarked). And in Germany the political discussion was developing into a latent civil war; in a civil war strong fists are superior to all speeches and convictions. Of course, the peaceable bourgeois is inferior in such a sort of combat.

Secondly, it needed a high degree of moral and intellectual superiority to rest quiet and patient in such a situation as the Germans experienced in 1931–1932, in the face of steadily growing millions of unemployed and of continual failures of foreign policy.

Thirdly, and more important, Hitler's demagogy was not restricted to negation alone. It gave the masses an admittedly indefinite conception of the future, but one which impressed them and aroused their enthusiasm. Hitler's criticism of existing powers was not designed to cause despair, but to prepare the way for what he named the regeneration of the state and the people.

The "chains of Versailles," he said, will be cast off as soon as Germany is regenerated from within, as soon as the will of the people really becomes assured, and thus permits a strong and definite leadership. The German people must put an end to the reign of numerous parties, must seize power from the November criminals, and place it in the hands of a national leadership; then Germany will be so great that the victorious powers of Versailles will be obliged to give her her "right to life" (*Lebensrecht*) without a struggle. Germany must be strong, so as to be indispensable to other countries; then she will not lack allies.

First of all, Germany must be set in order. A definite plan of action in the field of economics was hardly mentioned. But Hitler's hearers, dazzled by the vision of a new and more glorious Germany, scarcely noticed this omission. The appeal to instincts of hatred was covered up by declarations of idealist and patriotic sentiments—virile courage, discipline, selfless readiness to serve the community, the tendency of all forces towards one great end: spontaneous devotion to the whole, the social brotherhood of all classes.

As in Mussolini's Italy, the ideal of brotherhood at the front, where in the World War there were no party or class differences, was extremely important. Hitler also adopted the ideal of military leadership and discipline as the best means of creating an orderly state. For the people, however, to be led was to cooperate voluntarily and not to be commanded; his followers (*Gefolgschaft*) were governed by fidelity to the Führer, himself an official carrying out the will of the people, who undertook on his side to be faithful to his followers.

Thus was born the false image of a moral community, which concealed the future dictator's lust for power. He was able to appeal simultaneously to the highest and lowest instincts. This mixture is always the most effective in politics—good and evil, noble and vile, truth, lies, and half-truths. . . .

Eugene N. Anderson
THE NATIONAL ASPIRATIONS

The Germans accepted National Socialism as a last act of desperation. A nation which appreciated its own excellent qualities and high abilities thought its existence menaced by chaos. It could not understand the reason for this plight and refused to acquiesce. Millions of Germans from all classes and occupations felt the crisis to be so

From Gabriel A. Almond et al., *The Struggle for Democracy in Germany* (Chapel Hill, 1949). Reprinted by permission of the University of North Carolina Press.

acute that the Nazis were quickly transformed from a small group of crackpots into a mass party led by a messiah determined upon action to restore the vigor and the rightful glory of the German people. The ingredients of National Socialism were derived in sufficient strength from the German past to be acceptable as German. The *Führerprinzip* enjoyed the traditional prestige of centuries of absolute or strong monarchism, of Bismarckian authoritarianism, and of the traditions and habits of military and even bureaucratic command. It had been practiced, in an appropriate form, by Krupp, Stumm, and many other big industrialists. The new popular element in it was exalted as a sign of democratic equality and became immediately a powerful asset accepted even by the upper classes. The Germans also knew that in every crisis among every people the executive head becomes increasingly important as the instrument for quick and effective action. The relegation of parliament to an insignificant position seemed necessary and was fully approved by the millions of conservatives who had never liked representative government and by the middle classes and even many of the workers who cared less about it than about steady employment. Responsible representative government had had a short history, from 1919 to 1933, and had scarcely been crowned with success. The Germans were accustomed to a wide range of government authority, and in the crisis the individual wished the state to take even more responsibility away from him. The absence of tradition of private initiative and responsibility in civic affairs among most of the people and the dislike of politics and political parties as degrading influences led them to reject the potentialities of the Weimar Republic in favor of the wild promises of Nazism. They lacked democratic safeguards in the habits and standards of their private lives against the enticement of a seemingly easy way out of an unexpected and overwhelming crisis like that of the world economic depression. Certainly for some years until the destructive qualities of Nazism became apparent, few manifested any interest in defending moral principles against the nihilism of the National Socialist.

The qualities which German tradition regarded as the highest virtues became means of totalitarian domination. The Germans made a fetish of order, cleanliness, performance of duty, efficiency in craft or profession, concentration on the business in hand without interference in affairs about which they knew little, being obedient to officers and officials and to the law irrespective of the validity or morality of the order, ardent love of the nation, and supreme loyalty to it. All peoples of our civilization have these traits in varying degrees, but in Western democracies they are balanced by a strong sense of civic responsibility and of individual worth as a citizen. In no other country than Germany did such a combination of qualities obtain on such a broad scale, qualities which in favorable circumstances could be exploited to the ruin of a people.

One important line of German political and social philosophy for at least a century and a half had been basically concerned with the problem of the relation of the individual and the state. Scholars and popular writers at all levels of intelligence had discussed the subject. It permeated the cheap pamphlet literature which Hitler read as an embittered, unemployed ex-soldier. At times of prosperity the rights of the individual might be emphasized; but at every period of crisis— the Napoleonic era, 1848, the 1860s, the Bismarckian era, World War I, the economic depression of 1930–1931, the Nazi seizure of power—the belief in the subordination of the individual to the welfare of the nation-state became widespread. This exaggeration seems logical and understandable for a crisis situation where the individual finds no way to solve his problems alone and throws himself upon the mercy of the state. The view forms the core of nationalistic thought in every country, France, England, Italy, Russia, Germany, or any other. It is the peculiar fate of German history, however, that the idea, derived easily from a class society struggling to maintain hierarchy, suited nicely the needs of the upper classes, especially the monarchy and the aristocrats, in their effort to keep control over the rest of the population. Since they dominated, or believed that with a little more action they could restore their domination over the lower classes, they kept alive the ideal of the superior interests of the state over those of the individual.

When National Socialism arose, it adopted for its own purposes this rich tradition. For the first time in history a nation sought to organize and run itself according to the ideals of nationalism. The process of nationalism which characterized European history after the French Revolution thereby reached its culmination. As stated above, the National Socialists could have found most of their ideals in the nationalistic writings of any country; there is nothing peculiarly German in them. No other people, however, has attempted to realize these ideals, for in no other country has the combination of conditions, inherited and present, been comparable to that which gave National Socialism its opportunity. Only one further step is possible in the unfolding of nationalism and of authoritarianism. That step may be described as national bolshevism. Although one strong faction wished to go so far, the National Socialists were unable to force the German people into the final act of destruction of their social and institutional heritage.

It would be wrong to conclude that Nazism grew inevitably from the German past. This theory would imply a fatalism which is entirely out of place in any serious study of history. A careful analysis of the events of 1932–1933 shows that at that time a substantial majority of the German people favored an extraordinary increase in governmental authority necessary to solve their problems but opposed National Socialism, that this majority was increasing, and that the recession of the economic crisis would have entailed further losses of Nazi popular support. A relatively small group of Junkers, industrialists, and militarists actually achieved Hitler's appointment as chancellor and utilized the senility of President von Hindenburg to accomplish its purpose. The group expected to control the Nazis and to exploit the Nazi power for its own purposes; but the National Socialists proved too clever and too ruthless for it, giving the next twelve years their own imprint. It would also be wrong to equate the conservative authoritarianism of the Hohenzollerns, Bismarck, the Junkers, the big industrialists, and the army officers with National Socialist authoritarianism. The conservatives believed in and practiced authoritarianism as a means of preserving their social, economic, and political status, a status quite different from that of Nazism. Their way of life included respect for at least some of the Christian virtues and for the qualities of their own type of cultured personality. It implied a certain reasonableness and a disinclination on the whole to run desperate risks. Perhaps one may counter by asserting that totalitarianism in all its fulness and with its extreme ruthlessness lay dormant in these groups and awaited the utilization of a Hitler. The growing evidence does not bear out this accusation. Rather it points to a milder view that these conservatives sympathized strongly with a popular totalitarian movement, the full import of which they did not understand, that their nationalism and their craving for power induced them to take a chance with Hitler, and

FIGURE 2. Greetings from German Industry. In a typical propaganda shot, distributed throughout Germany in cigarette packets, a young worker salutes Hitler while his employers look approvingly on. (*Library of Congress*)

that the authoritarian forms of their own thinking and acting and of those of the German people made possible the easy acceptance of National Socialism. The obedience of the German conservatives and all other elements to the Nazis through twelve years of hell does not prove the identity of all the German people with National Socialism. It merely reveals how politically irresponsible two generations of conservative authoritarianism had left a great nation and how susceptible the people were to nationalistic and military success, how unable they were to distinguish between a form of authoritarianism in the old Christian tradition which might have helped to solve their problems without violating the ideals and standards of Western culture and the violent, sadistic ultranationalism of Nazi nihilism.

Few Germans seemed to regret the disappearance of freedom after 1933. The overwhelming majority of the population either joyfully accepted dictatorship or acquiesced in it. While history helps to explain this fact, it also offers the assurance that the Germans have not always approved authoritarianism, that they have not always been nationalistic, indeed, that a large percentage opposed vigorously the Hohenzollern authoritarianism and militarism and preferred the ideals of freedom. History shows that on several occasions the adherents to freedom were powerful enough almost to gain a decisive victory. Historical conditions differed markedly in Germany's development over the past century from those of Britain and France and produced the peculiar mixture of elements from the ancien régime, modern industrial capitalism, and mass social movements which reached its fullest authoritarian form in National Socialism. History offers the assurance that under new and favorable conditions the Germans have the elements of a liberal and even democratic tradition of sufficient strength to encourage and assist them in turning toward democracy. There is no historical reason to doubt that they are able and would be willing to learn the ways of living in social and political freedom; but it is equally clear that their experience since national unification does not offer them much positive guidance. Conservative authoritarianism provides no assurance against a resurgence of totalitarianism. The fate of the Weimar Republic demonstrates that democracy depends upon more than a free constitution and free political instruments; it must permeate likewise individual conduct and social relations. It is this conception of democracy that the Germans must for the first time and on a national scale learn how to practice. . . .

II THE PERSONALITY OF THE LEADER

Scarcely a publication appeared in Germany after 1933 which did not contain a flattering portrait of Adolf Hitler; and none failed to praise his qualities of leadership. He was above and beyond all else the Führer of his nation. What was there, then, about this man which found such resonance in the German people? The problem of the "great man" and his times is, of course, one of the old chestnuts of history. But in this instance it need not be considered in abstraction, since we now have access to some of the most intimate details of Hitler's private and public life.

Karl Dietrich Bracher strips away the layers of myth which surround Hitler's youth and soberly exposes the more banal reality. He takes careful account of the research of other scholars, but he refuses to elaborate far beyond what has actually been documented. This is a comparison of fantasy and fact, rather than a psychological probing. Yet Bracher acknowledges the psychopathic nature of Hitler's world view (Weltanschauung), and he attempts to delineate the sources of Hitler's racism and fanatic German nationalism.

Alan Bullock portrays the more mature Hitler and the baffling paradoxes of his character: self-deception and shrewd calculation, passion and intuition, cynicism and a sense of mission. In these ambiguities, Bullock believes, lay the secret of Hitler's immense personal charm and his unusual flair for propaganda. Here we can see the dictator at his best and at his worst, and we can recognize those qualities which made him both attractive and repulsive.

Ernst Nolte does not hesitate to expand on three traits of Hitler's personality—infantilism, monomania, and mediumism—which distinguished him from the other fascist leaders of Europe. Yet Nolte, too, stops short of claiming that a clinical analysis of Hitler's character is feasible or that, even so, this would suffice to explain the man and the magnetism he exercised on the masses who acclaimed him as their leader.

Robert G. L. Waite has ventured into the literature of psychobiography in order to fathom Hitler's emotional life. He concludes that the Führer was a man driven by feelings of guilt and inferiority, by fears about the "impurity" of his own blood and his warped sexuality. Hence Hitler's morbid concern with the possibility of defeat, the constant preoccupation with suicide and death, the predilection for religious imagery, and the rabid antipathy for all things Jewish. Waite remains perfectly aware of the speculative nature of psychoanalysis, yet he believes the serious student must confront these matters squarely, rather than leave them to salacious gossip.

Peter Loewenberg exemplifies a psychohistorical approach to the subject. By drawing on a variety of comparative, literary, and quantitative sources, he joins Waite in departing from the canons of conventional explanation. But he differs in drawing attention away from Hitler's unique personality, emphasizing instead the psychological profile of those who responded to him. Loewenberg sees the key to understanding the generation of the "Nazi youth cohort" in their common experience of material, nutritional, and familial deprivation during the First World War. This technique of inquiry may be easily caricatured—as if Nazism were the result of a decline in breast-feeding—but it is one which deserves careful consideration as a means of grasping the enthusiasm of the masses stirred by Hitler's oratory.

These selections leave no doubt as to the indispensability of Hitler to the Nazi movement. But they leave in question the adequacy of traditional biography to comprehend such a complex and devious personality. And, if it is inadequate, should we regard psychobiography and psychohistory as complementary or contradictory methods of analysis? The more stress is placed on the importance and idiosyncracy of one man, it would seem, the less compelling are causal explanations of generational conflict within the German population.

Karl Dietrich Bracher
FANTASY AND FACT

The triumph of National Socialism over the Weimar Republic and its realization in the Third Reich are so closely connected with the life of Adolf Hitler that one tends to equate the two. National Socialism has also been called "Hitlerism" and "nothing other than the projection of the will of the man Adolf Hitler into the realm of ideas and words," coming into existence with Hitler and also disappearing with him.[1] And the rise, triumph, and defeat of National Socialism undoubtedly cannot be divorced from Hitler. But National Socialism is more than the gigantic mistake of misguided followers, the product solely of the demonic powers of one individual. Some of the intellectual and political currents which fed National Socialism and made possible the emergence of a man like Hitler have already been mentioned. His life must be seen against the background of fin de siècle Austria, and his political rise falls within the framework of postwar Germany and Europe, burdened by grave intellectual and social problems.

Neither Hitler himself nor his closest collaborators, such as National Socialism's chief ideologist, Alfred Rosenberg, or the guiding spirit of Jewish extermination, Reinhard Heydrich, measured up to the prerequisites of the biological postulates of National Socialism: race and ancestry. Official data about Hitler were confined to scant information about his date of birth, scarcely detailed enough for that "small Aryan pass" which he later demanded of all his subjects. Whatever facts about his background have been unearthed give the lie to his story of the harsh early life of an ambitious genius frustrated by circumstances. Still more interesting are the many questions that remain unanswered,[2] beginning with the name and ancestry of the Austrian customs official Alois Hitler; Adolf Hitler, the fourth child of Alois's third marriage, was born on April 20, 1889, in the border town of Braunau am Inn. The name "Hitler" is possibly of Czech

From *The German Dictatorship*, Third Edition, by Karl Dietrich Bracher. Copyright © 1970 by Praeger Publishers, Inc., New York. Reprinted by permission of Praeger Publishers, Inc. and George Weidenfeld and Nicolson Ltd.

[1] Helmuth Heiber, *Adolf Hitler* (Berlin, 1960), p. 157.
[2] See, particularly, the special studies by Franz Jetzinger (*Hitler's Jugend* [Zurich, 1956]) and Werner Maser (*Die Frühgeschichte der NSDAP* [Frankfurt/Main, 1965]).

origin; the family originally came from the Waldviertel, an Austrian border region near Bohemia. But even this much is not certain, for Alois Hitler, the illegitimate son of a servant girl by the name of Maria Anna Schicklgruber, did not change his name to Hitler until 1876, when he was forty. The identity of Alois's father is not known; Maria Schicklgruber presumably had brought the child with her from the city where she had worked, and, five years after her return, at the age of forty-seven, had married a miller's helper by the name of Georg Hiedler. Almost thirty years after her and Hiedler's deaths, Alois Schicklgruber, with the help of a stepuncle and a gullible village priest, had his birth "legitimized," a step he believed essential to his career and one his stepuncle thought he owed his ambitious ward.

Thus, neither Adolf nor Alois could rightfully claim the name of Hitler. Later rumors and speculations, reaching the top echelons of National Socialism,[3] thought it highly probable that Hitler had a Jewish grandfather and ascribed the radicalization of anti-Semitism to Hitler's pathological eagerness to repress this fact. However, no conclusive evidence has thus far been turned up. Recent findings indicate that the name of Grandmother Schicklgruber's last employer in Graz was Frankenberger—by no means invariably a Jewish name—and his son might possibly have fathered her child.

Such digressions are as sensational as they are questionable and pointless, for, though well meaning, they are rooted in racist superstitions. Hitler's early years and development, particularly his Vienna period, offer ample explanation for his intellectual and psychological development. He grew up in the secure household of a minor civil servant, by no means as impoverished a home as later legend had it. The nice house of his birth, the family property, and his father's pension would indicate that Hitler's years of poverty were the result of his own failure. The father, contrary to his son's later claims, was not a chronic alcoholic, but, rather, a comparatively progressive man with a good job; the mother devoted herself to the care of her home and children. The only thing that seemed to be lacking was a sensible education. The note of self-pity struck by Hitler in making the sad fate of his early years responsible for his failures, culminating in the moving story of the young orphan who finally had to leave home to earn his living, is as contrived as it is untrue.

---

3 Thus, particularly, Hans Frank, *Im Angesicht des Galgens* (Munich, 1953), pp. 330ff.

In 1892, the family moved from Braunau to Passau (Bavaria) and in 1894, to Linz (Austria). Alois Hitler retired a year later, and for a while ran a farm in the Traun valley; in 1898, he purchased a house in Leonding near Linz. Thus, the symbolic significance which Hitler in *Mein Kampf* ascribed to his being born in Braunau, where in 1812 a patriotic bookdealer by the name of Palm was executed for anti-Napoleonic activities, also has little foundation, for Hitler spent part of his formative years in the Bavarian border town of Passau and the rest in Linz, the capital city of Upper Austria. His school career in Linz (he had to repeat his fifth year and was transferred to another school in his ninth) was a fiasco; Hitler was not only labeled indolent, but his performance in mathematics and shorthand as well as in German was considered unsatisfactory—a judgment borne out by his later style. Contrary to his claims in *Mein Kampf,* his grades in geography and history were only passing; his only above-average marks were in drawing and gymnastics. One of his teachers called him lopsidedly talented, uncontrolled, high-handed, dogmatic, ill-tempered, lacking in perseverance, and despotic.

After the death of his father (1903), his mother afforded the high-school dropout two-and-a-half years of idleness (1905–1907), which he spent daydreaming, occasionally drawing, and going to the theater. At this time, the sixteen-year-old began to manifest some of the traits that marked the later political fanatic and demagogue: utter self-involvement to the point of hysterical self-pity, a mania for untrammeled speechifying and equally grandiose and uncontrolled plan making, combined with listlessness and an inability to concentrate, let alone work productively. The serious lung disease which Hitler invoked to explain the way he lived is pure invention. A sentence in *Mein Kampf* about the end of his school career is most revealing: "Suddenly I was helped by an illness." The life he led after failing at school was exactly the sort of life that appealed to him. The irresponsible lack of restraint of his Vienna years may be seen as a direct consequence of his two years of idleness. It is simply not true that financial need was responsible for his life in Vienna. Even after the death of his overindulgent mother in late 1907, Adolf and his sister, Paula, were financially secure.

The Hitler myth has it that the seventeen-year-old, forced to earn his living, had to go to that decadent metropolis, Vienna. The fact is that in 1906, his mother treated him to a trip to Vienna, where he passed the time sightseeing and going to the theater, particularly to his beloved Wagner operas. The next year was spent in the protected setting of his mother's house. Neither school nor work was allowed to interrupt his routine. The only "work" he did was occasional drawings, and his grandiose plans for the rebuilding of Linz fore-shadowed the extravagant ideas of the master builder of the Third Reich. These youthful fantasies reemerged in the "monumental" designs he prepared after his entry into Linz in 1938. The pre-Vienna period of this "work-shy dreamer" already contained the seeds of the type of life and thoughts which have come to light in studies of Hitler's early years. An episode of 1906 is typical: he had an idea for a large-scale research project, complete with housekeeper and cook, which was to afford him and his musician friend August Kubizek the necessary leisure and comfort for the study of "German art" and the formation of a circle of "art lovers," said project to be realized through the purchase of a winning lottery ticket. According to his friend, "Adolf Hitler could plan and look into the future so beauti-fully that I could have listened to him forever."[4] Equally typical is the violence with which he reacted to the news that he had won neither the first nor any of the other lottery prizes: it was the fault of the "entire social order." This episode offers an almost uncanny preview of the later Hitler.

It is pointless to speculate about possible breakdowns suffered during his adolescence, Oedipal complexes, unrequited love, etc. Understandably enough, the relatives of the young man of leisure who refused to entertain any idea about simply "working for a living" began to pressure him to learn a trade. Having failed in his efforts to gain admission to the Vienna Academy of Art (September 1907), he gave no thought to the possibility of any other profession. He stayed on in Vienna, living the comfortable life of the "art student," without telling his ailing mother the truth. After his mother's death, he still was not under any immediate financial pressure; there was a substantial inheritance in addition to his orphan's allowance, which he continued to collect until his twenty-third year under the pretext of being enrolled at the Vienna Academy. Later, he also inherited a fairly substantial sum from an aunt. All these facts underscore the dishonesty of the piteous note struck in his autobiography.

[4] August Kubizek, *Adolf Hitler—mein Jugendfreund* (Graz, 1953); see also Jetzinger, *op. cit.*, pp. 166 ff.

The nineteen-year-old Hitler floundering in Vienna did not, contrary to the self-image of *Mein Kampf,* have any definite political orientation. His "nationalism" was in line with the national German tendencies prevalent in Linz, and his knowledge of history, in which he allegedly excelled at school, was limited. As late as the 1930s, his history instructor, Leopold Pötsch, of whom he speaks highly in *Mein Kampf,* did not want to be part of this myth. As to the "Jewish problem," Hitler also had little knowledge and no firm opinions. His family doctor was Jewish, and Hitler used to send him hand-painted postcards from Vienna. He also accepted money gifts from him, yet in 1938, after the Anschluss, the doctor was driven into exile. Against these facts we have Hitler's contention that while in Linz he had already learned "to understand and comprehend the meaning of history" and that the Austrian nationality conflict had taught him that the meaning of history was to be found in the battle for the "nation" (*Volkstum*) and in the victory of *"völkisch* nationalism" (*Mein Kampf,* pp. 8 ff.). Yet, some of the basic traits and thoughts which took shape during his five-and-a-half years in Vienna were, according to Kubizek, his patient audience, already to be found in the endless speeches and grandiose plans of his Linzer days. The experiences of Vienna, Munich, and World War I lent them substance and embellished them with the up-to-date content and impulses which so profoundly were to shape Hitler the political man.

He was driven to Vienna not by "need and harsh reality" but by the desire to escape work, the need to learn a trade, and the wish to continue the life-style of the "future artist," a pose which he was unable to maintain any longer under the watchful eyes of his relatives in Linz. He kept on urging his friend Kubizek to join him in Vienna. In the ensuing months, he was an almost daily visitor to the opera, went sightseeing, developed grandiose plans for a musical drama and for all sorts of building projects, while Kubizek, who had been as unaware of his friend's academic failure as the family, enrolled in the Vienna Conservatory. Hitler, as he proudly stated, was supreme master of his time. The harsh life of the "common laborer" who had to earn his "crust of bread" is one of the heart-rending myths of his autobiography. Between 1909 and 1913, the unsuccessful art student and self-designated "artist" and "writer" was introduced to the political ideas and currents that were to furnish the decisive concepts and stimuli for his later career. The political and social conflicts and emotions in the Vienna of that era offered material and food for a radical critique of society, and the unbridgeable gap between Hitler's wants, ambitions, and fantasies and naked reality made him accept and enlarge on this critique. It was the same impulse that later, in crisis-ridden postwar Germany, drove so large a segment of the lower middle class, its feelings of superiority threatened, into the arms of the radical-Right doctrine of salvation— a sociopolitical flight into an irrational political creed thriving on hatred and fear and demanding to be saved from conflict through the institution of a total "new order."

The rejection of Hitler's second application for admission to the Art Academy in the fall of 1908 seems to have been a turning point in his life. He broke off his friendship with Kubizek and became submerged in the shadowy world of public shelters (1908–1909) and homes for men (1910–1913), though the allowance and the gifts from relatives continued. Moreover, the "hard labor" referred to in *Mein Kampf* should have brought him additional funds. During this period, Hitler discovered the political and social slogans then in vogue, an encounter reminiscent of his earlier introduction to art. Contrary to his testimony, Hitler had read few books and had not really concerned himself with the political and social problems of his environment. A chance reading of books, occasional pamphlets, and generalizations based on subjective impressions combined to form the distorted political picture which, in almost pristine form, became the "weltanschauung" that dominated Hitler's future life and work.

The only work he did was an occasional copying of picture postcards which his fellow inmates of the men's home sold for him. He spent most of his time piecing together his weltanschauung from obscure sources. Its essence was extreme nationalism and a radical racial anti-Semitism. The literature which stimulated Hitler's interest in politics forms the subject of a comprehensive study.[5] Among his reading matter was a periodical with the resounding name of *Ostara,* the German goddess of spring, a publication which, from 1905 on, was widely sold in the tobacco kiosks of Vienna. It gave voice to the eccentric and bloodthirsty race mythology of Adolf Lanz (1874–1954), an ex-monk who called himself Lanz von Liebenfels. His program called for the founding oɪ a male order of blue-eyed, blond

5 Wilfried Daim, *Der Mann, der Hitler die Ideen gab* (Munich, 1958). On the religious background, see Friedrich Heer, *Der Glaube des Adolf Hitler* (Munich, 1968).

"Aryans." His headquarters were in a castle in Lower Austria which he had bought with the help of industrialist patrons. There Lanz hoisted the swastika banner in 1906 as the symbol of the Aryan movement. This pathological founding father of an "Aryan" hero cult was the author of *Theozoology* (1901), a work offering a particularly abstruse mixture of an extreme, pseudoreligious racism. Apparently, Hitler got in touch with Lanz personally in 1909, asking for copies of *Ostara* that were missing from his own collection. Lanz's views, and similarly fantastic notions from the "European underground," which later were to make their way into the Ludendorff movement, helped to shape Hitler's political ideology. Lanz's works disseminated the crass exaggerations of the Social Darwinist theory of survival, the superman and superrace theory, the dogma of race conflict, and the breeding and extermination theories of the future SS state. The scheme was simple: a blond, heroic race of "Arioheroes" was engaged in battle with inferior mixed races whose annihilation was deemed a historico-political necessity; "race defilement" was not to be tolerated, and the master race was to multiply with the help of "race hygiene," polygamy, and breeding stations; sterilization, debilitating forced labor, and systematic liquidation were to offer a final solution.

Such pamphlets were fatal reading for an unstable youth with few ideas of his own, even though, as Hitler himself confessed, his middle-class, liberal background initially led him to rebel against these teachings. This literature took on great significance against the background of impressions received by a footloose youth on the lowest rung of the social ladder in the capital city of a multinational monarchy. Hitler's acquaintance with Marxist socialism also was not the product of close study, as he claimed, but of obscure subjective impressions marked by the sort of class and cultural snobbery which was still part of him and which he now directed toward social and political issues. A passage in *Mein Kampf* (p. 25), precisely because of its exaggeration, throws interesting light on its author and the substance of his weltanschauung: "At that time I read ceaselessly and very thoroughly." (He never is specific about his reading matter; his "books," according to his own account of the genesis of his anti-Semitism [p. 59], are polemical pamphlets bought "for a few pennies.") The passage continues: "What free time I had left from my work was spent on my studies. In a few years I thus created for myself the basis of the knowledge on which I still feed. During that time I formed a picture of the world and an ideology which has become the granite foundation of my deeds. I only had to add a little more knowledge to that which I had acquired at that time; I did not have to revise anything."

Who else can say this of his impressions at the age of twenty? This passage is more revealing of the level of his Viennese "studies" (mostly, endless debates between the idle smart aleck and his fellow inmates at the shelter) and of the substance of the later National Socialist ideology than the most probing analysis. What Hitler "learned" in Vienna, and subsequently elevated to the status of a "constructive ideology," was that monomaniacal, obsessive, unseeing yet effective method of political argumentation which led from the evenings in the men's shelter of Vienna to the endless monologues of the demagogue.

In addition to inventing the story of the day laborer who while on the job had his eyes opened to Marxism and its Jewish "backers," Hitler also makes mention of the anti-Semitic movement of the Austro-Pan-German nationalist von Schönerer. The actual impact of this antimonarchist, anti-Marxist social movement, the Austrian version of a decidedly national "German socialism," is hard to assess, but its nationalist, völkisch battle cries undoubtedly are among the roots of National Socialism. They furnished the young Hitler with a political framework for his personal and social resentments against a society in which his adolescent daydreams and wants found neither response nor expression.

The substance of the ideas which Hitler made into the "granite foundation" of his future policies has been paraphrased repeatedly. It is nothing more than a sweeping rejection of and opposition to tolerance and cosmopolitanism, democracy and parliamentarianism, Marxism and Jewry, which, in primitive equation, were called the primary evils of the world. Even then, however, the core, probably the only "genuine" fanatically held and realized conviction of his entire life, was anti-Semitism and race mania. An enormously oversimplified scheme of good and evil, transplanted to the biological and racial sphere, was made to serve as the master key to the history of political thought. Hitler's fanatical hatred of the Jews defies all rational explanation; it cannot be measured by political and pragmatic gauges. The fact that an entire nation followed him and furnished a legion of executioners does demonstrate, however, that we are confronted not merely with the inexplicable dynamics of one man, but with a terrible disease of modern nationalism, whose desire for exclusivity and war against everything "alien" constitutes one of the root causes of anti-Semitism.

The psychopathic features of Hitler's weltanschauung were discernible even then: the social envy of the failure and the discrepancy between his exalted vision of personal prestige and the poverty of the unemployed man who held ordinary work in disdain both played a role. The much-abused Nietzsche once called anti-Semitism the ideology of the "those who feel cheated." Unconfirmed rumor has it that Hitler arrived at the "awareness" that the creative person—and he, being a painter, belonged to this category—gets cheated by the sly, worldly, aggressive Jewish trader after he himself had had an unpleasant experience with a Jewish art dealer. Such personal resentments may have contributed to the rationalization of his perverse anti-Semitism.

At about that time, Hitler had also become a "fanatical nationalist." At its highest pitch, nationalist ideology appeals to mass insanity, assuming the force of a collective psychosis in which the annihilation of the enemy spells one's own success and salvation. The anti-Semitic atmosphere of the Vienna of that time provided Hitler's new eclectic philosophy with the firm base on which militant nationalism could develop to its most extreme form and be carried to the point of absurdity. The Jews are the cause of all misfortune; ruthless battle against them holds the key to national if not universal salvation: this precept formed the base of Hitler's later nationalism and imperialism, which ultimately combined forcible expansion beyond the national boundaries with the missionary zeal of a German war on "world Jewry." After Hitler became chancellor, he confided to intimates that he had been compelled to resort to nationalism because of "the conditions of the times," but that he had always been convinced that "we have to get rid of this false conception" of democracy and liberalism and in its place "set up . . . the conception of race, which has not yet been politically used up."[6]

The "studies" and "harsh lessons" of his Vienna years, which Hitler said were the foundation of his entire career, thus provided the

[6] Hermann Rauschning, *Hitler Speaks: A Series of Political Conversations with Adolf Hitler on His Real Aims* (London, 1939), p. 229.

immature youth with the kind of banal, limited semieducation which is among the most dangerous impulses for the destructive forces of our time. Just as he failed to persevere in school and work, this rambling autodidact failed to gain real insight into the problems of the time. His tirelessly fundamental, global "debates" with Marxism and democracy, despite their manic repetition, also never went beyond generalities and platitudes. In *Mein Kampf,* he describes the method of reading and studying through which he acquired his pseudoeducation: he always knew how to separate the wheat from the chaff and to extract the true content of everything. In this way, he gathered a store of semi-information which he put to good use; his was a "pigeonhole mind" (*Heiber*), lacking the ability to see things in their context. But, at the same time, he satisfied his adolescent "striving for self-worth" (*Daim*) and also developed a set of ideas of whose simplicity he was to furnish proof. When, in 1924, Hitler proudly told a Munich court that by the time he left Vienna he had become "an absolute anti-Semite, a mortal enemy of the entire Marxist philosophy, Pan-German in my political convictions," he was probably telling the truth (*Mein Kampf,* pp. 130 ff.).

In May 1913, a year later than stated in *Mein Kampf,* Hitler suddenly turned up in Munich, after more than five years of obscurity. The reasons for his abrupt departure from Vienna are not clear. One might think he was telling the truth when he said that he was prompted by a dislike for the Habsburg Empire and a yearning for the Bavarian art capital, were it not for the recent revelation of an embarrassing episode. It seems that this future ideologist of combat, the "military genius," had evaded military service in 1909–1910, just as he had evaded all other duties, quite unlike those reviled "homeless" Marxists and Jews. Like all of Hitler's major "decisions"— leaving school, moving to Vienna, going to war, entering politics, again going to war, and, finally, his egocentric fall—the road to Munich was also an escape route, this time from military service. This is attested to also by the fact that the then twenty-four-year-old Hitler, who, in fact, remained a citizen of Austria until 1925, called himself "stateless." When arrested and extradited to Salzburg at the request of Austria, he fawningly told the court about his sad life, and, in fact, his poor physical condition saved him from punishment and conscription. Hitler's long letter of explanation (January 1914) to the Linz authorities hints at the legend of later years. When he writes, "I have never known the lovely word 'youth,'" it almost reads like a "draft for *Mein Kampf*" (Jetzinger). This shameful affair, the documents of which became the object of a feverish search after Hitler's invasion of Austria, testifies to his dishonesty and cowardice and to the mendacity of a weltanschauung whose rigorous precepts were valid only for others.

He fared no better in Munich than he had in Vienna. The sale of his bad paintings brought in little. The future looked no rosier in Germany. The outbreak of World War I almost seemed like salvation. A rare photograph of that time shows Hitler, wearing a dashing artist's hat, among the masses at the Odeonsplatz cheering the news that war had been declared. Carried away by the popular enthusiasm, he felt liberated from his unproductive, unsuccessful life. As a volunteer not expected to act or decide independently, freed from the purposeless existence of the occasional painter and coffeehouse habitué incapable of establishing personal relationships, he now found himself subject to a discipline which, unlike the disreputable camaraderie of the Vienna shelter, also satisfied his dreams of national and social grandeur. Hitler later justified and glorified the fact that he served in the German army rather than that of his homeland by denouncing the Habsburg Empire, however inconsistent this may have seemed with his critical attitude toward Wilhelmian Germany. The fact that once more he found himself in a male community indelibly affected his future life and ideas. "Destiny," which he liked to invoke, had pointed the way: "To me, those times were like a deliverance from the vexing emotions of my youth . . . so that, overcome by passionate enthusiasm, I fell to my knees and thanked heaven out of an overflowing heart" (*Mein Kampf,* p. 177). The war seemed to put an end to all problems of daily life in a society in which he had not been able to find his way and which, in typically egocentric fashion, he held responsible for his failure. This, not the dramatically stilted phrase of 1918 ("I, however, decided to become a politician"), was the decisive turning point; war as the transmutation of all values, battle as the father of all things, was the dominant force of Hitler's future life. Hence the eagerly sought-for prolongation of the war beyond the peace agreement into the crises and civil-war atmosphere of the Weimar Republic became the basis of Hitler's activities.

Little worth mentioning happened to Hitler during the war years. Though as a courier he remained a mere corporal, he did have occasion to distinguish himself. He remained a loner, nonsmoker, teeto-taler, and lover of sweets, a model patriot and tireless polemicist against Jews, Marxists, and defeatists; he had little in common with the ordinary soldier. The pronounced ascetic-heroic "idealism," the bent toward the undeviatingly radical, the rejection of "ordinary" and erotic pleasures, the feeling of superiority and the sacrificing of personal interests for a "higher ideal"—all these were already hinted at in his monologues and schemes in Linz. Later, Hitler per-mitted these tendencies to be magnified into an effective myth of a demigod free from ordinary human needs and failings. This, too, was, in effect, an escape, an "escape into legend" (Heiden).

It was the discipline of war and the "front-line acquaintance" with the clear and simple military hierarchy of order and values which were to shape Hitler's sense of values and turn this unstable dreamer unable to come to terms with the bourgeois world of work and order into the rigid fanatic with incredibly oversimplified ideas of war and order. This military male order was the model for the future armed party organizations, for the ideal of a "national community" ready for battle, and for the leader idea; it was elevated to the guiding principle of the political, social, and intellectual life of the country. Therefore Germany's defeat, news of which reached Hitler in the field hospital of Pasewalk, where he was being treated for gas poisoning, not only touched his patriotic feelings but affected his very existence: he was faced with the prospect of returning to his miserable prewar exis-tence. The war simply could not be over, and if, as Hitler was con-vinced, it had been lost because of defeatism on the home front and the Jewish-Marxist "stab in the back," then this conviction had to be validated by continuing the fight at home. This "national" neces-sity took on existential significance for Hitler. Ever since those liber-ating days of 1914, the private and now "professional" life of Hitler, a man with little education and no personal ties, had been based on perpetuating the state of war. It was this which lay at the root of the fanatical energy with which Hitler turned the war into his motivating principle. That is how he looked at politics as a career—as a means for gaining power which would make possible a new war, this one, however, fought according to his ideas until final victory was won.

Hitler's turn to politics also was not the logical outcome of his own decision and resolution, as the legend of *Mein Kampf* would have it. It, too, was an escape from regular work; once again, having returned to Munich, he let events force a decision on him, one, however, to which he held fast. But, initially, Hitler did little to translate into fact his alleged decision of November 9, 1918, "to get into politics." Fearing civilian life, he clung to the security of military service and witnessed, from his barracks, the brief turmoil of the Munich *Räterepublik* (April 1919). Only later was he given the opportunity, for the first time in his life, to exercise a political function. His "nationalistic" zeal in the service of a commission engaged in ferreting out revolutionary elements among the troops persuaded his superiors to make him an "information officer" responsible for the nationalist education and control of his comrades. Since this assignment involved contact with rightist groups, he found himself, in September 1919, as an observer at a meeting of one of the numerous new small right-wing parties, the German Workers' Party, in a Munich beer hall.

This chance happening was to make history and decide Hitler's career. Drexler's group of sectarians and beer-hall politicians gathered at this meeting to listen to a speech by the engineer Feder about the abolition of capitalism and the rule of finance capital; the speech was not very impressive. But Hitler felt at home in this uncritical assemblage, and so when informed some time later of his admission into the party, though he himself had never applied, he accepted. He became Party Comrade No. 55, and, simultaneously, the seventh member of the executive committee. Hitler may have been incapable of taking the initiative, let alone of founding a political party, but, once a decision had been made without his active help, he zealously threw himself into the new role of politician. In view of the disarmament provisions of the Versailles treaty, his days in the rump army were probably numbered anyway; now he found the framework which might possibly combine the ideas of his Vienna days with a wartime order, offering him a chance to use his modicum of "learning" to secure his existence and to compensate for his fear of the demands of a civilian life in which he had failed.

Alan Bullock
DECEPTION AND CALCULATION

The foundation of Hitler's success was his own energy and ability as a political leader. Without this, the help would never have been forth-coming, or would have produced insignificant results. Hitler's genius as a politician lay in his unequalled grasp of what could be done by propaganda, and his flair for seeing how to do it. He had to learn in a hard school, on his feet night after night, arguing his case in every kind of hall, from the smoke-filled back room of a beer cellar to the huge auditorium of the Zirkus Krone; often, in the early days, in the face of opposition, indifference, or amused contempt; learning to hold his audience's attention, to win them over; most important of all, learning to read the minds of his audiences, finding the sensitive spots on which to hammer. "He could play like a virtuoso on the well-tempered piano of lower middle-class hearts,"[1] says Dr. Schacht. Behind that virtuosity lay years of experience as an agitator and mob orator. Hitler came to know Germany and the German people at first hand as few of Germany's other leaders ever had. By the time he came to power in 1933 there were few towns of any size in the Reich where he had not spoken. Here was one great advantage Hitler had over nearly all the politicians with whom he had to deal, his immense practical experience of politics, not in the Chancellery or the Reichstag, but in the street, the level at which elections are won, the level at which any politician must be effective if he is to carry a mass vote with him.

Hitler was the greatest demagogue in history. Those who add "only a demagogue" fail to appreciate the nature of political power in an age of mass politics. As he himself said: "To be a leader, means to be able to move masses."[2]

The lessons which Hitler drew from the activities of the Austrian Social Democrats and Lueger's Christian Socialists were now tried

From *Hitler: A Study in Tyranny*, Completely Revised Edition, by Alan Bullock, pp. 68–71, 374–380, 384–385. Copyright © 1962 by Alan Bullock. Reprinted by permission of Harper & Row, Publishers, Inc. and The Hamlyn Publishing Group Limited. Foot-notes edited.

[1] Hjalmar Schacht, *Account Settled* (English translation of *Abrechnung mit Hitler*, London, 1949), p. 206.
[2] *Mein Kampf*, p. 474.

out in Munich. Success was far from being automatic. Hitler made mistakes and had much to learn before he could persuade people to take him seriously, even on the small stage of Bavarian politics. By 1923 he was still only a provincial politician, who had not yet made any impact on national politics, and the end of 1923 saw the collapse of his movement in a fiasco. But Hitler learned from his mistakes, and by the time he came to write *Mein Kampf* in the middle of the 1920s he was able to set down quite clearly what he was trying to do, and what were the conditions of success. The pages in *Mein Kampf* in which he discusses the technique of mass propaganda and political leadership stand out in brilliant contrast with the turgid attempts to explain his entirely unoriginal political ideas.

The first and most important principle for political action laid down by Hitler is: Go to the masses. "The movement must avoid everything which may lessen or weaken its power of influencing the masses . . . because of the simple fact that no great idea, no matter how sublime or exalted, can be realized in practice without the effective power which resides in the popular masses."[3]

> *Since the masses have only a poor acquaintance with abstract ideas, their reactions lie more in the domain of the feelings, where the roots of their positive as well as their negative attitudes are implanted. . . . The emotional grounds of their attitude furnish the reason for their extraordinary stability. It is always more difficult to fight against faith than against knowledge. And the driving force which has brought about the most tremendous revolutions on this earth has never been a body of scientific teaching which has gained power over the masses, but always a devotion which has inspired them, and often a kind of hysteria which has urged them into action. Whoever wishes to win over the masses must know the key that will open the door to their hearts. It is not objectivity, which is a feckless attitude, but a determined will, backed up by power where necessary.[4]*

Hitler is quite open in explaining how this is to be achieved. "The receptive powers of the masses are very restricted, and their understanding is feeble. On the other hand, they quickly forget. Such being the case, all effective propaganda must be confined to a few bare necessities and then must be expressed in a few stereotyped formulas."[5] Hitler had nothing but scorn for the intellectuals who are always

---

[3] Ibid., p. 101.
[4] Ibid., p. 283.
[5] Ibid., p. 159.

looking for something new. "Only constant repetition will finally succeed in imprinting an idea on the memory of a crowd."[6] For the same reason it is better to stick to a program even when certain points in it become out of date: "As soon as one point is removed from the sphere of dogmatic certainty, the discussion will not simply result in a new and better formulation, but may easily lead to endless debates and general confusion."[7]

When you lie, tell big lies. This is what the Jews do, working on the principle, "which is quite true in itself, that in the big lie there is always a certain force of credibility; because the broad masses of a nation are always more easily corrupted in the deeper strata of their emotional nature than consciously or voluntarily, and thus in the primitive simplicity of their minds they more readily fall victims to the big lie than the small lie, since they themselves often tell small lies in little matters, but would be ashamed to resort to large-scale falsehoods. It would never come into their heads to fabricate colossal untruths and they would not believe that others could have the impudence to distort the truth so infamously. . . . The grossly impudent lie always leaves traces behind it, even after it has been nailed down."[8]

Above all, never hesitate, never qualify what you say, never concede an inch to the other side, paint all your contrasts in black and white. This is the "very first condition which has to be fulfilled in every kind of propaganda: a systematically one-sided attitude towards every problem that has to be dealt with. . . . When they see an uncompromising onslaught against an adversary, the people have at all times taken this as proof that right is on the side of the active aggressor; but if the aggressor should go only halfway and fail to push home his success . . . the people will look upon this as a sign that he is uncertain of the justice of his own cause."[9]

Vehemence, passion, fanaticism, these are "the great magnetic forces which alone attract the great masses; for these masses always respond to the compelling force which emanates from absolute faith in the ideas put forward, combined with an indomitable zest to fight for and defend them. . . . The doom of a nation can be averted only

6 Ibid., p. 163.
7 Ibid., p. 383.
8 Ibid., pp. 198–9.
9 Ibid., pp. 160–1, 283.

FIGURE 3. The Picture of Determination. Although Hitler's oratorical skills and gestures were carefully rehearsed, his ability to sway crowds finally depended on his earnestness and self-conviction. (*Library of Congress*)

by a storm of glowing passion; but only those who are passionate themselves can arouse passion in others."[10]

Hitler showed a marked preference for the spoken over the written word. "The force which ever set in motion the great historical avalanches of religious and political movements is the magic power of the spoken word. The broad masses of a population are more amenable to the appeal of rhetoric than to any other force."[11] The employment of verbal violence, the repetition of such words as "smash," "force," "ruthless," "hatred," was deliberate. Hitler's gestures and the emotional character of his speaking, lashing himself up to a pitch of near hysteria in which he would scream and spit out his resentment, had the same effect on an audience. Many descriptions have been given of the way in which he succeeded in communicating passion to his listeners, so that men groaned or hissed and women sobbed involuntarily, if only to relieve the tension, caught up in the spell of powerful emotions of hatred and exaltation, from which all restraint had been removed.

It was to be years yet before Hitler was able to achieve this effect on the scale of the Berlin Sportpalast audiences of the 1930s, but he had already begun to develop extraordinary gifts as a speaker. It was in Munich that he learned to address mass audiences of several thousands. In *Mein Kampf* he remarks that the orator's relationship with his audience is the secret of his art. "He will always follow the lead of the great mass in such a way that from the living emotion of his hearers the apt word which he needs will be suggested to him and in its turn this will go straight to the hearts of his hearers."[12] A little later he speaks of the difficulty of overcoming emotional resistance: this cannot be done by argument, but only by an appeal to the "hidden forces" in an audience, an appeal that the orator alone can make.

*   *   *

The conversations recorded by Hermann Rauschning for the period 1932–1934, and by the table talk at the Führer's H.Q. for the period 1941–1942,[13] reveal Hitler in another favorite role, that of visionary and prophet. This was the mood in which Hitler indulged, talking far

[10] Ibid., pp. 317, 100.
[11] Ibid., p. 100.
[12] Ibid., pp. 391–2.
[13] *Hitler's Table Talk* (London, 1953).

into the night, in his house on the Obersalzberg, surrounded by the remote peaks and silent forests of the Bavarian Alps; or in the Eyrie he had built six thousand feet up on the Kehlstein, above the Berghof, approached only by a mountain road blasted through the rock and a lift guarded by doors of bronze.[14] There he would elaborate his fabulous schemes for a vast empire embracing the Eurasian Heartland of the geopoliticians; his plans for breeding a new elite biologically preselected; his design for reducing whole nations to slavery in the foundation of his new empire. Such dreams had fascinated Hitler since he wrote *Mein Kampf.* It was easy in the late 1920s and early 1930s to dismiss them as the product of a disordered and overheated imagination soaked in the political romanticism of Wagner and Houston Stewart Chamberlain. But these were still the themes of Hitler's table talk in 1941–1942 and by then, master of the greater part of Europe and on the eve (as he believed) of conquering Russia and the Ukraine, Hitler had shown that he was capable of translating his fantasies into a terrible reality. The invasion of Russia, the SS extermination squads, the planned elimination of the Jewish race; the treatment of the Poles and Russians, the Slav *Untermenschen*— these, too, were the fruits of Hitler's imagination.

All this combines to create a picture of which the best description is Hitler's own famous sentence: "I go the way that Providence dictates with the assurance of a sleepwalker."[15] The former French ambassador speaks of him as "a man possessed"; Hermann Rauschning writes: "Dostoevsky might well have invented him, with the morbid derangement and the pseudo-creativeness of his hysteria";[16] one of the defense counsel at the Nuremberg trials, Dr. Dix, quoted a passage from Goethe's *Dichtung und Wahrheit* describing the Demoniac and applied this very aptly to Hitler. With Hitler, indeed, one is uncomfortably aware of never being far from the realm of the irrational.

But this is only half the truth about Hitler, for the baffling problem about this strange figure is to determine the degree to which he was swept along by a genuine belief in his own inspiration and the degree

---

[14] It is typical of Hitler that, according to the secretary whose account has already been quoted, he rarely visited the pavilion on the Kehlstein, except to impress foreign visitors like M. François-Poncet.

[15] In a speech at Munich on 15 March, 1936, just after the successful reoccupation of the Rhineland, against the experts' advice, had triumphantly vindicated his power of intuition.

[16] Hermann Rauschning, *Hitler Speaks,* pp. 253–4.

to which he deliberately exploited the irrational side of human nature, both in himself and others, with a shrewd calculation. For it is salutary to recall, before accepting the Hitler Myth at anything like its face value, that it was Hitler who invented the myth, assiduously cultivating and manipulating it for his own ends. So long as he did this he was brilliantly successful; it was when he began to believe in his own magic, and accept the myth of himself as true, that his flair faltered.

So much has been made of the charismatic nature of Hitler's leadership that it is easy to forget the astute and cynical politician in him. It is this mixture of calculation and fanaticism, with the difficulty of telling where one ends and the other begins, which is the peculiar characteristic of Hitler's personality: to ignore or underestimate either element is to present a distorted picture.

The link between the different sides of Hitler's character was his extraordinary capacity for self-dramatization. "This so-called *Wahnsystem,* or capacity for self-delusion," Sir Nevile Henderson, the British ambassador, wrote, "was a regular part of his technique. It helped him both to work up his own passions and to make his people believe anything that he might think good for them."[17] Again and again one is struck by the way in which, having once decided rationally on a course of action, Hitler would whip himself into a passion which enabled him to bear down all opposition, and provided him with the motive power to enforce his will on others. An obvious instance of this is the synthetic fury, which he could assume or discard at will, over the treatment of German minorities abroad. When it was a question of refusing to listen to the bitter complaints of the Germans in the South Tyrol, or of uprooting the German inhabitants of the Baltic States, he sacrificed them to the needs of his Italian and Russian alliances with indifference. So long as good relations with Poland were necessary to his foreign policy he showed little interest in Poland's German minority. But when it suited his purpose to make the "intolerable wrongs" of the Austrian Nazis, or the Germans in Czechoslovakia and Poland, a ground for action against these states, he worked himself into a frenzy of indignation, with the immediate— and calculated—result that London and Paris, in their anxiety for

17 Sir N. Henderson, *Failure of a Mission* (London, 1940), p. 229.

peace, exerted increased pressure on Prague or Warsaw to show restraint and make further concessions to the German demands.

One of Hitler's most habitual devices was to place himself on the defensive, to accuse those who opposed or obstructed him of aggression and malice, and to pass rapidly from a tone of outraged innocence to the full thunders of moral indignation. It was always the other side who were to blame, and in turn he denounced the Communists, the Jews, the Republican government, or the Czechs, the Poles, and the Bolsheviks for their "intolerable" behavior which forced him to take drastic action in self-defense.

Hitler in a rage appeared to lose all control of himself. His face became mottled and swollen with fury, he screamed at the top of his voice, spitting out a stream of abuse, waving his arms wildly and drumming on the table or the wall with his fists. As suddenly as he had begun he would stop, smooth down his hair, straighten his collar and resume a more normal voice.

This skillful and deliberate exploitation of his own temperament extended to other moods than anger. When he wanted to persuade or win someone over he could display great charm. Until the last days of his life he retained an uncanny gift of personal magnetism which defies analysis, but which many who met him have described. This was connected with the curious power of his eyes, which are persistently said to have had some sort of hypnotic quality. Similarly, when he wanted to frighten or shock, he showed himself a master of brutal and threatening language, as in the celebrated interviews with Schuschnigg and President Hacha.

Yet another variation in his roles was the impression of concentrated willpower and intelligence, the leader in complete command of the situation and with a knowledge of the facts which dazzled the generals or ministers summoned to receive his orders. To sustain this part he drew on his remarkable memory, which enabled him to reel off complicated orders of battle, technical specifications, and long lists of names and dates without a moment's hesitation. Hitler cultivated this gift of memory assiduously. The fact that subsequently the details and figures which he cited were often found to contain inaccuracies did not matter: it was the immediate effect at which he aimed. The swiftness of the transition from one mood to another was startling: one moment his eyes would be filled with tears and pleading, the next blazing with fury, or glazed with the faraway look of the visionary.

Hitler, in fact, was a consummate actor, with the actor's and orator's facility for absorbing himself in a role and convincing himself of the truth of what he was saying at the time he said it. In his early years he was often awkward and unconvincing, but with practice the part became second nature to him, and with the immense prestige of success behind him, and the resources of a powerful state at his command, there were few who could resist the impression of the piercing eyes, the Napoleonic pose, and the "historic" personality.

Hitler had the gift of all great politicians for grasping the possibilities of a situation more swiftly than his opponents. He saw, as no other politician did, how to play on the grievances and resentments of the German people, as later he was to play on French and British fear of war and fear of communism. His insistence upon preserving the forms of legality in the struggle for power showed a brilliant understanding of the way to disarm opposition, just as the way in which he undermined the independence of the German army showed his grasp of the weaknesses of the German Officer Corps.

A German word, *Fingerspitzengefühl* ("finger-tip feeling"), which was often applied to Hitler, well describes his sense of opportunity and timing.

> *No matter what you attempt [Hitler told Rauschning on one occasion], if an idea is not yet mature you will not be able to realize it. Then there is only one thing to do: have patience, wait, try again, wait again. In the subconscious, the work goes on. It matures, sometimes it dies. Unless I have the inner, incorruptible conviction: this is the solution, I do nothing. Not even if the whole Party tries to drive me into action.*[18]

Hitler knew how to wait in 1932, when his insistence on holding out until he could secure the chancellorship appeared to court disaster. Foreign policy provides another instance. In 1939 he showed great patience while waiting for the situation to develop after direct

---

[18] Hermann Rauschning, *Hitler Speaks,* p. 181. The present author shares the view of Professor Trevor-Roper that Rauschning's account of his conversations with Hitler in this book has been vindicated by the evidence of Hitler's views which has been discovered since its publication and that it is an important source for any biography of Hitler.

negotiations with Poland had broken down and while the Western powers were seeking to reach a settlement with Soviet Russia. Clear enough about his objectives, he contrived to keep his plans flexible. In the case of the annexation of Austria and of the occupation of Prague, he made the final decision on the spur of the moment.

Until he was convinced that the right moment had come Hitler would find a hundred excuses for procrastination. His hesitation in such cases was notorious: his refusal to make up his mind to stand as a presidential candidate in 1932, and his attempt to defer taking action against Röhm and the SA in 1934, are two obvious examples. Once he had made up his mind to move, however, he would act boldly, taking considerable risks, as in the reoccupation of the Rhineland in 1936, or the invasion of Norway and Denmark just before the major campaign in the west.

Surprise was a favorite gambit of Hitler's, in politics, diplomacy, and war: he gauged the psychological effect of sudden, unexpected hammer-blows in paralyzing opposition. An illustration of his appreciation of the value of surprise and quick decision, even when on the defensive, is the second presidential campaign of 1932. It had taken Goebbels weeks to persuade Hitler to stand for the presidency at all. The defeat in the first ballot brought Goebbels to despair; but Hitler, now that he had committed himself, with great presence of mind dictated the announcement that he would stand a second time and got it onto the streets almost before the country had learned of his defeat. In war the psychological effect of the blitzkrieg was just as important in Hitler's eyes as the strategic: it gave the impression that the German military machine was more than life-size, that it possessed some virtue of invincibility against which ordinary men could not defend themselves.

No regime in history has ever paid such careful attention to psychological factors in politics. Hitler was a master of mass emotion. To attend one of his big meetings was to go through an emotional experience, not to listen to an argument or a program. Yet nothing was left to chance on these occasions. Every device for heightening the emotional intensity, every trick of the theater was used. The Nuremberg rallies held every year in September were masterpieces of theatrical art, with the most carefully devised effects. "I had spent six years in St. Petersburg before the war in the best days of the old Russian ballet," wrote Sir Nevile Henderson, "but for grandiose beauty I have never seen a ballet to compare with it."[19] To see the films of the Nuremberg rallies even today is to be recaptured by the hypnotic effect of thousands of men marching in perfect order, the music of the massed bands, the forest of standards and flags, the vast perspectives of the stadium, the smoking torches, the dome of searchlights. The sense of power, of force, and unity was irresistible, and all converged with a mounting crescendo of excitement on the supreme moment when the Führer himself made his entry. Paradoxically, the man who was most affected by such spectacles was their originator, Hitler himself, and, as Rosenberg remarks in his memoirs, they played an indispensable part in the process of self-intoxication.

Hitler had grasped as no one before him what could be done with a combination of propaganda and terrorism. For the complement to the attractive power of the great spectacles was the compulsive power of the Gestapo, the SS, and the concentration camp, heightened once again by skillful propaganda. Hitler was helped in this not only by his own perception of the sources of power in a modern urbanized mass society, but also by possession of the technical means to manipulate them. This was a point well made by Albert Speer, Hitler's highly intelligent minister for armaments and war production, in the final speech he made at his trial after the war.

Hitler's dictatorship [Speer told the court] differed in one fundamental point from all its predecessors in history. His was the first dictatorship in the present period of modern technical development, a dictatorship which made complete use of all technical means for the domination of its own country.

Through technical devices like the radio and the loud-speaker, eighty million people were deprived of independent thought. It was thereby possible to subject them to the will of one man. . . .

Earlier dictators needed highly qualified assistants, even at the lowest level, men who could think and act independently. The totalitarian system in the period of modern technical development can dispense with them; the means of communication alone make it possible to mechanize the lower leadership. As a result of this there arises the new type of the uncritical recipient of orders. . . . Another result was the far-reaching supervision of the citizens of the State and the maintenance of a high degree of secrecy for criminal acts.

---

[19] Henderson, p. 71.

*The nightmare of many a man that one day nations could be domi-
nated by technical means was all but realized in Hitler's totalitarian system.*[20]

In making use of the formidable power which was thus placed in
his hands Hitler had one supreme, and fortunately rare, advantage:
he had neither scruples nor inhibitions. He was a man without roots,
with neither home nor family; a man who admitted no loyalties, was
bound by no traditions, and felt respect neither for God nor man.
Throughout his career Hitler showed himself prepared to seize any
advantage that was to be gained by lying, cunning, treachery, and
unscrupulousness. He demanded the sacrifice of millions of German
lives for the sacred cause of Germany, but in the last year of the
war was ready to destroy Germany rather than surrender his power
or admit defeat.

Wary and secretive, he entertained a universal distrust. He admitted no one to his counsels. He never let down his guard, or gave
himself away. "He never," Schacht wrote, "let slip an unconsidered
word. He never said what he did not intend to say and he never
blurted out a secret. Everything was the result of cold calculation."[21]

*   *   *

. . . Cynical though he was, Hitler's cynicism stopped short of
his own person: he came to believe that he was a man with a mission,
marked out by Providence, and therefore exempt from the ordinary
canons of human conduct.

Hitler probably held some such belief about himself from an early
period. It was clear enough in the speech he made at his trial in 1924,
and after he came out of prison those near him noticed that he began
to hold aloof, to set a barrier between himself and his followers. After
he came to power it became more noticeable. It was in March 1936
that he made the famous assertion already quoted: "I go the way
that Providence dictates with the assurance of a sleep-walker."[22] In
1937 he told an audience at Würzburg:

However weak the individual may be when compared with the omnipotence

---

[20] Final statement by Speer (N.P., Part XXII, pp. 406–7).
[21] Schacht, p. 219.
[22] Hitler's speech at Munich, 15 March 1936.

and will of Providence, yet at the moment when he acts as Providence would have him act he becomes immeasurably strong. Then there streams down upon him that force which has marked all greatness in the world's history. And when I look back only on the five years which lie behind us, then I feel that I am justified in saying: That has not been the work of man alone.[23]

Just before the occupation of Austria, in February 1938, he declared in the Reichstag:

Above all, a man who feels it his duty at such an hour to assume the leadership of his people is not responsible to the laws of parliamentary usage or to a particular democratic conception, but solely to the mission placed upon him. And anyone who interferes with this mission is an enemy of the people.[24]

It was in this sense of mission that Hitler, a man who believed neither in God nor in conscience ("a Jewish invention, a blemish like circumcision"), found both justification and absolution. He was the Siegfried come to reawaken Germany to greatness, for whom morality, suffering, and "the litany of private virtues" were irrelevant. It was by such dreams that he sustained the ruthlessness and determination of his will. So long as this sense of mission was balanced by the cynical calculations of the politician, it represented a source of strength, but success was fatal. When half Europe lay at his feet and all need of restraint was removed, Hitler abandoned himself entirely to megalomania. He became convinced of his own infallibility. But when he began to look to the image he had created to work miracles of its own accord—instead of exploiting it—his gifts deteriorated and his intuition deluded him. Ironically, failure sprang from the same capacity which brought him success, his power of self-dramatization, his ability to convince himself. His belief in his power to work miracles kept him going when the more skeptical Mussolini faltered. Hitler played out his "world-historical" role to the bitter end. But it was this same belief which curtained him in illusion and blinded him to what was actually happening, leading him into that arrogant overestimate of his own genius which brought him to defeat. The sin which Hitler committed was that which the ancient Greeks

[23] Hitler at Würzburg, 27 June 1937 (Baynes: vol. I, p. 411).
[24] Hitler before the Reichstag, 20 February 1938 (Baynes: vol. II, pp. 1,381–2).

called hybris, the sin of overweening pride, of believing himself to be more than a man. No man was ever more surely destroyed by the image he had created than Adolf Hitler.

Ernst Nolte

INFANTILISM, MONOMANIA, MEDIUMISM

No one is likely to query the statement that Hitler was even more essential to National Socialism than Maurras was to the Action Française or Mussolini to Italian Fascism. He also did not create his movement from nothing, of course, and objective factors of great significance combined with a thousand favorable circumstances to work to his advantage; nevertheless, it is very much easier to imagine Fascism without Mussolini than National Socialism without Hitler.

The fact that right from the start Hitler was a more extreme figure than Mussolini or Maurras is accounted for only in small part by the circumstances and events of his youth. Indeed, there are as many analogies here as deviations.

In common with Maurras and Mussolini, Hitler came from the provincial lower middle class of a Catholic country, although he alone lived under the shadow of the dreaded unknown factor in his family history. He too had a nonbelieving father and a pious and beloved mother. At fourteen he also was a "freethinker," but, unlike Mussolini, he was not offered a coherent system of political faith as a substitute.

As a young man he went to the distant capital to devote himself to an artistic profession; in helpless rage he looked upon the strangeness around him, typified for him—as for Maurras—by the Jew. He became acquainted with poverty and even, like Mussolini, tried begging. But his ideas did not develop, as Maurras's did, under the critical eye of a literary public; he lectured on his weltanschauung to the inmates of men's hostels and shelters for the destitute; he did not, as did Mussolini, receive any vocational training. He left school

From *Three Faces of Fascism,* by Ernst Nolte. Translated by Leila Vennewitz. Copyright © 1965 by R. Piper & Co. Verlag, Munich. Reprinted by permission of Holt, Rinehart and Winston, Inc. and George Weidenfeld and Nicolson Ltd.

early and lived for two years in his mother's house without a job; then, until he was twenty-five, he wandered around Vienna and Munich, eking out a meager living by painting postcards. The Dreyfus affair made a politician out of Maurras—a not entirely unknown writer who enjoyed the esteem of friends who were celebrities; World War I confronted Mussolini, a party leader of considerable standing, with the most important decision of his career; the war was a cataclysmic experience for Hitler too, but even though it brought him for the first time face to face with an overwhelming reality to which he enthusiastically responded, it merely cast him from the nothingness of bourgeois existence into the nothingness of the obscure common soldier, and when in 1918 he decided to enter politics the material foundation of his life was still nothingness.

The differences in the circumstances surrounding their lives were therefore not so much objective facts as the products of differing reactions. Maurras and Mussolini came to terms with the intellectual premises and random happenings of their lives with a similar prompt and clear-cut decisiveness. There were some things to which Hitler did not react at all—hence his inertia, his aimless drifting, his inconsistency—as against others which provoked an extremely sharp reaction. A psychological description of Maurras and Mussolini was superfluous; references to the outstanding intelligence and literary bent of the one, and the "impressionability" of the other, merely served to indicate normal characteristics intensified to a supranormal degree.

Hitler was different. In his case certain dominant traits came to the fore which, although they cannot immediately be dubbed "abnormal," did approach the abnormal and are best described in psychopathological terms. In view of the unchanging nature of character and convictions which Hitler shared with Maurras, it is permissible to cite examples . . . from all periods of his life.

The fact that, according to August Kubizek, the friend of his youth, Hitler's favorite stories were legends of German heroes, that he steeped himself in the world of those ancient times and identified himself with their heroes, was no doubt something he had in common with innumerable boys of his age. The fact that he designed a magnificent house in the Renaissance style for the woman he silently adored from afar merely put him on a level with a smaller group of young men. But that he should plan, down to the last detail, a luxurious apartment for himself and his friend in the firm hope of winning a lottery, that he should mentally engage an "exceptionally refined, elderly lady" as receptionist and tutor for the two art students, that after the disillusionment of the lottery drawing he should passionately and in all seriousness inveigh against the lottery in particular and the world in general—this must have removed him some considerable distance from the majority of even the most fanciful of his age group.

Moreover, this extraordinary capacity for wishful thinking, this mingling of reality and dream, did not diminish with time. Scarcely had one of his companions in a Vienna men's hostel described certain technical plans, of direct concern to him as a future engineer, than Hitler already saw himself part owner of the firm "Greiner & Hitler, Airplane Construction." In *Hitler's Table Talk* (published in America as *Hitler's Secret Conversations*), Hitler speaks of the poverty of that period of his life. "But in my imagination I dwelled in palaces." It was during that time, he said, that he drew up the first plans for the remodeling of Berlin.

There are many witnesses to the fact that during his time of struggle he was already living in the Third Reich, untouched by doubts of any kind, impervious to counsels of moderation, devoid of any desire for sober assessment and calculation. Hermann Rauschning's *Gespräche mit Hitler* provide what is probably the most vivid picture of the utter lack of restraint of this inordinate imagination.

When he was in the throes of remodeling Berlin and Linz, his plans were far from exhausted. The new Reich Chancellery had to be so vast that all would recognize it immediately as the seat of the "master of the world," and by comparison St. Peter's would seem a mere toy. No turn of events in the war could shake the power of this desire, this vision, nor was its force of conviction affected by the fact that this dream was just as divorced from reality as it had been during his youth.

In January 1945, the Gauleiter of Danzig came to Hitler, disheartened and full of defiant resolve to confront Hitler with the whole truth about the desperate situation of his city. He left the room, according to the secretary, a changed man, miraculously cheered and encouraged: the Führer had promised him relief. There was no relief anywhere in sight, but Hitler saw it in his mind's eye and was able to convince a man with perfect vision that he was blind.

As late as March 1945, his secretary saw him standing interminably in front of the wooden model of the future city of Linz. He was still dreaming the dreams of his youth.

The dominant trait in Hitler's personality was infantilism. It explains the most prominent as well as the strangest of his characteristics and actions. The frequently awesome consistency of his thoughts and behavior must be seen in conjunction with the stupendous force of his rage, which reduced field marshals to trembling nonentities. If at the age of fifty he built the Danube bridge in Linz down to the last detail exactly as he had designed it at the age of fifteen before the eyes of his astonished boyhood friend, this was not a mark of consistency in a mature man, one who has learned and pondered, criticized and been criticized, but the stubbornness of the child who is aware of nothing except himself and his mental image and to whom time means nothing because childishness has not been broken and forced into the sober give-and-take of the adult world. Hitler's rage was the uncontrollable fury of the child who bangs the chair because the chair refuses to do as it is told; his dreaded harshness, which nonchalantly sent millions of people to their death, was much closer to the rambling imaginings of a boy than to the iron grasp of a man, and is therefore intimately and typically related to his profound aversion to the cruelty of hunting, vivisection, and the consumption of meat generally.

And how close to the sinister is the grotesque! The first thing Hitler did after being released from the Landsberg prison was to buy a Mercedes for 26,000 marks—the car he had been dreaming of while serving his sentence. Until 1933 he insisted on passing every car on the road. In Vienna alone he had heard *Tristan and Isolde* between thirty and forty times, and had time as chancellor to see six performances of *The Merry Widow* in as many months. Nor was this all. According to Otto Dietrich he reread all Karl May's boys' adventure books during 1933 and 1934, and this is perfectly credible since in *Hitler's Table Talk* he bestowed high praise on this author and credited him with no less than opening his eyes to the world. It is in the conversations related in *Hitler's Table Talk* that he treated his listeners to such frequent and vindictive schoolboy reminiscences that it seems as if this man never emerged from his boyhood and completely lacked the experience of time and its broadening, reconciling powers.

The monomaniacal element in Hitler's nature is obviously closely related to his infantilism. It is based largely on his elemental urge toward tangibility, intelligibility, simplicity. In *Mein Kampf* he expressed the maxim that the masses should never be shown more than *one* enemy. He was himself the most loyal exponent of this precept, and not from motives of tactical calculation alone. He never allowed himself to face more than one enemy at a time; on this enemy he concentrated all the hatred of which he was so inordinately capable, and it was this that enabled him during this period to show the other enemies a reassuring and "subjectively" sincere face. During the crisis in Czechoslovakia he even forgot the Jews over Beneš. His enemy was always concrete and personal, never merely the expression but also the cause of an obscure or complex event. The Weimar system was caused by the "November criminals," the predicament of the Germans in Austria by the Habsburgs, capitalism and Bolshevism equally by the Jews.

A good example of the emergence and function of the clearly defined hate figure, which took the place of the causal connection he really had in mind, is to be found in *Mein Kampf.* Here Hitler draws a vivid picture of the miseries of proletarian existence as he came to know it in Vienna—deserted, frustrated, devoid of hope. This description seems to lead inevitably to an obvious conclusion: that these people, if they were not wholly insensible, were bound to be led with compelling logic to the socialist doctrine, to their "lack of patriotism," their hatred of religion, their merciless indictment of the ruling class. It should, however, have also led to a self-critical insight: that the only reason he remained so aloof from the collective emotions of these masses was because he had enjoyed a different upbringing, middle-class and provincial, because despite his poverty he never really worked, and because he was not married. Nothing of the kind! When he was watching spellbound one day as the long column of demonstrating workers wound its way through the streets, his first query was about the "wirepullers." His voracity for reading, his allegedly thorough study of Marxist theories, did not spur him on to cast his gaze beyond the frontier and realize that such demonstrations were taking place in every city in Europe, or to take note of the "rabble-rousing" articles of a certain Mussolini, which he would doubtless have regarded as "spiritual vitriol" like those in the *Arbeiterzeitung.*

What Hitler discovered was the many Jewish names among the

leaders of Austrian Marxism, and now the scales fell from his eyes—
at last he saw who it was who, besides the Habsburgs, wanted to wipe
out the German element in Austria. Now he began to preach his conclusions to his first audiences; now he was no longer speaking, as
until recently he had spoken to Kubizek, to hear the sound of his own
voice: he wanted to convince. But he did not have much success. The
management of the men's hostel looked on him as an insufferable
politicizer, and for most of his fellow inmates he was a "reactionary
swine." He got beaten up by workers, and in conversations with
Jews and Social Democrats he was evidently often the loser, being
no match for their diabolical glibness and dialectic. This made the
image of the archenemy appear all the more vivid to him, all the
more firmly entrenched. Thirty years later the most experienced
statesmen took him for a confidence-inspiring statesman after meeting him personally; hard-bitten soldiers found he was a man they
could talk to; educated supporters saw in him the people's social
leader. Hitler himself, however, made the following observations in
the presence of the generals and party leaders around his table:
though Dietrich Eckart had considered that from many aspects
Streicher was a fool, it was impossible to conquer the masses without
such people, . . . though Streicher was criticized for his paper, *Der
Stürmer;* in actual fact Streicher idealized the Jew. The Jew was far
more ignoble, unruly, and diabolical than Streicher had depicted him.

Hitler rose from the gutter to be the master of Europe. There is no
doubt that he learned an enormous amount. In the flexible outer layer
of his personality he could be all things to all men: a statesman to
the statesmen, a commander to the generals, a charmer to women, a
father to the people. But in the hard monomaniacal core of his being
he did not change one iota from Vienna to Rastenburg.

Yet if his people had found that he intended after the war to pro-
hibit smoking and make the world of the future vegetarian it is
probable that even the SS would have rebelled. There are thousands
of monomaniacal and infantile types in every large community, but
they seldom play a role other than among their own kind. These two
traits do not explain how Hitler was able to rise to power.

August Kubizek tells a strange story which there is little reason to
doubt and which sheds as much light on the moment when Hitler decided to enter politics as on the basis and prospects of that decision.
After a performance of *Rienzi* in Linz, Kubizek relates, Hitler had

taken him up to a nearby hill and talked to him with shining eyes and trembling voice of the mandate he would one day receive from his people to lead them out of servitude to the heights of liberty. It seemed as if another self were speaking from Hitler's lips, as if he himself were looking on at what was happening in numb astonishment. Here the infantile basis is once again unmistakable. The identification with the hero of the dramatic opera bore him aloft, erupted from him like a separate being. There were many subsequent occasions testifying to this very process. When Hitler chatted, his manner of talking was often unbearably flat; when he described something, it was dull; when he theorized, it was stilted; when he started up a hymn of hate, repulsive. But time and again his speeches contained passages of irresistible force and compelling conviction, such as no other speaker of his time was capable of producing. These are always the places where his "faith" finds expression, and it was obviously this faith which induced that emotion among the masses to which even the most hostile observer testified. But at no time do these passages reveal anything new, never do they make the listener reflect or exert his critical faculty: all they ever do is conjure up magically before his eyes that which already existed in him as vague feeling, inarticulate longing. What else did he express but the secret desires of his judges when he declared before the People's Court: "The army we have trained is growing day by day, faster by the hour. It is in these very days that I have the proud hope that the hour will come when these unruly bands become battalions, the battalions regiments, the regiments divisions, when the old cockade is raised from the dust, when the old flags flutter again on high, when at last reconciliation takes place before the eternal Last Judgment, which we are prepared to face."

His behavior at a rally has often been described: how, uncertain at first, he would rely on the trivial, then get the feel of the atmosphere for several minutes, slowly establish contact, score a bull's-eye with the right phrase, gather momentum with the applause, finally burst out with words which seemed positively to erupt through him, and at the end, in the midst of thunderous cheering, shout a vow to heaven or, amid breathless silence, bring forth a solemn Amen. And after the speech he was as wet as if he had taken a steambath and had lost as much weight as if he had been through a week's strict training.

He told every rally what it wanted to hear—yet what he voiced was not the trivial interests and desires of the day but the great universal, obvious hopes: that Germany should once again become what it had been, that the economy should function, that the farmer should get his rights, likewise the townsman, the worker, and the employer, that they should forget their differences and become one in the most important thing of all—their love for Germany. He never embarked on discussion, he permitted no heckling, he never dealt with any of the day-to-day problems of politics. When he knew that a rally was in a critical mood and wanted information instead of weltanschauung, he was capable of calling off his speech at the last moment.

There should be no doubt as to the mediumistic trait in Hitler. He was the medium who communicated to the masses their own, deeply buried spirit. It was because of this, not because of his monomaniacal obsession, that a third of his people loved him long before he became chancellor, long before he was their victorious supreme commander. But mediumistic popular idols are usually simpletons fit for ecstasy rather than fulfillment. In the turmoil of postwar Germany it would have been *impossible* to love Hitler had not monomaniacal obsession driven the man on and infantile wishful thinking carried him beyond the workaday world with its problems and conflicts. Singly, any one of these three characteristics would have made Hitler a freak and a fool; combined, they raised him for a brief time to be lord and master of his troubled era.

A psychological portrait of Hitler such as this must, however, give rise to doubts in more ways than one. Does the portrait not approach that overpolemical and oversimplified talk of the "madman" or the "criminal"? There is no intention of claiming that this represents a clinical diagnosis. It is not even the purpose of this analysis to define and categorize Hitler as an "infantile mediumistic monomaniac." What has been discussed is merely the existence of infantile, mediumistic, and monomaniacal traits. They are not intended to exhaust the nature of the man Hitler, nor do they of themselves belong to the field of the medically abnormal. Rather do they represent individually an indispensable ingredient of the exceptional. There can be few artists without a streak of infantilism, few ideological politicians without a monomaniacal element in their make-up. It is not so much the potency of each element singly as the combination of all three which gives Hitler his unique face. Whether this combination is pathological in the clinical sense is very doubtful, but there can be no doubt that it excludes historical greatness in the traditional sense.

A second objection is that the psychological description prevents the sociological typification which from the point of view of history is so much more productive. Many attempts have been made to understand Hitler as typical of the angry petit bourgeois. The snag in this interpretation is that it cannot stand without a psychologizing adjective and almost always suggests a goal which is obviously psychological as well as polemical. What this theory tries to express is that Hitler was "actually only a petit bourgeois," in other words, something puny and contemptible. But it is precisely from the psychological standpoint that the petit bourgeois can best be defined as the normal image of the "adult": Hitler was exactly the reverse. What is correct, however, is that, from the sociological standpoint, bourgeois elements may be present in an entirely nonbourgeois psychological form. It remains to be shown how very petit bourgeois was Hitler's immediate reaction to Marxism. However, it was only by means of that "form" which cannot be deduced by sociological methods that his first reaction underwent its momentous transformation.

The third objection is the most serious. The historical phenomenon of National Socialism might be considered overparticularized if it is based solely on the unusual, not to say abnormal, personality of one man. Does not this interpretation in the final analysis even approach that all too transparent apologia which tries to see in Hitler, and only in him, the *"causa efficiens* of the whole sequence of events"? But this is not necessarily logical. It is only from one aspect that the infantile person is more remote from the world than other people; from another aspect he is much closer to it. For he does not dredge up the stuff of his dreams and longings out of nothing; on the contrary, he compresses the world of his more normal fellow men, sometimes by intensifying, sometimes by contrasting. From the complexity of life, monomaniacal natures often wrest an abstruse characteristic, quite frequently a comical aspect, but at times a really essential element. However, the mediumistic trait guarantees that nothing peripheral is compressed, nothing trivial monomaniacally grasped. It is not that a nature of this kind particularizes the historical, but that this nature is itself brought into focus by the historical. Although far from being a true mirror of the times—indeed, it is more of a monstrous distortion—nothing goes into it that is pure invention; and what does go into it arises from certain traits of its own. Hitler sometimes compared himself to a magnet which attracted all that was brave and heroic; it would probably be more accurate to say that certain extreme characteristics of the era attracted this nature like magnets, to become in that personality even more extreme and visible. Hence . . . there [should] be little mention of Hitler's psyche, but all the more of the conditions, forces, and trends of his environment to which he stood in some relationship. For whether he merely interpreted these conditions or intervened in them, whether he placed himself on the side of these forces or opposed them, whether he let himself be borne along by these trends or fought them: something of this force or this trend never failed to emerge in extreme form. In this sense Hitler's nature may be called a historical substance.

Robert G. L. Waite
GUILT FEELINGS AND PERVERTED SEXUALITY

A major problem in dealing with the life of Adolf Hitler is that of determining the extent to which he had confidence in himself as a person and as a political leader. This essay will discuss one aspect of his remarkably complex personality and will show that one of history's most ruthless rulers was beset by feelings of guilt and the need for self-punishment.

In public and private speech, Hitler revealed his concern by talking repeatedly about unworthiness, guilt, and conscience. He worried, for example, about his own worthiness in the sight of God and attempted to quiet his doubts in two ways. He protested too much that

From Robert G. L. Waite, "Adolf Hitler's Guilt Feelings: A Problem in History and Psychology," *The Journal of Interdisciplinary History* 1 (Winter 1971): 229–249, by permission of *The Journal of Interdisciplinary History* and The M.I.T. Press, Cambridge, Massachusetts. Copyright © 1971 by the Massachusetts Institute of Technology. Footnotes omitted.

he really was worthy, saying, typically, "The Great Judge of all time . . . will always give victory to those who are the most worthy [*würdig*]." And again, "I carry my heavy burdens with dutiful thanks to Providence which has deemed me *worthy*. . . ." Another way of silencing his own doubts was to insist that, while he certainly was worthy, others were not. Thus the Jews were unworthy to be citizens of his Reich and must die. By 1945 he reached the conclusion that the entire German people had proved unworthy of him; they too should perish.

Over and over again he showed that he was bothered by conscience and felt the need of dulling its demands:

> *Only when the time comes when the race is no longer overshadowed by the* consciousness of its own guilt *then will it find internal peace.*

> Conscience *is a Jewish invention. It is a blemish like circumcision.* . . .

> *I am freeing men from* . . . *the* dirty and degrading *modification of a chimera called* conscience and morality.

> *We must distrust the intelligence and the* conscience. . . .

> *We must be ruthless* . . . *we must regain our* clear conscience *as to ruthlessness. . . . Only thus shall we* purge our people.

Hitler was even convinced that dogs suffer from a "bad conscience."

The Führer felt guilty about something. But when a historian attempts to give the precise reasons for those guilt feelings, he is reminded again of Trevelyan's trenchant admonition to those who would try to make of history a science: "in the most important part of its business, history is . . . an imaginative guess."

Aided by the insights of psychoanalysis, let us set forth here our best guesses as to the causes of Hitler's feelings of guilt. One possibility can quickly be eliminated. Hitler felt no remorse whatever over the calculated murder of millions of "racially inferior" people, or the holocaust of war, or the annihilation of the village of Lidice, or the planned destruction of the Fatherland and the burning of Paris, or the squandered lives of young German soldiers. Atrocities did not disturb Hitler. Other guesses are needed.

Hitler seems to have felt unworthy of being the Führer of a racially pure Germany because he suspected that he himself might have been "guilty of having Jewish blood"—as the barbarous expression ran in the Third Reich. He had been so shaken in 1930 when he heard dark hints that his own grandfather might have been a Jew that he sent his personal lawyer, Hans Frank, to investigate. Frank's report was not reassuring. It said that Hitler's father was born out of wedlock to a certain Maria Anna Schicklgruber who had worked as a domestic in Graz, Austria, "in the home of a Jewish family by the name of Frankenberger." That Frank's investigations may have been in error does not alter the crucial fact that Hitler *believed that they might be correct* and was haunted by the fear that he himself might be "part Jewish." He testified to this fear in various ways. He took special pains to dictate the precise language of the Nuremberg Racial Laws of 1935 and gave orders that not one word should be changed. The wording of Article 3 is particularly interesting. Of all the civil disabilities for Jews he might have ordered, he set forth this one: "Jews may not employ female household servants of German or related blood who are under 45 years of age." Hitler's own grandmother had been forty-two when she gave birth to Hitler's father.

Anxiety about a Jewish grandfather was also shown when he projected his own fears onto Matthias Erzberger, a leader of the Center party whom Hitler accused of betraying Germany by accepting the Versailles treaty: "Matthias Erzberger . . . *the illegitimate son of a servant girl and a Jewish employer,* was the German negotiator who set his name to the document which had the deliberate intention of bringing about the destruction of Germany." The servant girl in a Jewish household was still on his mind years later. In one of his nightly monologues during 1942 he told his entourage about "a country girl who had a place in Nuremberg in the household of Herr Hirsch," who had raped her.

Hitler projected guilt feelings about the impurity of his own blood in another way. He sought to lessen his personal anxiety by universalizing the guilt, saying that all Germans were at fault. Thus he insisted that "*All of us* are suffering from . . mixed, corrupted blood. How can we purify ourselves and make atonement?"

There is further evidence that Hitler suspected his own blood was tainted. Just two months after taking over Austria in March 1938, Hitler had a survey made of the lovely little farming village of Döllersheim—the village where his father had been born and his grandmother buried. The purpose of the survey was to determine the suitability of the area for an artillery range for the German army. The commanding general of Wehrkreis XVII was given orders directly from

Hitler to make the area ready "as soon as possible" for that purpose. The inhabitants were evacuated, the village was demolished by artillery fire, and the graves of the cemetery were rendered unrecognizable. Why? There are thousands of empty acres in this part of Lower Austria. Hitler must have chosen this particular village as an artillery range because he felt a great compulsion to wipe out—quite literally—the suspicion of his own Jewish blood by obliterating the birthplace of his father and the grave of his grandmother whom he considered guilty of contaminating him.

In the so-called "Gestapo Reports" of the Main Archives of the party, there are records of several separate investigations of Hitler's own family background. The most thorough of these inquiries was made in 1942—just prior to the onset of the massacres which killed about 6 million Jews. Why were these special investigations undertaken? Hitler rarely talked about his own family. Why then did he have this remarkable concern about his ancestors unless he was anxiously hoping to prove that he was a "pure Aryan"—or at least as Aryan as his own racial laws required?

Hitler also manifested his concern about "racial contamination" in both his public and private life. Racial purity was, of course, absolutely basic to the whole theory of National Socialism, and in public speeches he often spoke about "blood baths," "the blood order," and "the blood flag." But his concern about blood went beyond that. He worried about his own blood and seems to have been convinced that there was something wrong with it. He became a vegetarian partly because he thought that a vegetable diet would purify his blood. And he regularly got rid of his blood by letting leeches suck it from him. Later, his quack doctor, Theodor Morell, drew it from him, and preserved it in test tubes, so that Hitler could gaze at it apprehensively.

The feeling that his own blood was impure contributed to his sense of unworthiness and inadequacy in performing the role of mighty Führer of a racially pure Reich. Hence he often looked anxiously into a mirror and asked his valet for assurance, saying, "I really do look like the Führer. Don't I, Linge?" As a young man he had been teased about looking Jewish, and the suggestion continued to bother him.

Hitler also seems to have felt guilty about incestuous desires. His relations with both his mother and his niece were very close indeed, and the word incest was often on his mind. Whether or not he actually

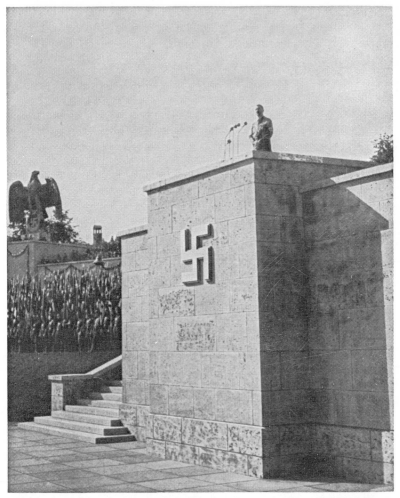

FIGURE 4. Alone at Last. With a cast of millions Hitler staged the most epic production in history. Might it all have been different had this one man never existed? (*Library of Congress*)

acted out his incestuous feelings is not very important psychologically. As Freud showed us long ago, fantasies can be as psychically formative as realities.

It is also possible that acute feelings of unworthiness, guilt, and self-loathing were a consequence of a massively masochistic sexual perversion. Hitler gained sexual satisfaction by having a young woman—as much younger than he as his mother was younger than his father—squat over him to urinate or defecate on his head.

When confronted with data such as these, a biographer of Adolf Hitler has at least three options. He can ignore such evidence as sensational, embarrassing, and quite beneath the dignity of a serious historian. He can use some of the data selectively as unusual sidelights, showing the eccentricities of his subject. Or he can try to show how a discussion of Hitler's psychological abnormalities had historical consequences and can help in a fuller understanding of him as a person. With appropriate trepidation—and trepidation is certainly appropriate here—let us suggest some historical results in Hitler's personal feelings of guilt and unworthiness.

Most obviously, he sought relief from his burden of guilt by an elaborate system of defenses. Indeed he displayed virtually all the major mechanisms Anna Freud has described in her classical work on the subject. He relied heavily, for example, upon reaction formation. Thus his perversion and voyeurism were masked behind ostentatiously prudish behavior. He appeared a moral and ascetic person who forbade the telling of off-color stories in his presence, who did not swear, who denied himself alcohol and tobacco, and who objected when women wore lipstick. He complained that it was manufactured from French urine. He showed that he was disturbed by the filth of his perversion in the number of times the words urine, filth, and dirt were on his mind, saying, typically, that he would free men from "the dirty and degrading" aspects of conscience, or that Jews were "filthy," "unclean," "like a maggot in a rotting corpse." His reaction formation against filth was appropriately extreme and took the form of excessive cleanliness. He washed his hair at least once a day, bathed and changed his underwear twice daily, and scrubbed his hands frequently. He was greatly concerned about his body odors. One of the reasons he became a vegetarian was because— like Benjamin Franklin—he believed that eating meat increased the objectionable odor of flatulation, a chronic complaint of Hitler's which he sought to alleviate by taking enormous quantities of "Dr. Köster's Antigas Pills." These efforts to make his body odors less objectionable were linked to his fear that he might be part Jewish. Jews, he insisted, had a peculiar and objectionable odor.

Hitler also sought to lessen his feelings of guilt through self-punishment—hence his abstentious habits and the masochism of his perversion. It is even conceivable that he actually punished himself physically to the point of partial self-castration. And time and again he promised to commit suicide, the ultimate masochistic dissolution. Among the many childish games he played was a form of substitute suicide. Hitler disliked tying his own necktie and ordered his valet to do it for him. He would hold his breath during the process and count slowly to ten. If Linge could finish the knot before Hitler had finished counting, the Führer was greatly relieved.

Adolf Hitler also indulged in a form of self-punishment which may have had important historical consequences. As McRandle was first to suggest, Hitler punished himself by unconscious desires for failure and defeat. Of course, his life can be seen quite differently, as a re-markable success story, with an unlikely hero played by a neurotic dropout of Linz and Vienna who had failed in all his undertakings and been jailed at the start of his political career, but who, within a decade, became the master of Germany and then arbiter of Europe. Historians are clearly justified in dwelling on Hitler's extraordinary gifts and brilliant victories. And yet there is a curious pattern of behavior that also needs to be noted in attempting to understand this very complex personality. Throughout his life, Adolf Hitler flirted with failure and involved himself unnecessarily in situations that were fraught with danger to himself and his movement.

During his first years in elementary school, Adolf had had an excellent record, but he failed to get a diploma from Realschule and ran away to Vienna. He failed his first examination for the academy of art, and, when given a second chance, he did not apply himself and failed a second time. His first bid for power in 1923 shows a similar pattern of choosing the alternatives least likely to succeed. Through-out the summer of 1923 he made no plans for seizing political power. He gratuitously insulted the leading military figures of Bavaria and Germany, Generals Franz Ritter von Epp, Otto von Lossow, and Hans von Seeckt—men whose support or neutrality was indispensable to him if he planned a coup. Having failed to make preparations, he suddenly called forth a great national revolution which had no chance of success, loudly promising either total victory or suicide. Instead, he ran away and hid in the summer home of a Harvard graduate, "Putzi" Hanfstaengl. Arrested and confronted by political disaster, he extricated himself by brilliant demogoguery.

Hitler's record during the "seizure of power" in 1920–1933 is usually considered brilliant, perhaps because it was successful. And surely there were signs of both enormous energy and political acumen. But there is also evidence of political mistakes so glaring as to suggest an unconscious desire for failure. He went out of his way, for example, to alienate the one great political force he needed to mollify, and ran for the presidency against President Field-Marshal Paul von Hindenburg. Hitler's success in 1933 was due at least as much to the stupidities and failures of Weimar's political leaders as it was to his own efforts.

Similarly, however one interprets his foreign policy, it can be viewed as an invitation to disaster. Three differing interpretations may be considered. First, if A. J. P. Taylor is right in insisting that all Hitler really wanted was a negotiated revision of Versailles, then the methods he employed to attain that end were indeed "singularly inappropriate." Second, if we are to suppose that Hitler wanted only a limited war against Poland to gain Danzig and the corridor, certainly his bellicose speeches against the Western powers, his atrocities against the Jews and other minorities, and his broken promises to Chamberlain show him proceeding in ways unlikely to isolate Poland and most likely to assure his victim of strong allies. Finally, let us suppose he really plotted the great war of European conquest that he had promised in *Mein Kampf,* again in 1925, in his second book of 1928, and in a dozen speeches. If so, he made inadequate preparations for fighting such a war. He got himself involved in a general conflict against the Western powers and still promised total victory or total destruction. Once more, largely through intuition, skill, and luck, he was victorious in the West. Then he decided to attack Russia at the very time that it was trying desperately to appease him by shipping Germany thousands of tons of supplies. While his offensive against the USSR faltered and failed, Hitler suddenly declared war on the United States, the greatest industrial power on earth. Thus it was Hitler who took the initiative in bringing about the kind of global war he could not conceivably win. And during those titanic years from 1941–1944 Hitler dawdled and dithered over the crucial question of a war economy for Germany. Economic mobilization was not really declared until the autumn of 1944, that is, until well after "Fortress Europa" had been breached from the West and Russia was counterattacking along a thousand miles of the Eastern front. Only then, when it was much too late, did Hitler hesitatingly move in the direction of full economic mobilization. But he could never bring himself to give clear orders for a complete war economy.

In the end, as he had done so often in his life, he ran away and hid, this time in his air-raid shelter in Berlin. He killed himself by taking poison and having his bride perform the coup de grâce.

Throughout his career, Hitler seldom contemplated a line of action without thinking of defeat. The disjunctives which characterized his thought almost invariably included the possibility of failure and of suicide. Typically, in the midst of the Beer Hall Putsch, he turned to Gustav von Kahr, Lossow, and Hans von Seisser and said, "You must be victorious with me or die with me. If things go wrong, I have four bullets in my pistol: three for my fellow workers if they desert me, the last bullet is for me." He contemplated failure and suicide on many other occasions: while hiding at the Hanfstaengl summer home in 1923; upon his arrival in 1924 at Landsberg; in 1931 after the suicide of his niece, "Geli" Raubal; in 1932 if he were not appointed chancellor; in 1936 if the occupation of the Rhineland failed; and on many other occasions.

Even at the very height of prewar success he was concerned about failure. On November 10, 1938, for example, he addressed the German press in what should have been a moment of triumph. His first big pogrom against the Jews in the *Kristallnacht* had been executed with the acquiescence of the German people. During the preceding months he had enjoyed a series of other victories: the reintroduction of universal military training; the reoccupation of the Rhineland; the highly successful plebiscite approving his withdrawal from the League of Nations; Anschluss with Austria; and most recently the triumph of the Munich agreement. And yet his speech of November 10 is studded with foreboding. The words *Angst, Rückschlag, Niederlage,* and *Misserfolg* were very much on his mind:

> *I must tell you that I often have one single* misgiving . . . *I become almost anxious. . . . I have had nothing but successes, but what would happen if I were to suffer a* failure? *Yes, Gentlemen, even that can happen. . . . How would [the masses] act if we ever had a* failure? *Formerly, Gentlemen, it was my greatest pride that I built up a party that* even in time of defeat *stood behind me. . . .*

Certainly in sending first his lawyer and then the Gestapo to investigate the racial purity of his own family he was taking an enormous risk. Psychologically he had based his very identity as a person on the projection of his own feelings of guilt, inadequacy, failure, and perversion onto the Jews; politically, he had staked his entire career on the principle of Aryan superiority and the terrible threat of the "Jewish Peril" from which he was defending Western civilization. If his investigators had found that Hitler's own grandfather had been a Jew, he could have been ruined by this disaster to both his psyche and his life work.

Incidents surrounding the launching of World War II also suggest preoccupation with prospects of failure. Albert Speer recalls that on the night of August 24, 1939, when Hitler's pact with Stalin—which gave him a free hand to attack the West—was announced, the Führer met with a small group of intimates at his "Eagle's Nest" overlooking Berchtesgaden. The group stood out on the balcony to watch a spectacular display of northern lights as they pulsated and throbbed above the Bavarian Alps. The dominant color was red, and the skies and mountains and the faces and hands of the watchers were washed in scarlet. Hitler saw an omen in the eery and foreboding light. He turned apprehensively to his military aide and said: "This time *we won't make it* without using force."

The complexities and contradictions of Hitler's personality are shown clearly in his conduct of the war. He displayed a great capacity for innovation in his use of armor and airpower; and his military campaigns against Poland and the West were smashing triumphs. Further, Hitler's successes as a tactician were, in the early years of the war, matched by remarkable strategic insight. Indeed, a distinguished British military analyst has concluded that "no strategist in history has been more clever in playing on the minds of his opponents—which is the supreme art of strategy."

All this is true. Hitler, it bears repeating, could act with devastating effectiveness, and his military abilities and victories should not be disparaged. Yet here too are suggestions that his remarkable career was beset by unconscious desires to punish himself in the very midst of success. There was the curious refusal to press his advantage at Dunkirk. There was the long hesitation and inaction after the fall of France—a time when "the wave of conquest broke on the shoals of delay and indecision." Month after month during the critical summer of 1940, Hitler continued to violate the cardinal principle of Clausewitz, an authority he had studied so avidly: "Once the great victory

is gained there should be no talk of rest, of getting breath, or of consolidation, etc., but only of pursuit . . . of attacking. . . ."

Instead of concentrating his forces against his only remaining
enemy, an isolated and desperately wounded England, Hitler turned
to court his Nemesis. He sent his armies—without winter issue—
marching into Russia. That he set the date for invasion in 1941 on the
precise anniversary of Napoleon's ill-fated campaign (June 22) is perhaps coincidental, but why did he choose the code name of "Barbarossa"? It is true that Hitler saw himself, like Frederick Barbarossa,
as a crusader whose mission it was to destroy an infidel Eastern
enemy; but, as an avid reader of history, Hitler knew that the most
notable thing about Barbarossa was that he was a failure. He had
failed in five campaigns against the Lombard towns; he had failed to
centralize the Holy Roman Empire; he had failed to obtain his objectives during the Third Crusade. And he had died by drowning. Adolf
Hitler was pathologically afraid of the water, and had nightmares
about loss of breath and strangulation. Moreover, the words Hitler
used in announcing the invasion of Russia are worth remembering.
"The world," he said, "will hold its breath." When Adolf Hitler held
his breath and counted to ten while his valet tied his tie, he was
symbolically enacting suicide and self-destruction.

Hitler also sought to dull his feelings of guilt by a kind of "introjec-
tion" in which he took upon himself the role of a great moral and religious leader. He saw himself as a messiah who was establishing a
new religion and leading a great crusade against the cosmic forces
of evil, that is, the incarnate evil of "the international Jewish conspiracy." It is not surprising, therefore, to find Hitler very seriously
comparing himself to Jesus. He said on one occasion, as he lashed
about him with a whip, "In driving out the Jews I remind myself of
Jesus in the temple"; and on another, "Like Christ, I have a duty to
my own people. . . ." He considered himself betrayed by Ernst Röhm
in 1934 and drew the analogy to the betrayal of Jesus, saying, "Among
the twelve apostles, there was also a Judas. . . ."

That he saw himself as the special agent of God and identified with
Him was made manifest on many occasions:

> *I go the way that Providence dictates for me with all the assurance of a
> sleepwalker.*

God has created this people and it has grown according to His will. And according to our will [nach unserem Willen] it shall remain and never shall it pass away.

I believe that it was God's will that from her [Austria] a boy was sent into the Reich and that he grew up to become the Leader of the nation.

By warding off the Jews, I am fighting for the Lord's work.

Hitler patterned the organization of his party and his Reich after the Roman Catholic church, which had impressed him so much as a young boy. He saw himself as a political pope with an apostolic succession when he announced to a closed meeting of the faithful in the Brown House during 1930, "I hereby set forth for myself and my successors in the leadership of the National Socialist Democratic Party the claim of political infallibility. I hope the world will grow as accustomed to that claim as it has to the claim of the Holy Father." The oath of direct obedience to the Führer was strikingly reminiscent of the special oath the Jesuits swore to the pope, and Hitler spoke of his elite SS, who wore the sacred *⚡⚡* and dressed in black, as a Society of Jesus, from which, he said, he had learned so much.

The bolts of excommunication and anathema which Hitler hurled against nonbelievers and heretics were not unlike those of a Gregory VII:

Woe to them who do not believe. These people have sinned . . . against all of life. . . . It is a miracle of faith that Germany has been saved. Today more than ever it is the duty of the Party to remember this National Socialist Confession of Faith [Glaubensbekenntnis] and to bear it forward as our holy [heiliges] sign of our battle and our victory.

Hitler chose a cross as the symbol and sign of his movement.

The Nazis, like the Catholics, had their prophets, saints, and martyrs. Hitler's followers who fell during the Beer Hall Putsch were sanctified by Hitler when he said, in dedicating their memorial, that their death would bring forth "a true belief in the Resurrection of their people . . . the blood that they shed has become the baptismal water of the Third Reich." The annual Nazi march on November 9 from the Bürgerbraükeller to the Feldherrnhalle was a studied reenactment of the stations of the cross combined with the Passion Play. The analogy was made clear by the stress on "the blood that was shed for the redemption of the Fatherland."

Hitler's holy reliquary was the Brown House which contained the sacred Blood Flag which had been born by the martyrs of November 9. It was Hitler and Hitler alone who could perform the priestly ritual of touching the Blood Flag to the standards of the Brownshirts.

Hitler substituted Nazi high holy days for traditional religious holidays. They included January 30, the day Hitler came to power in the year he referred to as "the Holy Year of our Lord, 1933," and April 20, the leader's own birthday and the day when the Hitler Youth were confirmed in the faith. The holiest day, however, and one which served as a kind of Nazi Good Friday was November 9, celebrated as the Blood Witness [*Blutzeugen*] of the movement.

Religions require devils. For National Socialism, the Jewish people played that part, and Hitler insisted that the German people could achieve salvation only after they had destroyed the Jew who was, in Hitler's words, *"the personification of the Devil"* and the "symbol of all evil." The concept was made unmistakably vivid in the childish rhyme:

> *Wer kennt den Jude*
> *Kennt den Teufel.*

Hitler also provided a sacred book for his new religion, and *Mein Kampf* replaced the Bible as the traditional wedding present given to all young Aryans. The close parallel between Christian commitment to God and the sacred oath of allegiance to Hitler is best seen in a description of public oath-taking recorded in the Nazi newspaper, *Westdeutscher Beobachter:* "Yesterday witnessed the profession of the Religion of the Blood in all its imposing reality. . . . Whoever has sworn his oath of allegiance to Hitler has pledged himself unto death to this sublime idea."

It is true that Hitler sometimes told his intimates that he did not wish to be deified, but he did little to stop his followers from exalting him as savior and messiah. Indeed, he directly approved the patent paganism and Führer worship of the Warthegau church as a model for the church he planned after the war. And he did not object to the following version of the Lord's Prayer which was recited by the League of German Girls:

> *Adolf Hitler, you are our great leader*
> *Thy name makes the enemy tremble.*

*Thy Third Reich comes, thy will alone is law
upon earth. Let us hear daily thy voice and
order us by thy leadership, for we will obey
to the end, even with our lives.
We praise thee! Heil Hitler!*

It is to be noted that prayers were given not only for the Führer, but to him as a deity.

In speeches and soliloquies, and in ways he may not have been aware, Hitler himself spoke in the very words of Christ and the scriptures—thereby revealing a considerable knowledge of the Bible. A few examples will suffice here: in dedicating the House of German Art in Munich he observed, "Man does not live by bread alone." In talking to the Brownshirts on January 30, 1936, he echoed the words of Jesus to his disciples as recorded in St. John's Gospel, saying, "I have come to know thee. Who thou art, thou art through me, and all I am, I am through thee." He reminded one of his disciples that "I have not come to Germany to bring peace but a sword." In a public speech in Graz in 1938 he announced, "God Almighty has created the Nation. And what the Lord has joined together let not Man set asunder."

He was particularly prone to Biblical quotations when talking to the Hitler Youth. On September 5, 1934, he told them, "You are flesh of our flesh and blood of our blood." In 1932 he advised them either to be "hot or cold, but the lukewarm should be damned and spewed from your mouth." The phrasing is too close to the New Testament to be coincidental. The Revelation of St. John reads: "I know thy works, that thou art neither cold nor hot; I would thou wert cold or hot. So then, because thou art lukewarm, and neither cold nor hot, I will spew thee out of my mouth."

During one of the last suppers with his followers, Hitler invited them to eat of their leader's body, asking them if they would like some blood sausage made from his own blood. In effect he was saying, "Take, eat: this is my body, which is broken for you. . . ."

The defense mechanism used by Adolf Hitler that had the greatest historical consequence was that of projection. Hitler made his own feelings of guilt more bearable by shifting the finger of guilt away from himself and pointing it at Jews. Allport has given a succinct description of the process and has shown the connection between guilt and self-hatred with the need for projection:

> *The hated scapegoat is merely a disguise for persistent and unrecognized self-hatred. A vicious circle is established. The more the sufferer hates himself, the more he hates the scapegoat, the less sure he is of his . . . innocence; hence the more guilt he has to project.*

It needs to be emphasized that in Hitler's case both the degree of self-hatred and the corresponding amount of projected hatred were of truly monumental proportions. He hated Jews for many reasons and accused them of every conceivable crime. But never did he become "so emotional, so arbitrary and so absurd" as when he fulminated against Jewish sex crimes, incest, and perversion—precisely those sexual aberrations about which he felt personally so guilty. The direct projection onto the Jews of guilt felt as the result of his own perversions is shown in an incident in 1938 involving the dismissal of General Werner von Blomberg as minister of defense. Hitler expressed outraged shock at the disclosure that the general had married a former prostitute. He used the scandal as an excuse for dismissing an uncooperative general, and had the Gestapo collect incriminating evidence against Frau General Blomberg. They supplied him with photographs which showed her plying her profession by participating in various forms of deviant sexual activity. A man who has seen the photographs says that they were of "the most shocking depravity." What concerns us here is Hitler's instinctive reaction upon first seeing the pictures. He said at once that the male partner in the photographs "*must have been* of Jewish extraction." He then became "absolutely convulsed by the wildest anti-Semitic outpouring he had ever given vent to in his entire life."

Thus did the Jews become the hated personal enemy of Hitler and his Reich. In destroying the Jewish people, Adolf Hitler was not only "doing the work of the Lord." He was destroying the evil thing which he felt within himself. This would seem to be the meaning of the curious comment he once made to Rauschning: "The Jew is always within us" [*Der Jude sitzt immer in uns*].

The historical importance of this projection is clear: the racial anti-Semitism which lay at the very core of German fascism and which produced the greatest mass horror of history was, among other things, a direct consequence of Adolf Hitler's personal feelings of guilt and self-hatred.

Peter Loewenberg
THE APPEAL TO YOUTH

The historical relationship between the events of World War I and its catastrophic aftermath in Central Europe and the rise of National Socialism has often been postulated. The causal relationship is usually drawn from the savagery of trench warfare on the western front, the bitterness of defeat and revolution, to the spectacular series of National Socialist electoral victories beginning in 1930, as if such a relationship were historically self-evident. It is the thesis of this paper that the relationship between the period from 1914 to 1920 and the rise and triumph of National Socialism from 1929 to 1935 is specifically generational. The war and postwar experiences of the small children and youth of World War I explicitly conditioned the nature and success of National Socialism. The new adults who became politically effective after 1929 and who filled the ranks of the SA and other paramilitary party organizations such as the Hitler-Jugend and the Bund-Deutscher-Madel were the children socialized in the First World War.

This essay examines what happened to the members of this generation in their decisive period of character development—particularly in early childhood—and studies their common experiences in childhood, in psychosexual development, and in political socialization that led to similar fixations and distortions of adult character. The specific factors that conditioned this generation include the prolonged absence of the parents, the return of the father in defeat, extreme hunger and privation, and a national defeat in war, which meant the loss of the prevailing political authority and left no viable replacement with which to identify.

Most explanations for the rise of National Socialism stress elements of continuity in German history. These explanations point to political, intellectual, social, diplomatic, military, and economic factors, all of which are important and none of which should be ignored. The historian and social scientist studying Nazism should be conversant with and well versed in these categories of explanation.

From Peter Loewenberg, "The Psychohistorical Origins of the Nazi Youth Cohort," *American Historical Review* 76, no. 5 (December 1971). Reprinted by permission of the author. Footnotes edited.

The study of political leadership is also of unquestioned importance for the understanding of the dynamics of totalitarianism, and it should be intensively developed by historians as an approach to that understanding.

This essay, however, will focus not on the leader but on the followers, not on the charismatic figure but rather on the masses who endow him with special superhuman qualities. It will apply psychoanalytic perceptions to the problem of National Socialism in German history in order to consider the issues of change rather than continuity in history, to deal with social groups rather than individual biography, and to focus on the ego-psychological processes of adaptation to the historical, political, and socioeconomic context rather than on the instinctual biological drives that all men share.

The rapid political ascendancy of the NSDAP in the period from 1928 to 1933 was marked by particularly strong support from youth. Since this generation experienced childhood deprivation in World War I, the argument becomes a psychoanalytical one of taking seriously the developments of infancy and childhood and their effect on behavior in adulthood. I wish to offer an added factor, one to be included as an explanation in addition to rather than instead of the other explanatory schemata of history. Both history and psychoanalysis subscribe to overdetermination in causation. It would be a poor historian who sought to attribute a war or a revolution to only a single cause. Similarly in psychoanalytic theory every symptom and symbol is psychically overdetermined and serves multiple functions. When the subject of study is a modern totalitarian mass movement it requires analysis utilizing all the tools for perceiving and conceptualizing irrational and affective behavior that the twentieth century has to offer, including psychoanalysis and dynamic psychology.

No genuine historical understanding is possible without the perspective of self-understanding from which the historian can then move forth to deal with historical materials. Likewise there can be no measure of historical understanding if we research what men said and did and fail to understand why they acted. The twentieth century has experienced the gross magnification of political and personal irrationality correlative to the exponential increment in the power of modern technology. No history will speak with relevance or accuracy to the contemporary human condition if it fails to assess realistically the profound capacity of the irrational to move men. . . .

FIGURE 5. The Nazi Youth Cohort. Hitler returns the firm look of the generation which would later follow him to disaster. Behind the Führer, also hatless, are Rudolf Hess and Hitlerjugend-leader Baldur von Schirach. (*Library of Congress*)

Rather than proceeding with the story of the Nazi youth cohort chronologically and beginning with its origins, this essay will use what Marc Bloch termed the "prudently retrogressive" method of looking at the outcome first, and then tracking down the beginnings or "causes" of the phenomenon. This, of course, corresponds to the clinical method of examining the "presenting complaints" first and then investigating etiology. The outcome of the story in this case is the related and concomitant economic depression, the influx of German youth to the ranks of National Socialism, the political decline of the Weimar Republic, and the Nazi seizure of power.

The Great Depression hit Germany harder than any other country, with the possible exception of the United States. Germany's gross national income, which rose by 25 percent between 1925 and 1928, sank 43 percent from 71 billion RM in 1929 to 41 billion RM in 1932. The production index for industry in 1927–1928 was halved by 1932–1933. In the critical area of capital goods, production in 1933 was one-third of what it had been five years earlier. The very aspect of Nazi success at the polls in the elections of 1930 accelerated the withdrawal of foreign capital from Germany, thus deepening the financial crisis.

The greatest social impact of the economic crisis was in creating unemployment. By 1932 one of every three Germans in the labor market was without a job. This meant that even those who held jobs were insecure, for there were numerous workers available to take the place of every employee. The young people were, of course, the most vulnerable sector of the labor market. New jobs were non-existent, and the young had the least seniority and experience with which to compete for employment. To this must be added that the number of apprenticeships was sharply diminishing for working-class youths. For example, apprenticeships in iron, steel, and metal-working declined from 132,000 in 1925 to 19,000 in 1932. University graduates had no better prospects for finding employment. They soon formed an underemployed intellectual proletariat that looked to National Socialism for relief and status.

The electoral ascendancy of the Nazi party in the four years between 1928 and 1932 constitutes one of the most dramatic increments of votes and political power in the history of electoral democracy. In the Reichstag elections of May 20, 1928, the National Socialists received 810,127 votes, constituting 2.6 percent of the total vote and 12 Reichstag seats. In the communal elections of 1929 the Nazis made decisive gains. With this election Germany had its first Nazi minister in Thuringia in the person of Wilhelm Frick, a putschist of 1923. In the next Reichstag elections of September 14, 1930, the National Socialists obtained 6,379,672 votes, for 18.3 percent of the total and 107 seats. At the election of July 31, 1932, the National Socialists became the largest party in the country and in the Reichstag with 13,765,781 votes, giving them 37.4 percent of the total vote and 230 parliamentary seats.

This extremely rapid growth of Nazi power can be attributed to the participation in politics of previously inactive people and of those who were newly enfranchised because they had reached voting eligibility at 20 years of age. There were 5.7 million new voters in 1930. The participation of eligible voters in elections increased from 74.6 percent in 1928 to 81.41 percent in 1930, and 83.9 percent in 1932. In the elections of March 5, 1933, there were 2.5 million new voters over the previous year and voting participation rose to 88.04 percent of the electorate.

The German political sociologist, Heinrich Streifler, makes the point that not only were new, youthful voters added at each election, but there were losses from the voting rolls due to deaths that must be calculated. He shows that 3 million voters died in the period between 1928 and 1933. The increment of first-time, new voters in the same period was 6.5 million.

In the elections of 1928, 3.5 million young voters who were eligible did not participate in the voting. "This," says Streifler, "is a reserve that could be mobilized to a much greater extent than the older non-voters." He goes on to suggest that these young nonvoters were more likely to be mobilized by a radical party that appealed to passions and emotions than to reason.

The Nazis made a spectacular and highly successful appeal to German youth. An official slogan of the party ran "National Socialism is the organized will of youth" *(Nationalsozialismus ist organisierter Jugendwille)*. Nazi propagandists like Gregor Strasser skillfully utilized the theme of the battle of the generations. "Step down, you old ones!" *(Macht Platz, ihr Alten!)* he shouted as he invoked the names of the senior political leaders from Left to Right and associated them with the disappointments of the generation of the fathers and the deprivations of war, defeat, and revolution.

Whether they are named Scheidemann and Wels, whether Dernburg or Koch, whether Bell and Marx, Stresemann and Riesser, whether Hergt and Westarp—they are the same men we know from the time before the war, when they failed to recognize the essentials of life for the German people; we know them from the war years, when they failed in the will to leadership and victory; we know them from the years of revolution, when they failed in character as well as in ability, in the need of an heroic hour, which, if it had found great men, would have been a great hour for the German people—who, however, became small and mean because its leading men were small and mean.

The Nazis developed a strong following among the students, making headway in the universities in advance of their general electoral successes. National Socialism made its first visible breakthrough into a mass sector of the German people with its conquest of academic youth. The student government (ASTA) elections of 1929 were called a "National Socialist storm of the universities" by the alarmed opposition press. The Nazi Student Organization (Nationalsozialistische Deutsche Studentenbund) received more than half the votes and dominated the student government in 1929 at the universities of Erlangen and Greifswald. In the 1930 student election it also captured absolute majorities in the universities of Breslau, Giessen, Rostock, Jena, Königsberg, and the Berlin Technische Hochschule. Both of these student elections preceded the Reichstag elections of 1930 in which the Nazis made their decisive breakthrough into the center of national political life. Developments toward National Socialism among the university students anticipated by four years the developments in German society at large.

The comparative age structure of the Nazi movement also tells a story of youthful preponderance on the extreme Right. According to the Reich's census of 1933, those 18 to 30 constituted 31.1 percent of the German population. The proportion of National Socialist party members of this age group rose from 37.6 percent in 1931 to 42.2 percent a year later, on the eve of power. "The National Socialist party," says the sociologist Hans Gerth, "could truthfully boast of being a 'young party.'" By contrast, the Social Democratic party, second in size and the strongest democratic force in German politics, had only 19.3 percent of its members in the 18 to 30 age group in 1931. In 1930 the Social Democrats reported that less than 8 percent of their membership was under 25, and less than half was under 40.

"National Socialism," says Walter Laqueur, the historian of the German youth movement, "came to power as the party of youth." The Nazi party's ideology and organization coincided with those of the elitist and antidemocratic elements of the German youth movement. The Wandervogel, while essentially nonpolitical, retreated to a rustic life on the moors, heaths, and forests where they cultivated the bonds of group life. The Nazi emphasis on a mystical union of blood and soil, of *Volk,* nation, language, and culture, appealed to the romanticism of German youth *Bünde.*

The Hitler Youth adopted many of the symbols and much of the content of the German youth movement. The Nazis incorporated the uniform, the Führer principle and authoritarian organization (group, tribe, *gau*), the flags and banners, the songs, and the war games of the *Bünde*. The National Socialists were able to take over the youth movement with virtually no opposition. On April 15, 1933, the executive of the Grossdeutsche Jugenbund voted to integrate with the Nazi movement. On June 17, 1933, the Jugenbund was dissolved and Baldur von Schirach was appointed the supreme youth leader by Hitler.

A number of scholars have interpreted the radicalization of newly enfranchised German youth in the years of the rise of National Socialism. The Nazification of the youth has also been variously attributed to the spirit of adventure and idealism, a lust for violence and military discipline, the appeal of an attack on age and established power, and the quest for emotional and material security. . . .

There is ample evidence that this generation of German youth was more inclined toward violent and aggressive, or what psychoanalysts call "acting-out," behavior than previous generations. At this point the explanations offered for this phenomenon are inadequate in their one-dimensionality. To say that the youth craved action or that they sought comfort in the immersion in a sheltering group is to beg the question of what made this generation of German youth different from all previous generations. What unique experiences did this group of people have in their developmental years that could induce regression to infantile attitudes in adulthood? One persuasive answer lies in fusing the knowledge we have of personality functioning from psychoanalysis—the most comprehensive and dynamic theory of personality available to the social and humanistic sciences today—with the cohort theory of generational change from historical demography and with the data on the leadership and structure of the Nazi party that we have from the researches of political scientists, historians, and sociologists.

In the half century prior to World War I Germany was transformed from an agricultural to an industrial economy, and her population grew from an agriculturally self-sufficient 40 million to 77 million by 1913. This mounting industrial population made her increasingly dependent on the importation of foreign foodstuffs. In the decade preceding World War I, five-sixths of Germany's vegetable fats, more than half of her dairy goods, and one-third of the eggs her people consumed were imported. This inability to be self-sufficient in foodstuffs made the German population particularly susceptible to the weapon of the blockade. The civilian population began to feel the pressure of severe shortages in 1916. The winter of 1916–1917 is still known as the infamous "turnip winter," in which hunger and privation became widespread experiences in Germany. Getting something to eat was the foremost concern of most people. The official food rations for the summer of 1917 were 1,000 calories per day, whereas the health ministry estimated that 2,280 calories was a subsistence minimum. From 1914 to 1918 three-quarters of a million people died of starvation in Germany.

The armistice of November 11, 1918, did not bring the relief that the weary and hungry Germans anticipated. The ordeal of the previous three years was intensified into famine in the winter of 1918–1919. The blockade was continued until the Germans turned over their merchant fleet to the Allies. The armistice blockade was extended by the victorious Allies to include the Baltic Sea, thus cutting off trade with Scandinavia and the Baltic states. Although the Allies undertook responsibility for the German food supply under Article 26 of the Armistice Agreement, the first food shipment was not unloaded in Hamburg until March 26, 1919. On July 11, 1919, the Allied Supreme Economic Council decided to terminate the blockade of Germany as of the next day, July 12. Unrestricted trade between the United States and Germany was resumed three days later, on July 15.

The degree of German suffering under the postwar Allied blockade is a matter on which contemporary opinions differed. Some Allied diplomats and journalists charged that the German government exaggerated the plight of her people in order to increase Allied food deliveries. Today the weight of the historical evidence is that there was widespread extreme hunger and malnutrition in the last three years of the war, which was intensified by the postwar blockade. We may concur with the evaluation of two American historians that "the suffering of the German children, women, and men, with the exception of farmers and rich hoarders, was greater under the continued blockade than prior to the Armistice."

Among the documents that Matthias Erzberger, the chairman of the German Armistice Commission in 1918, requested from the Reichsgesundheitsamt (Reich's public health service) was a memorandum discussing the effects of the blockade on the civilian population. The memorandum, entitled "Damage to the Strength of the

German People due to the Enemy Blockade Which Contravenes International Law," was submitted on December 16, 1918. This document is of special psychological interest because it consists of statistics giving increases in deaths, disease, stillbirths, and loss of strength in the labor force, all of which bear sums indicating monetary losses per individual and to the nation. The most remarkable set of figures are those that conclude that, on the basis of a population of 50 million with an average weight of 114.4 pounds, who have each lost one-fifth of their weight, the German people have lost 520,000 tons of human mass (*Menschenmasse*). The memorandum goes on to estimate that 1.56 million to 1,768,000 tons of food would be necessary to restore the flesh (*Fleische*) that had been lost according to the previous calculation.

The demographic and statistical data constitute an overwhelming case that the German civil population, particularly infants and children, suffered widely and intensively during the war and blockade. Public health authorities and medical researchers have compiled population studies indicating damage to health, fertility, and emotions from 1914 to 1920. These are quantifiable indexes of physical deprivation from which the equally damaging but much more difficult to measure facts of emotional deprivation may be inferred.

On the grossest level the figures show a decline in the number of live births from 1,353,714 in 1915 to 926,813 in 1918. The birth rate per 1,000 population, including stillbirths, declined from 28.25 in 1913 to 14.73 in 1918. The number of deaths among the civilian population over one year old rose from 729,000 in 1914 to 1,084,000 in 1918. While there was a decline in deaths from causes related to nutrition and caloric intake, such as diabetes mellitus, alcoholism, obesity, diseases of the gastrointestinal tract, as well as a decrease in suicides, the gross mortality of the German population increased due to malnutrition, lack of heating, and consequent weakened resistance to disease. Specific causes of death that increased sharply during the war were influenza, lung infections and pneumonia, tuberculosis, diseases of the circulatory system, diphtheria, typhus, dysentery, and diseases of the urinary and reproductive organs. All these diseases indicate a population whose biological ability to maintain health and to counter infection had been seriously undermined in the war years.

Upon looking at the comparative statistics for neonates and infants, we find a decline in weight and size at birth, a decline in the ability of mothers to nurse, a higher incidence of disease, particularly rickets and tuberculosis, as well as an increase in neurotic symptoms such as bed-wetting and an increment in the death rate. In the third year of the war the weight of neonates was 50 to 100 grams less at birth than before the war. In one Munich clinic in the year 1918 the females averaged 50 grams and the males 70 grams less at birth than in peacetime.

During the first year of the war more mothers nursed babies and the period of breast feeding was longer than previously, but by the winter of 1915 a decline in breast feeding had set in that was to continue through 1919. This is attributed to the war work of mothers and the "prolonged malnutrition and the damaged body of the mother due to psychic insult." One chemical analysis done in Berlin found a marked decline in the quantity and quality of mother's milk resulting in the retarded development of breast-fed children and a delay in their normal weight gain. Infants fed on cow's milk also received milk that was short of nutriments, butterfat, and vitamins because of the lack of feed for the milk cows and the skimming off of cream for butter production. To the shortage and inferior quality of milk must be added the almost total absence of fresh vegetables and fruit, important sources of vitamins, in the diets of children during the war and postwar period. . . .

World War I was the first total war in history—it involved the labor and the commitment of full energies of its participant peoples as no previous war had. The men were in the armed services, but a modern war requires a major industrial plant and increased production of foodstuffs and supplies to support the armies. Yet the number of men working in industry in Germany dropped 24 percent between 1913 and 1917. In the state of Prussia in 1917 the number of men working in plants employing over ten workers was 2,558,000, including foreigners and prisoners of war, while in 1913 the total of men employed had been 3,387,000.

In Germany this meant a shift of major proportions of women from the home and domestic occupations to war work. In the state of Prussia alone the number of women engaged in industrial labor rose by 76 percent, from 788,100 in 1913 to 1,393,000 in 1917. For Germany as a whole 1.2 million women newly joined the labor force in medium- and large-sized plants during the war. The number of women workers in the armaments industry rose from 113,750 in 1913 to

702,100 in 1917, a gain of 500 percent. The number of women laborers who were covered under compulsory insurance laws on October 1, 1917, was 6,750,000. The increase of adult female workers in Prussia in 1917 was 80.4 percent over 1913. The number of women railroad workers in Prussia rose from 10,000 in 1914 to 100,000 in 1918, an increase of 1,000 percent.

Another new factor in the labor force was the youthful workers. The number of adolescents aged 14 to 16 employed in chemical manufacturing increased 225 percent between 1913 and 1917. For heavy industry the corresponding figure was 97 percent. Many of these were young girls aged 16 to 21. This age group constituted 29 percent of all working women.

That German women were massively engaged in war work was recognized as having resulted in the neglect of Germany's war children and damage to the health of the mothers. Reports came from government offices of increased injuries to children of ages 1 to 5 years due to lack of supervision. S. Rudolf Steinmetz evaluates the demoralization of youth between 1914 and 1918 as an indirect consequence of the war. He ascribes to "the absence of many fathers, the war work of many mothers" the damaged morals and morality of youth.

Many of the war-related phenomena under discussion were not unique to the Central European countries. The factor of a chauvinistic atmosphere of war propaganda was certainly present in all belligerent countries. The absence of the parents in wartime service was also not unique to Germany or Austria. The children of other countries involved in the war too had absent parents and were often orphaned. French and British families undoubtedly experienced the sense of fatherlessness and desertion by the mother as much as did German and Austrian families. Two added factors, however, make the critical difference in the constellation of the child's view of the world: the absence of German and Austrian parents was coupled with extreme and persistent hunger bordering in the cities on starvation, and when the German or Austrian father returned he came in defeat and was unable to protect his family in the postwar period of unemployment and inflation. Not only was the nation defeated, but the whole political-social world was overturned. The kaiser of Germany had fled, and the kaiser of Austria had been deposed. Some Germans would say that the kaiser had deserted his people, to be replaced by

an insecure and highly ambivalent republic under equivocating socialist leadership. Much more than an army collapsed—an entire
orientation to the state and the conduct of civic life was under assault in 1918–1919. These national factors unique to Central Europe
exacerbated the familial crisis of the absence of parents and made
of this wartime experience a generational crisis. . . .

When a child who is struggling with his aggressive and destructive
impulses finds himself in a society at war, the hatred and violence
around him in the outer world meet the as yet untamed aggression
raging in his inner world. At the very age when education is beginning to deal with the impulses in the inner environment the same
wishes receive sanction and validation from a society at war. It is impossible to repress murderous and destructive wishes when fantasied
and actual fighting, maiming, and killing are the preoccupation of all
the people among whom the child lives. Instead of turning away from
the horrors and atrocities of war, he turns toward them with primitive excitement. The very murderous and destructive impulses that he
has been trying to bury in himself are now nourished by the official
ideology and mass media of a country at war.

The power of his aroused inner fantasies of violence is anxiety-
producing for the child. It is as though an inner signal alerts him to
beware of the danger of losing control. When, in addition, the child
is not with his family, he will often develop the symptoms of ner-
vousness, bed-wetting, fecal incontinence, stealing, truancy, and de-
linquency that Winnicott describes.

Many political scientists and historians have pointed to the function of National Socialism as a defense against emotional insecurity.
Harold Lasswell, in contrast to those who have interpreted Hitler as
a father or a son symbol, develops precisely the theme of Hitler's maternal function for the German people, suggesting that Nazism was a
regressive attempt to compensate for mothering and family life that
had been inadequate. Lasswell stresses the imagery of cleanliness
and pollution of the anal phase.

*There is a profound sense in which Hitler himself plays a maternal role
for certain classes in German society. His incessant moralizing is that of
the anxious mother who is totally preoccupied with the physical, intellectual and ethical development of her children. He discourses in public, as
he has written in his autobiography, on all manner of pedagogical problems, from the best form of history teaching to the ways of reducing the*

> *ravages of social disease. His constant preoccupation with "purity" is consistent with these interests; he alludes constantly to the "purity of the racial stock" and often to the code of personal abstinence or moderation. This master of modern Galahadism uses the language of Protestant puritanism and of Catholic reverence for the institution of family life. The conscience for which he stands is full of obsessional doubts, repetitive affirmations, resounding negations and stern compulsions. It is essentially the bundle of "don'ts" of the nursemaid conscience.*

Similarly, research indicates that paternal deprivation in childhood, which assumes increasing importance in later years as the child approaches and works through his Oedipal conflict, also has a profound impact on the personality and ideas of youth concerning father images, political authority, and sources of power. In a study comparing father-separated from father-at-home elementary school children, George R. Bach found that "father separated children produce an idealistic fantasy picture of the father" that "seem[s] to indicate the existence of strong drives for paternal affection." In turn, then, "the severely deprivated [*sic*] drive for paternal affection provides strong instigation for the idealistic, wish-fulfilling fantasies." The absent father is idealized. This is in part a reaction formation—that is, a defense against hatred toward the father by replacing these repressed hostile feelings with their conscious opposite.

Psychoanalytic theory and clinical evidence tell us that prolonged absence of the father results in intensified closeness to the mother. This in turn will heighten Oedipal conflict for the son in latency. Stimulated incestuous fantasies will increase the fear of punishment for the forbidden longings. The sharpened castration anxiety of the boy left alone with his mother results in strengthened identification with the absent idealized father and in homosexual longings for him. The homosexual feelings for the distant father are a love for him shared with the mother and a defense against heightened incestuous feelings for her.

The emancipation of women, which was accelerated greatly in World War I by the needs of a total war economy, gave to women what had been traditionally men's vocational roles and familial responsibilities. In such circumstances, in her own eyes and in the eyes of her children, the woman who works in industry and agriculture is now doing "man's" work. Thus the mother who manages the affairs of the family may acquire a "phallic" or masculine image to her children. As she is not accustomed to bearing the full responsibility for the family welfare and discipline, she might tend to become anxious. This anxiety is further exacerbated by her sexual and emotional frustration and concern for her husband. Anxieties of all kinds are immediately and inevitably communicated to children, who then become anxious as well. In her uncertainty a mother will often be more punitive than she would be under normal circumstances, both to ward off her own sexual feelings and because of anxiety about her role as disciplinarian. This heightens the passive masochism and castration anxiety in young boys.

Boys who become homosexuals are often those who were left alone with their mothers and formed an intense attachment to them that was unmediated by the father's presence and protection. The struggle against feminine identification and the regression to narcissistic object choice—that is, choosing someone who is like himself, what he was, or what he would like to be—are all generally intensified in boys raised without fathers. . . .

*   *   *

We must seek the widest possible type and range of clinical material, cultural documentation, and quantitative statistical data in our quest for historical evidence. This essay will present three bodies of historical materials, some from each of these categories of data: comparative, qualitative, and quantitative. All varieties of historical evidence have an important and complementary function in generating new hypotheses, contributing new insight, and demarking future areas for exploration. . . .

A study such as the present one, which attempts to assess the impact on children of a catastrophe like a war, should use the best clinical observations in comparative historical situations when these are available. If wartime deprivation has profound emotional effects on young children, these effects should not be limited to one time and place in the modern world. The findings in Germany should also be evident in another industrial land and for other twentieth-century wars, such as for England in World War II.

The British experience is especially valuable to the historian who would consider the emotional effect of war on children because many English children were evacuated from their homes and families in

London and the other big cities during World War II, and they were helped through this trying experience by the expert guidance of such specialists in the psychology of children as Anna Freud, Dorothy T. Burlingham, and D. W. Winnicott. These psychoanalysts carried out close residential observation of the evacuated children and published detailed studies of the children's responses and adaptations to the breakup of families in wartime. These were "normal" children, they were not hospitalized, nor were they juvenile offenders. They were not so heavily traumatized by their experience that their regressive defenses resisted all modification, as is the case with most of the children who survived concentration camps. The blitzed English children were provided with a homelike environment and encouraged in every way toward normal development. The fact that they were out of their homes and away from their families provides a degree of objectivity to the observations. The data were not filtered through reports of the parents; they are first-hand observations by trained professionals.

Anna Freud and Burlingham found that while a child will accept mother substitutes in the absence of its own mother, "there is . . . no father substitute who can fill the place which is left empty by the child's own father." "The infant's emotional relationship to its father begins later in life than that of its mother," they write, "but certainly from the second year onward it is an integral part of its emotional life and a necessary ingredient in the complex forces which work towards the formation of its character and its personality."

The researchers found that absent parents were greatly idealized. Their letters were carried around and had to be read to the children innumerable times. When the father was away in the armed services he was spoken of by his child in terms of endearment and admiration. Especially children who were in reality rejected or disappointed by their fathers formed passionate, loving, and admiring relationships to them. When a child had never known his father he would invent an idealized fantasy father who sanctioned his forbidden greedy and destructive wishes, who loved him and gave him security.

When a father came home on leave, however, and thereby encroached on the existing close mother-child relationship, he was met with resentment and hostility by the child. The father was viewed as an intruder who separated the mother and son. One little boy said: "Do write to my Daddy, I don't want him to come here. I don't want to have lunch with him. Somebody else can have my Daddy." But the same son and his father were best of friends when they were left alone without the mother.

When in some cases the ultimate disaster struck, Anna Freud and Burlingham report a complete inability of the children to accept their father's death. All the orphaned children talked about their dead fathers as if they were still alive. They denied the fact of death with fantasies of the father's rebirth and return from heaven.

The most original psychoanalytical approach to National Socialist youth, and the one that I find conceptually most perceptive and useful, is Martin Wangh's excellent analysis of 1964. He structures the psychodynamics of the First World War German children who came to the age of political effectiveness with the rise of Hitler with precision and insight. A preoccupation with guilt, Wangh points out, is also an unrecognized self-reproach for unresolved aggression against the father. Aggression toward the absent father-rival is expressed in gleeful ideas concerning his degradation and defeat. But the hostility is coupled with a longing for the idealized father that exacerbates childish homosexual wishes. Those homosexual longings offer a way out of the Oedipal conflict that is heightened for sons left alone with their mothers. In these circumstances the woman is often rejected, and the incestuous wish is ascribed to someone else. These mental defenses, Wangh suggests, were renewed in the Nazi movement's deification of the Führer and its infernalization of the Jew. Homosexual tension was relieved through submission to an all-powerful leader, through turning women into "breeders" of children, and by persecuting Jews as "incestuous criminals" and "defilers of the race." The passive-masochistic inclinations that develop when boys are brought up and disciplined by mothers who are anxious and punitive may be defended against by preference for submission to a man, as this is less threatening and less castrating than submission to a woman. Self-humiliation and self-contempt were displaced onto the Jews and other supposedly inferior people, thereby assuaging feelings of unworthiness and masochistic fantasies of rejection. Since the former wartime enemies were for the time being unassailable, the Jew, who was defenseless and available, became by the mechanism of displacement the victim of those who needed a target for regressive action. . . .

Among the richest sources for the expression of the experience of young Germans during the war and postwar years is the literature of the period, which more than held its place amid the cultural fecundity of the Weimar epoch. Sometimes literary expression can capture for historians the essence of a generation's experience both graphically and with a depth of emotional subtlety that cannot be conveyed by statistics or quantitative data. Many qualitative affects cannot be statistically comprehended or documented. It is possible to see, identify, and demonstrate father identification and castration anxiety without necessarily being able to computerize them. This is the appeal to the historian of both clinical insight and literary sensibility. Can one measure or compare quantitatively, for example, the degree of suffering, mourning, loss, or rage a subject feels? For this kind of emotional evidence we must rely on that most sensitive of our cultural materials—the subjective written word of literature.

When this has been said, it is nevertheless astonishing to experience the great autobiographical pacifist novel *Jahrgang 1902* by Ernst Glaeser (1902–1963), which describes the author's feelings with such intensity and pathos that it often reads more like the free associations of a patient in psychoanalysis than a novel. The critic William Soskin ranked *Jahrgang 1902* with *Sergeant Grisha* and *All Quiet on the Western Front* as one of the most significant works on the First World War. This book ran through six German printings during the winter of 1928–1929. It sold 70,000 copies in Germany and was translated into twenty-five languages.

The book takes its title from the year of the author's birth, which also automatically became the year of his military-service class. The class of 1902 was not to experience the war of 1914–1918 on the front.[1] For that they were too young, but as Glaeser pointedly noted,

[1] For a sardonic expression from among the youngest class that went to war, see Erich Kästner, "The Class of 1899," in his *Bei Durchsicht meiner Bücher* . . . (Zurich: Atrium Verlag, 1946), 97–98. "We took the women to bed, / While the men stood in France. / We had imagined that it would be much more wonderful. / We were merely confirmants. / Then they took us to the army, / For nothing more than cannon fodder. / The benches at school were emptied, / Mother wept at home. / Then we had a bit of revolution / And potato chips came raining down. / Then came the women, just like they used to / And then we caught the clap. / Meanwhile the old man lost his money, / So we became night-school students / By day we worked in an office / And dealt with rates of interest. / Then she almost had a child. / Whether by you or by me—who knows! / A friend of ours scraped it out. / And the next thing you know we will be thirty. / We even passed an examination / And have already forgotten most of it. / Now we are alone day and night / And have nothing decent to eat! / We looked the world straight in the snout, / Instead of playing with dolls / We spit at the rest of the world, / Insofar as we were not killed at Ypres. /

"The war did not establish a moratorium on puberty." The book, he said, deals with "the tragedy of murdered minds and souls and diseased temperaments in the noncombatant social body."

As the war began the fathers left to join their regiments and the twelve-year-old boy observes that "life in our town became quieter." The boys played war games in which the French and Russians were always soundly beaten. The fathers were sorely missed. They were quickly idealized and glorified. Glaeser describes the process of overestimation and identification with the father who is absent at war:

> We thought only of our fathers in these days. Overnight they had become heroes. . . . We loved our fathers with a new sublime love. As ideals. And just as we formerly used to express our admiration for the Homeric heroes or the figures of the Wars of Liberation by token symbols of clothing such as golden helmets of tin foil or Lützow caps, so we now also began, but in far greater measure, to turn ourselves symbolically into the idealized figures of our fathers.

The boys of the village went to the barber to have their hair cut in the close-cropped military style like their fathers.

> We had our hair cut. Bare. Smooth. Three millimeters high. For this is how we had seen it on our fathers as they left for the front. None of them had hair to part now.
>
> One evening late in September a group of fifteen determined boys went to the barber. We stood according to height and let the instrument pass over our heads. As the barber was sweeping up our hair with a broom an hour later, he said: "Now you look like recruits."
>
> We were proud of this distinction and enthusiastically paid 40 pfennigs each.

By the winter of 1916 the privation of the war began to be felt in the daily lives of the boys. They were always hungry. There was never enough to eat. The steady diet of turnip soup became inedible. City folk bribed and bartered away precious possessions in order to get nourishing food from the farmers. The mother gave Kathinka, the maid, one of her finest blouses so that she would bring back food when she visited her peasant parents. Faithfully Kathinka smuggled

They made our bodies or our spirit / A wee bit too weak / They threw us into world history too long, / Too fast, and too much. / The old folks maintained that the time has come / For us to sow and to reap. / But wait a moment. Soon we will be ready. / Just a moment. Soon we will be there! / Then we will show you what we have learned!"

butter past the gendarmes in her woolen bloomers. Field gendarmes and controllers appeared on the roads and at the stations to search travelers for contraband foodstuffs. The children developed tactics for deceiving the gendarmes and smuggling forbidden foodstuffs home. One boy would serve as a decoy to draw the gendarme's attention while the other raced home across the fields with a sack of flour or a ham.

This progression within two years from idealism to hunger and the struggle for survival is vividly described by Glaeser.

> *The winter remained hard until the end. The war began to burst over the fronts and to strike the people. Hunger destroyed our unity; in the families children stole each other's rations. . . . Soon the women who stood in gray lines in front of the shops talked more about the hunger of their children than of the death of their husbands. The sensations of war had been altered.*
>
> *A new front existed. It was held by women. The enemies were the entente of field gendarmes and uncompromising guards. Every smuggled pound of butter, every sack of potatoes gleefully secreted by night was celebrated in the families with the same enthusiasm as the victories of the armies two years earlier. . . . It was wonderful and inspiring to outwit the gendarmes and after successfully triumphing to be honored by one's mother as a hero.*

Oedipal longings were heightened for the sons left alone with their mothers during years of war. Starvation led to the mobilization of unconscious wishes for a return to the oral comforts of early mother-child units. Occasionally the prolonged hunger was broken by feasting on an illegally slaughtered pig or a smuggled goose that the father sent home from the eastern front. Then an orgy of feeding took place. Gluttony reigned and undernourished bellies got sick on the rich food. The windows had to be stuffed to keep the neighbors from smelling the meat. The adolescent boy and his mother consumed almost an entire twelve-pound goose in one night. A stolen drumstick for his girlfriend was to her the convincing symbol of love. Glaeser writes, "We scarcely spoke of the war any more, we only spoke of hunger. Our mothers were closer to us than our fathers."

The fathers were not present to shield the sons from maternal seduction. One young adolescent in the novel is seduced by a motherly farmer's wife with the promise of a large ham. But, much as the pangs of his stomach and his mother's pleading letters argued for bringing the ham home, he could not do it. The great succulent ham had become an incestuous object. He had earned it from the farm wife by taking her husband's place. Now he was too guilty and too anxious to permit himself and his family to enjoy it. The pangs of guilt were stronger than the pains of hunger. As if he could "undo" his Oedipal crime, the boy laid the ham on the farm wife's bed and left. He was tearful and depressed, feelings he rationalized as being due to his injured feelings because he was really only a substitute (*Ersatz*) for the husband. He climbed into bed with his boy comrade. In the stillness of the dawn they embraced, keeping each other warm, and he shared his story of seduction and sexual discovery. In this episode we see fully elaborated the heightened Oedipal conflict when the father is absent, the increased guilt and fear of retribution, and finally the rejection of the woman as a sexual object and an exacerbation of adolescent homosexuality arising from the emotional effects of the war.

By the winter of 1917 the fathers had become aliens to their sons. But they were not only unknown men, they were feared and threatening strangers who claimed rights and control over the lives of their sons. They had become distant but powerful figures who could punish and exact a terrible price for disobedience and transgressions. Glaeser recounts his reaction as a fifteen-year-old to a letter from his father on the Russian front in terms of intense castration anxiety. The adolescent boy's Oedipal victory in having displaced his father would now be terribly expiated and revenged by a towering, castrating monster of his guilt-laden fantasies. Glaeser attempts to deny that his father has any legitimate claim to control over him at all. But his father would know where to find him and the inevitable retribution would be inexorable.

> *We were frightened. That was the voice of the front. That was the voice of those men who formerly were once our fathers, who now, however, removed from us for years, were strangers before us, fearsome, huge, overpowering, casting dark shadows, oppressive as a monument. What did they still know of us? They knew where we lived, but they no longer knew what we looked like and thought.*

It is of biographical interest for the thesis of this essay that Glaeser went into emigration from Germany after 1933, living in Prague, Zurich, and Paris. In Zurich in 1939 he wrote a newspaper article condoning Hitler's policies and condemning his fellow émigrés. Within days he received a contract from a Berlin publisher. He returned to Germany and joined the war effort, becoming a war reporter for the Luftwaffe and the editor of the military newspaper, *Adler im Suden.*

Thus, as did so many others of his cohort, Glaeser was two decades later to choose to wear a uniform and to identify with his distant and glorified father. The identification with the father who went out to war served to erase the memory of the feared and hated strange father who came home in defeat. By being a patriot and submitting to authority, the ambivalence of the young boy who gleefully observed his father's humiliating defeat and degradation was denied and expiated. Now he would do obeisance to an idealized but remote leader who was deified and untouchable. . . .

The third variety of data I wish to examine is quantitative. It is a series of autobiographical essays collected in 1934 by Theodore Abel, a sociologist at Columbia University, in an essay contest offering cash prizes for "the best personal life history of an adherent of the Hitler movement."

In reading the essays one is often struck by their didactic quality. Some writers say outright that they are delighted to write down their experiences for the benefit of American researchers at Columbia University. As the essays were solicited by a bulletin at all local headquarters of the NSDAP and by announcements in the party press, and as the writers were not anonymous, one may infer that the writers suspected that party organs would be informed of any criticism and political or personal deviance in the essays. In some cases one senses that a local party functionary may have encouraged the writers to respond to the essay contest. Some contributions bear the NSDAP Abteilung Propaganda stamp. Many tiresomely repeat propaganda slogans about Jewish war profiteering, Red vandalism in the revolution of 1918–1919, and so forth.

All these caveats notwithstanding, these nearly 600 essays constitute a valuable historical source. In the first place it is a contemporary source. No set of interviews of ex-Nazis thirty-seven years later could possibly elicit the same material. The Abel autobiographies may be utilized, not as a statistical sample for generalizations, but as bases for theory building. They will serve as a cognitive prism for drawing attention to necessary variables of political behavior rather than as a monolithic statistical sample that can produce conclusive findings for the population of the Nazi party. They can tell us, however, what excited and stimulated the writers, what preoccupied their fantasies and imaginations, how they viewed themselves, their childhoods and homes, and their enemies. These data can then become referents for further theoretical conceptualization and behavioral model-building, particularly with respect to emotional connotations that are not censored by the writers because they appear to be apolitical and therefore unimportant.

The most striking emotional affect expressed in the Abel autobiographies are the adult memories of intense hunger and privation from childhood. A party member who was a child of the war years recollects, "Sometimes I had to scurry around eight to ten hours—occasionally at night—to procure a few potatoes or a bit of butter. Carrots and beets, previously considered fit only for cattle, came to be table luxuries." Another man's memory is vivid in its sense of abandonment and isolation expressed in language that makes a feeling of maternal deprivation very clear.

> *Hunger was upon us. Bread and potatoes were scarce, while meat and fats were almost non-existent. We were hungry all the time; we had forgotten how it felt to have our stomachs full.*
>
> *All family life was at an end. None of us really knew what it meant—we were left to our own devices. For women had to take the place of their fighting men. They toiled in factories and in offices, as ostlers and as commercial travelers, in all fields of activity previously allotted to men—behind the plow as well as on the omnibus. Thus while we never saw our fathers, we had only glimpses of our mothers in the evening. Even then they could not devote themselves to us because, tired as they were, they had to take care of their household, after their strenuous day at work. So we grew up, amid hunger and privation, with no semblance of decent family life.*

A study of the Abel autobiographies focused on a sample from the birth cohorts 1911 to 1915, who were small children during the war, indicates the presence of the defensive mechanisms of projection, displacement, low frustration tolerance, and the search for an idealized father. For example, the essays of two sisters born in 1913 and 1915, whose father fell in 1915, clearly demonstrate that Hitler served as an idealized father figure for them. Their earliest memories are of their mother crying a great deal and of all the people wearing black. They relate their excitement at first hearing the Führer speak in person at a rally in Kassel in 1931. The sisters were so exhilarated that neither of them could sleep all night. They prayed for the protection of the Führer, and asked forgiveness for ever having doubted him. The sisters began their Nazi party activities by caring for and feeding SA men.

Some of the men in the Abel Collection who lost their fathers early in life and were separated from their mothers especially valued the comradeship of the SA. One such man wrote, "It was wonderful to belong to the bond of comradeship of the SA. Each one stood up for the other." Massive projection of ego-alien impulses is evident in many of the essays. One man says that bejeweled Jewesses tried to seduce him politically with cake. Many of the SA men who engaged in street brawls and violence blamed others, such as the police and the Communists, for instigating the fighting and for persecuting them. One man displays remarkable projection and displacement of his own murderous feelings toward a younger brother when he relates the death of that brother in an unnecessary operation performed by a Jewish doctor. "Since I especially loved my dead brother," he writes, "a grudge arose in me against the doctor, and this not yet comprehensible hatred increased with age to become an antagonism against everything Jewish."

*   *   *

The demographic factors of massive health, nutritional, and material deprivation and parental absence in Central Europe during World War I should lead the historian to apply theoretical and clinical knowledge of the long-term effects of such a deprived childhood on personality. The anticipation of weakened character structure manifested in aggression, defenses of projection and displacement, and inner rage that may be mobilized by a renewed anxiety-inducing trauma in adulthood is validated in the subsequent political conduct of this cohort during the Great Depression when they joined extremist paramilitary and youth organizations and political parties. In view of these two bodies of data for which a psychoanalytic understanding of personality provides the essential linkage, it is postulated that a direct relationship existed between the deprivation German children experienced in World War I and the response of these children and adolescents to the anxieties aroused by the Great Depression of the early 1930s. This relationship is psychodynamic: the war generation had weakened egos and superegos, meaning that the members of this generation turned readily to programs based on facile solutions and violence when they met new frustrations during the depression. They then reverted to earlier phase-specific fixations in their child development marked by rage, sadism, and the defensive idealization of their absent parents, especially the father. These elements made this age cohort particularly susceptible to the appeal of a mass movement utilizing the crudest devices of projection and displacement in its ideology. Above all it prepared the young voters of Germany for submission to a total, charismatic leader.

But fantasy is always in the end less satisfying than mundane reality. Ironically, instead of finding the idealized father they, with Hitler as their leader, plunged Germany and Europe headlong into a series of deprivations many times worse than those of World War I. Thus the repetition was to seek the glory of identification with the absent soldier-father, but like all quests for a fantasied past, it had to fail. Hitler and National Socialism were so much a repetition and fulfillment of the traumatic childhoods of the generation of World War I that the attempt to undo that war and those childhoods was to become a political program. As a result the regressive illusion of Nazism ended in a repetition of misery at the front and starvation at home made worse by destroyed cities, irremediable guilt, and millions of new orphans.

A return to the past is always unreal. To attempt it is the path of certain disaster. There was no glorified father who went to war and who could be recaptured in Hitler. He existed only in fantasy, and he could never be brought back in reality. There are no ideal mothers and fathers; there are only flawed human parents. Therefore, for a World War I generation seeking restitution of a lost childhood there was to be only bitter reality in the form of a psychotic charlatan who skillfully manipulated human needs and left destruction to Germany and Europe. What the youth cohort wanted was a fantasy of warmth, closeness, security, power, and love. What they recreated was a repetition of their own childhoods. They gave to their children and to Europe in greater measure precisely the traumas they had suffered as children and adolescents a quarter of a century earlier.

III POLITICS, INDUSTRY, AND THE ARMY

The political role of elites is important to any evaluation of Nazism. The support or acquiescence of business and military leaders was crucial to the solidification and expansion of Nazi Germany. How did Hitler secure their cooperation, and specifically what responsibility did they share in the Nazi acquisition of power?

Franz Neumann insists that Germany's economic recovery in the mid-1920s was something of an illusion, since it depended so heavily on foreign capital. Likewise, the political structure of the Weimar Republic—a dubious attempt to reconcile democratic political institutions with monopolistic economic practices—was defective. The Great Depression did not create these inherent flaws; it did seriously deepen them. Neumann indicates, therefore, that the short-sighted and essentially antidemocratic ambition of German capitalists was a central factor in the collapse of the republic and the success of the Nazis.

Wolfgang Sauer sees fascism in general, and German National Socialism in particular, as the refuge of those who suffered most from industrialization; it was "a movement of losers" and, as such, was actually antithetical to the interests of modern capitalism. Sauer attempts to unravel the paradoxical nature of Nazism as both reactionary and revolutionary. It perhaps follows from his interpretation that the German elites cannot be directly blamed as witting accomplices of Nazism: the advance of an industrializing society could not avoid producing an antimodernist current.

George W. F. Hallgarten moves to a less theoretical level. He argues that a coincidence of interests between Hitler and Germany's industrial elite resulted in an uneasy alliance, which gave the Nazi movement sufficient financial backing when it was most needed. If the affluence of German capitalists did not create the Nazi movement, Hallgarten contends, it did sustain Hitler's drive to power long enough for him to gain the chancellorship. From there it was but one step to a dictatorship that seemed to promise handsome economic returns for prior political investment.

Henry A. Turner, Jr. disputes the assertion that Hitler received major *political and financial support from heavy industry before 1933. He believes the industrialists were frightened by the radical implications of Nazism and continued to place their influence, such as it was, behind the conservative politicians. The relatively light contributions by large business firms to the Nazi party afford little evidence of an early collusion between capitalists and fascists—although Turner hastens to add that once Hitler gained control of the state, circumstances quickly changed in his favor.*

Gordon A. Craig indicts German military leadership, particularly General von Schleicher, in a detailed reconstruction of the political intrigues which enabled Hitler to take the final step to power. He presumes this would have been impossible without the active assistance of certain officers and the benign indulgence of many others. Craig's assessment is accusatory, since he regards the situation as fluid and the outcome uncertain. A concerted opposition within the officer corps might, therefore, have blocked Hitler altogether from political dominance.

Gerhard Ritter adopts a broader view and a more apologetic tone. He explains German militarism as the natural outgrowth of a precarious geopolitical situation. He denies, moreover, that the officer corps as such played a significant part in the Nazi seizure of power. Ritter states that their acknowledgment of Hitler's leadership once it was legitimized led to a reversal, rather than to a continuation, of the historical relationship between civil and military authority. Thus the major responsibility lies with the overwhelming force of a political tidal wave, not the alleged influence or collaboration of the military elite.

Nowhere else in the literature on Nazism are the issues so sharply drawn or the alternatives so diametrically opposed. As a consequence, the entire character of historical judgment is called into question: Does a decisive opinion have special merit, so long as presuppositions and qualifications are frankly exposed; or does wisdom ordinarily dictate a standpoint midway between two contradictory hypotheses, granting a certain validity to each? In either case the reader would do well to remain sensitive to the ideological implications of his own position as well as that of the historian.

Franz Neumann
DEMOCRACY AND MONOPOLY

The strong man of the Social Democratic party, Otto Braun, Prussian prime minister until June 20, 1932, when he was deposed by the Hindenburg-Papen coup d'état, attributes the failure of the party and Hitler's successful seizure of power to a combination of Versailles and Moscow. This defense is neither accurate nor particularly skillful. The Versailles treaty naturally furnished excellent propaganda material against democracy in general and against the Social Democratic party in particular, and the Communist party unquestionably made inroads among Social Democrats. Neither was primarily responsible for the fall of the republic, however. Besides, what if Versailles and Moscow had been the two major factors in the making of National Socialism? Would it not have been the task of a great democratic leadership to make the democracy work in spite of and against Moscow and Versailles? That the Social Democratic party failed remains the crucial fact, regardless of any official explanation. It failed because it did not see that the central problem was the imperialism of German monopoly capital, becoming ever more urgent with the continued growth of the process of monopolization. The more monopoly grew, the more incompatible it became with the political democracy. . . .

The efficient and powerfully organized German system of our time was born under the stimulus of a series of factors brought into the forefront by the First World War. The inflation of the early '20s permitted unscrupulous entrepreneurs to build up giant economic empires at the expense of the middle and working classes. The prototype was the Stinnes empire and it is at least symbolic that Hugo Stinnes was the most inveterate enemy of democracy and of Rathenau's foreign policy. Foreign loans that flowed into Germany after 1924 gave German industry the liquid capital needed to rationalize and enlarge their plants. Even the huge social-welfare program promoted by the Social Democracy indirectly strengthened the centralization and concentration of industry, since big business could far more easily as-

From *Behemoth: The Structure and Practice of National Socialism* by Franz Neumann. Published in 1963 by Octagon Books. Copyright 1942, 1944 by Oxford University Press. Reprinted by permission of Farrar, Strauss & Giroux, Inc.

sume the burden than the small or middle entrepreneur. Trusts, combines, and cartels covered the whole economy with a network of authoritarian organizations. Employers' organizations controlled the labor market, and big business lobbies aimed at placing the legislative, administrative, and judicial machinery at the service of monopoly capital.

In Germany there was never anything like the popular anti-monopoly movement of the United States under Theodore Roosevelt and Woodrow Wilson. Industry and finance were of course firmly convinced that the cartel and trust represented the highest forms of economic organization. The independent middle class was not articulate in its opposition, except against department stores and chains. Though the middle class belonged to powerful pressure groups, like the Federal Union of German Industries, big business leaders were invariably their spokesmen.

Labor was not at all hostile to the process of trustification. The Communists regarded monopoly as an inevitable stage in the development of capitalism and hence considered it futile to fight capital concentration rather than the system itself. Ironically enough, the policy of the reformist wing of the labor movement was not significantly different in effect. The Social Democrats and the trade unions also regarded concentration as inevitable, and, they added, as a higher form of capitalist organization. Their leading theorist, Rudolf Hilferding, summarized the position at the party's 1927 convention: "Organized capitalism means replacing free competition by the social principle of planned production. The task of the present Social Democratic generation is to invoke state aid in translating this economy, organized and directed by the capitalists, into an economy directed by the democratic state." By economic democracy the Social Democratic party meant a larger share in controlling the monopolist organizations and better protection for the workers against the ill effects of concentration.

The largest trusts in German history were formed during the Weimar Republic. The merger in 1926 of four large steel companies in western Germany resulted in the formation of the Vereinigte Stahlwerke (the United Steel Works). The Vereinigte Oberschlesische Hüttenwerke (the United Upper Silesian Mills) was a similar combination among the steel industries of Upper Silesia. The I. G. Farbenindustrie (the German Dye Trust) arose in 1925 through the merger of the six largest corporations in this field, all of which had previously been combined in a pool. In 1930 the capital stock of the Dye Trust totaled 1.1 billion marks and the number of workers it employed reached 100,000.

At no time in the republic (not even in the boom year of 1929) were the productive capacities of German industry fully, or even adequately, utilized. The situation was worst in heavy industry, especially in coal and steel, the very fields that had furnished the industrial leadership during the empire and that still dominated the essential business organizations. With the Great Depression, the gap between actual production and capacity took on such dangerous proportions that governmental assistance became imperative. Cartels and tariffs were resorted to along with subsidies in the form of direct grants, loans, and low interest rates. These measures helped but at the same time they intensified another threat. The framework of the German government was still a parliamentary democracy after all, and what if movements threatening the established monopolistic structure should arise within the mass organizations? As far back as November 1923, public pressure had forced the Stresemann cabinet to enact a cartel decree authorizing the government to dissolve cartels and to attack monopolistic positions generally. Not once were these powers utilized, but the danger to privileges inherent in political democracy remained and obviously became more acute in times of great crisis. . . .

Even before the beginning of the Great Depression, therefore, the ideological, economic, social, and political systems were no longer functioning properly. Whatever appearance of successful operation they may have given was based primarily on toleration by the antidemocratic forces and on the fictitious prosperity made possible by foreign loans. The depression uncovered and deepened the petrification of the traditional social and political structure. The social contracts on which that structure was founded broke down. The Democratic party disappeared; the Catholic Center shifted to the right; and the Social Democrats and Communists devoted far more energy to fighting each other than to the struggle against the growing threat of National Socialism. The National Socialist party in turn heaped abuse upon the Social Democrats. They coined the epithet

November criminals: a party of corruptionists and pacifists responsible for the defeat in 1918, for the Versailles treaty, for the inflation.

The output of German industry had dropped sharply. Unemployment was rising: 6 million were registered in January 1932, and there were perhaps 2 million more of the so-called invisible unemployed. Only a small fraction received unemployment insurance and an ever larger proportion received no support at all. The unemployed youth became a special problem in themselves. There were hundreds of thousands who had never held jobs. Unemployment became a status, and, in a society where success is paramount, a stigma. Peasants revolted in the north while large estate owners cried for financial assistance. Small businessmen and craftsmen faced destruction. Houseowners could not collect their rents. Banks crashed and were taken over by the federal government. Even the stronghold of industrial reaction, the United Steel Trust, was near collapse and its shares were purchased by the federal government at prices far above the market quotation. The budget situation became precarious. The reactionaries refused to support a large-scale works program lest it revive the declining power of the trade unions, whose funds were dwindling and whose membership was declining. . . .

By joining the concert of the Western European powers the Weimar government hoped to obtain concessions. The attempt failed. It was supported neither by German industry and large landowners nor by the Western powers. The year 1932 found Germany in a catastrophic political, economic, and social crisis.

The system could also operate if the ruling groups made concessions voluntarily or under compulsion by the state. That would have led to a better life for the mass of the German workers and security for the middle classes at the expense of the profits and power of big business. German industry was decidedly not amenable, however, and the state sided with it more and more.

The third possibility was the transformation into a socialist state, and that had become completely unrealistic in 1932 since the Social Democratic party was socialist only in name.

The crisis of 1932 demonstrated that political democracy alone without a fuller utilization of the potentialities inherent in Germany's industrial system, that is, without the abolition of unemployment and an improvement in living standards, remained a hollow shell.

The fourth choice was the return to imperialist expansion. Imperialist ventures could not be organized within the traditional democratic form, however, for there would have been too serious an opposition. Nor could it take the form of restoration of the monarchy. An industrial society that has passed through a democratic phase cannot exclude the masses from consideration. Expansionism therefore took the form of National Socialism, a totalitarian dictatorship that has been able to transform some of its victims into supporters and to organize the entire country into an armed camp under iron discipline. . . .

Wolfgang Sauer
CAPITALISM AND MODERNITY

Fascism can be defined as a revolt of those who lost—directly or indirectly, temporarily or permanently—by industrialization. Fascism is a revolt of the déclassés. The workers and industrialists do not fall under this definition; it applies mainly to most of the lower middle class as defined above. They indeed suffered, or feared they would suffer, from industrialization—peasants who opposed the urbanizing aspects of industrialism; small businessmen and those engaged in the traditional crafts and trades that opposed mechanization or concentration; white-collar workers (at least as long as they felt the loss of economic independence); lower levels of the professions, especially the teaching profession, which opposed changing social values; and so forth. Also the military joins here, with opposition against the industrialization of war, which tended to destroy traditional modes of warfare and which by its increasing destructiveness intensified pacifism and antimilitarism. On the other hand, groups like the aristocracy, the large landlords, the higher bureaucrats, and so on, who lost also by industrialization, generally did not turn to fascism. In continuing the counterrevolutionary position, they defended hier-

From Wolfgang Sauer, "National Socialism: Totalitarianism or Fascism?" *American Historical Review* 73, no. 2 (December 1967). Reprinted by permission of the author. Footnotes omitted.

archical society and abhorred, therefore, the egalitarian elements in fascism. In exact distinction, then, fascist movements represented the reaction of the lower-class losers, while the upper-class losers tended to react in a nonfascist way, but were potential allies of fascist regimes.

Such an analysis seems to be a way of explaining the intriguing paradox of a revolutionary mass movement whose goals were anti-revolutionary in the classical sense. As a movement of losers, it turned against technological progress and economic growth; it tried to stop or even to reverse the trend toward industrialization and to return to the earlier, "natural" ways of life. In this respect the movement was reactionary, but, as a movement of the lower classes, its means were necessarily revolutionary. In defining fascism as a revolt of losers, we can also understand better both fascist atavism and fascist opportunism. Since the process of industrialization as a whole is irresistible, the existence of civilization is inextricably bound to it. Fascist revolt against industrialization must, therefore, eventually turn against civilization too. This was most evident in Germany, where Nazism developed into full-fledged neobarbarism, but it is also true of the other fascist movements, though for various reasons neo-barbarism remained, there, more or less underdeveloped. Such a definition of fascism as a neobarbaric revolt against civilization seems to describe in more concrete terms what Nolte calls the resistance against the "transcendence."

The same condition led to fascist opportunism. Since fascists acted, as losers, essentially from a position of weakness, they were compelled, in spite of their tendency toward violence, to compromise with their environment, even with their industrial enemy. This accounts for the contradiction that fascist regimes often fostered indus-trialization and yet insisted, ultimately, upon setting the clock back. The dialectic that resulted from this condition led eventually to a point at which the movement assumed suicidal proportions. Industrial-ization was sought in order to destroy industrial society, but since there was no alternative to industrial society, the fascist regime must eventually destroy itself. This was the situation of Nazism. The Nazis built an industrial machinery to murder the Jews, but once in opera-tion the machine would have had to continue and would have ruined, indirectly at least, first the remnants of civilized society and then the fascist regime. Industrialization of mass murder was, thus, the only logical answer Nazism had to the problems of industrial society.

The analysis of fascism in terms of economic growth also offers a way to define more precisely the fallacy in the Marxist-Leninist concept of fascism. The fallacy lies in that Marxism blurs the distinction between early commercial and late industrial capitalism. Fascism indicated a conflict within capitalism, between traditional forms of commercialism and the modern form of industrialism. The fact that the former had survived in the twentieth century only on the lower levels of the middle classes accounted for the social locus of fascism. It is true, therefore, that fascism was capitalist by nature; it is not true that it was industrial. It is also true that fascist regimes often were manipulated in varying ways and degrees, but the share of industrialists in manipulation was rather small. Fetscher shows convincingly that the share was indeed larger in industrially underdeveloped Italy than it was in industrially advanced Germany.

On the other hand, the difference between fascism and Bolshevism appears, in light of this analysis, more fundamental than the totalitarianism analysis would admit. Neither V. I. Lenin nor Joseph Stalin wished to turn the clock back; they not merely wished to move ahead, but they wished to jump ahead. The Bolshevik revolution had many elements of a development revolution not unlike those now under way in the underdeveloped countries. One of the striking differences between the two systems appears in the role of the leaders. The social and political order of bolshevism is relatively independent from the leadership; it is, so to speak, more objective. Fascist regimes, by contrast, are almost identical with their leaders; no fascist regime has so far survived its leader. This is why Bullock's interpretation of Hitler in terms of traditional tyranny has some bearing. The limits of this approach would become evident, I believe, if scholars could be persuaded to balance their interest in Hitler's secret utterances and political and military scheming by also stressing his role as a public speaker. The Nazi mass rallies with their immediate, ecstatic communication between leader and followers were, indeed, what might be called a momentary materialization of the Nazi utopia, at least so far as the "Nordic race" was concerned.

Finally, it is plain from an analysis in terms of economic growth that the degree of radicalization must somehow be related to the degree of industrialization. The more highly industrialized a society, the more violent the reaction of the losers. Thus Germany stood at the top, Italy lagged behind, and Spain and others were at the bottom. In Germany, fascism gained sufficient momentum to oust its allies. By the dismissal of Schacht, Werner von Blomberg, Werner von Fritsch, and Konstantin von Neurath in 1937–1938, the Nazis assumed control over the economy, the army, and the diplomacy, those exact three positions that their conservative allies of January 30, 1933, had deemed it most important to maintain. In Italy a fairly stable balance was sustained between the movement and its various allies until the latter, relying on the monarchy and assisted by Fascism's defeat in war, finally ousted the Fascists. In Spain, a borderline case, the allies assumed control from the outset and never abandoned it. Similar observations can be made with the many cases of pre-, proto-, and pseudofascist regimes in Central, Eastern, and Southeastern Europe.

The thesis of the parallel growth of industrialization and fascist radicalization seems to conflict, however, with the evidence of some highly industrialized societies such as France and England where fascist opposition never gained much momentum. The problem can be solved only by adding a broader historical analysis involving the specific national, social, and cultural traditions that industrialization encountered in individual societies. It is perhaps not accidental that the industrialization process ran relatively smoothly in West European nations whose political rise concurred with the rise of modern civilization since the late Middle Ages. Fascist opposition, by contrast, was strongest in the Mediterranean and Central European regions where the premodern traditions of the ancient Roman and the medieval German and Turkish empires persisted. The religious division between Protestantism and Catholicism may also have some relevance: one remembers both Max Weber's thesis on the correlation of Protestantism and capitalism and the recent controversy on the attitude of Pope Pius XII toward Fascism and Nazism. In other words, fascism emerged where preindustrial traditions were both strongest and most alien to industrialism and, hence, where the rise of the latter caused a major break with the past and substantial losses to the nonindustrial classes.

This definition is still incomplete, however, since it does not tell why fascism emerged rather simultaneously throughout Europe though the countries affected were on different levels of economic growth. We face here the question of the "epoch" of fascism, raised but not answered by Nolte. The general conditions of fascism as defined above existed, after all, earlier. In Germany, for example, lower-middle-class opposition against industrialization had already emerged in the mid-nineteenth century and accompanied economic growth in varying degrees through all its stages. Why did it not turn into fascism prior to 1914, though it did so on parallel stages of growth in Italy and Spain after the First World War? At this point the importance of the military element for the analysis of fascism becomes apparent again: Only after total war had militarized European societies and had created large military interests were the conditions required for fascism complete. The First World War had tremendously strengthened industrialization in technical terms, but it had diverted it from production to destruction. After the war the victorious nations of the West managed, on the whole, to stabilize industrial society and to return to production, but the defeated nations and those industrially underdeveloped found it extremely difficult to follow the same course. When they met with economic crises, many of them abandoned whatever advance they had made toward democracy and turned to fascism.

This breakdown occurred roughly along the social and cultural lines defined above. If we examine the geographical distribution of fascist regimes in Europe between the two world wars, we find that they emerged mainly in three areas: the Mediterranean coast; the regions of Central, Eastern, and Southeastern Europe; and Germany. In the first area, the original and highly developed Mediterranean urban and commercial civilization that reached back to antiquity faced destruction by the invasion of industrialism as released or accelerated by World War I. Defeat, either imagined as in the case of Italy or real as in the case of Spain at the hands of Abd-el-Krim at Anual in 1921, played an additional role. In the second area, an old feudal civilization struggled with the problems arising out of sudden liberation from Habsburg or tsarist dominations as well as from competition with both Western industrialism and Eastern Bolshevism. Both regions were predominantly Catholic. In the third area, a technologically fully developed industrial society clashed violently with the stubborn resistance of surviving remnants of preindustrial forms of society over who was to pay for defeat and economic crises. Catholicism played, here, a dual and partly contradictory role. On the one hand, it seems to have influenced indirectly Nazism as such top Nazi leaders as Hitler, Himmler, and Goebbels were Catholic by origin, and the Vatican was quick to compromise with the Hitler regime. On the other hand, the vast majority of the Catholic population was relatively immune to Nazi temptations. Significantly enough, Protestantism also split, though along somewhat different lines.

These differentiations suggest a division into three subtypes of fascism: the Mediterranean as the "original" one; the various and not too long-lived regimes in Central, Eastern, and Southeastern Europe as a mixed, or not full-fledged, variation; and German Nazism as a special form.

The "epoch" of fascism starts, thus, with the aftermath of the First World War, but when does it end? Eugen Weber and Lipset agree with many scholars who believe that there is no epoch of fascism, that fascism is a general condition of modern society contingent upon crises in liberal democracy. This is certainly indisputable as far as fascist attitudes and movements are concerned; it is quite another problem, however, whether fascist regimes will emerge again. This emergence seems unlikely for two reasons. First, the socioeconomic development in the highly industrialized societies of the West generally rules out the reemergence of the historical condition of fascism—a disarrangement of society in which the rise of large masses of déclassés coincides with the rise of a sizable group of military desperadoes. There are no longer economic losers of industrialization, at least not on a mass scale, and Charles de Gaulle's victory over the rebellious French military shows that military desperadoes alone will not get very far. In addition, the horrible experience of neobarbarism puts a heavy burden on all attempts at imitation. If the success of fascism under modern, Western conditions is unlikely, there remain, theoretically, the underdeveloped countries as possible breeding grounds of fascism. Yet it is doubtful whether opposition against industrialization will assume there the form of fascism since these countries lack the specific traditions of the ancient and medieval civilizations that conditioned the antimodernist revolt in Europe. The second reason working against fascist regimes is, thus, that fascism is inseparable from its Central and South European conditions; it is, in fact, one of the products of the dialectical movement of European civilization.

Some remarks on specific characteristics of Nazism and its German origins may be added as a conclusion to this discussion of fascism. The specialty of the German case may be seen, in light of this analysis, in that Germany was the only highly industrialized society in which a fascist regime emerged. Some authors have tried to explain this by pointing to the dominant role the state played in German industrialization. Yet Gerschenkron has convincingly shown that a relatively strong role of the state is a general characteristic of industrialization under conditions of "relative backwardness." We must look, therefore, for other causes, and it seems that they can be found in social rather than in political conditions of industrialization. A comparison with developments in France and Russia shows that the state in these countries changed its social basis by revolutionary means either prior to or during the process of industrialization; in Germany, however, preindustrial social traditions proved so strong and so flexible that they maintained influence on, if not control over, the state up to and beyond the stage of what Rostow calls industrial maturity. The ambivalent social structure that resulted from this twisted process was so fragile that it broke apart under the impact of the series of severe crises from World War I to the Great Depression.

One of the conditions that complicated German industrialization may be seen in the fact that Wilhelm von Humboldt's reform of the German educational system favored, at the very moment when Germany began to industrialize, an aesthetic-aristocratic idea of culture over an idea of civilization compatible with industrialism. The tensions resulting from this divergence are reflected in German nineteenth-century intellectual history and its complex relationship to the intellectual roots of Nazism. Fritz Stern and George L. Mosse, among others, have recently made important contributions to this subject. Mosse has taken up the issue of the völkisch ideology and has convincingly shown how deeply it had penetrated into German society already prior to 1914. In focusing on the völkisch ideology alone, Mosse has, however, by-passed what appears to be the real problem. Parallel to the rise of the völkisch ideology, Germany experienced one of the greatest intellectual flowerings in its history during the first three decades of this century. In many cases it reached the level of the classical period around 1800, and it certainly surpassed it in breadth. The real question is, then, why this parallelism occurred and why the völkisch ideology eventually triumphed. As far as intellectual history is concerned, there was, in fact, no gradual decline toward Nazism; there was a clear rupture in 1933.

Stern's study is less ambitious and more penetrating. Its results might lend some support to Nolte's thesis of metaphysical despair, but they are valuable especially because they draw attention to the crisis of self-confidence in the academic establishment. This seems to correspond to Allen's findings that indicate a deep and violent resentment on the "grass root" level of the Nazi party against the "educated" classes, and both studies together may hint at some reasons for the triumph of the völkisch ideology analyzed by Mosse. Synthesized in this way, the results of the three authors may draw attention to one of the unduly neglected class divisions in Germany: between the educated and the uneducated. In the classical country of *Bildung* where the professor held and still holds one of the top positions in public prestige, such a division was highly important in itself. It became still more important, even in a political sense, when the aristocracy partially adopted during the nineteenth century the bourgeois ideal of *Bildung.* Most telling in this respect is the rise of the idea of the army as a "school of the nation," indicating that even the Prussian army felt advised after 1848 to engage in a competition for education with the bourgeoisie. The civil bureaucracy had already adopted the educational ideal earlier; now, the military and part of the aristocracy followed in an attempt to maintain their position and to provide for the cooptation of "suitable" bourgeois elements.

In view of these facts, the hypothesis seems to arise that the division between the educated and uneducated may have developed in the nineteenth century into the true dividing line between the ruling oligarchy and its subjects. If this is true, subjects seeking emancipation had two ways to respond: either forming a subculture or resorting to barbarism. The first was the solution of the socialist labor movement; the second was the way of the Nazis, and it was the true revolutionary way. Evidence suggests that Hitler's prestige with the masses did not rest exclusively on economic and foreign-policy successes; it also appears to have been supported by the fact that Hitler succeeded again and again in defeating and humiliating the members of the old oligarchy. Hitler's frequent invectives against this class in his speeches are usually explained as motivated merely by his own personal resentments. The motive may well have been more sophisticated, however. Such considerations must lead to the perplexing question of whether the Nazi movement did involve some elements of a completion, terribly distorted indeed, of Germany's age-old unfinished revolution. This would open some new perspectives on the resistance movement, and it would perhaps explain the intriguing fact that the Nazi regime, in contrast to the Hohenzollern monarchy in 1918 and to the Fascist regime in Italy in 1943–1944, was not overthrown by a mass upheaval from within. The question cannot be answered here, but it is crucial. The answer will determine not only our understanding of the nature of Nazism in terms of the problem of fascism, but also our interpretation of Nazism as an element in German history.

George W. F. Hallgarten
THE COLLUSION OF CAPITALISM

Down to the time of the depression, the German bankers and the captains of industry had not shown much interest in sponsoring fascism or Nazism proper. While hardly less eager to check communism than anybody else in the Reich, they felt they could do so most efficiently by continuing the policy of cooperation with the German trade unions which Hugo Stinnes, the later so-called "king of the Ruhr," and the union leader Carl Legien had inaugurated in the defeat-clouded autumn of 1918. To be sure, heavy industry and its affiliates had not always followed this line too meticulously. During the months of social radicalism which followed the outbreak of the German Revolution in November 1918 a group of the Reich's most prominent businessmen, comprising Stinnes, Albert Vögler (then director of the Gelsenkirchen Mining Co., Ltd.), Carl Friedrich von Siemens, Felix Deutsch (of German General Electric), Director Mankiewitz, of the Deutsche Bank, and Director Salomonsohn, of the

From George W. F. Hallgarten, "Adolf Hitler and German Heavy Industry, 1931–1933," *Journal of Economic History* 12 (Summer 1952). Reprinted by permission of the publisher, New York University Press, and of the author.

Diskontogesellschaft, financed the movement of a Hitler forerunner, one Dr. Eduard Stadtler, who demanded the establishment of a German National Socialist state and who was instrumental in the smashing of communism in Berlin—then called Spartacism—and in the killing of its leaders, Karl Liebknecht and Rosa Luxemburg. In the Ruhr, Stadtler's movement was backed by the very same steel producers who, as will be shown, later backed Hitler: Emil Kirdorf, the venerated but dreaded God Wotan of German heavy industry, Albert Vögler, Fritz Springorum, of the Hoesch steel group, and also by Paul Reusch, of the Haniel group, and August Thyssen, father of Hitler's later financier Fritz Thyssen. But as soon as actual street fighting stopped, the industrialists dropped Stadtler and returned to their political cooperation with union labor.

Hitler who originally was nothing but the chief of an insignificant nationalist South German group could not hope to change this basic line followed by the Ruhr industrialists. Down to 1929 his party appears to have lived, in the main, on membership dues and individual gifts, mainly from local South German producers. A donation by Fritz Thyssen in 1923 remained an isolated fact. Even the party's increasing intimacy with Emil Kirdorf did not change the picture. A survivor of the period when the Reich, under Bismarck's leadership, had tried to solve the workers' question by a mixture of benevolent despotism and brutality, Kirdorf was considered out-of-date by everybody but the Nazis. Even the fact that he opened to the party access to the funds of the Bergbaulicher Verein and the Federation Eisen Nord West should not be overrated. Compared to the increasing indebtedness of the party which by 1933 rose to ca. 12 million RM, these payments were only a drop in the bucket. For the same reason, it is not too important to determine the exact amount that Hitler received at this and other occasions, as even the highest figures mentioned remained far behind the party's expenditures. What mattered was the fact that such amounts came in at all. They were like shots in the arm which proved to the millions of Hitler's followers that their Führer was "in" with the right type of people and thus deserved credit, politically and economically. After 1929 Hitler's chances in both fields improved rapidly. Favored by the increasing depression and by the funds he received from Alfred Hugenberg, leader of the conservative German Nationalist party in the Reichstag, the chief of the Nazis managed to raise the number of Nazi voters within two years from 800,000 to far over 6 millions. The Reichstag elections of September 14, 1930, gave the Nazis 107 seats, which made them the second largest party. The following year, with its bank crashes and public scandals which led in the summer to the closing of the German stock exchange and to the establishment of currency control, widened the Nazis' chances of success. From this time on, Hitler had dozens of meetings with business leaders, to gain support.

The depreciation of the British currency, on September 20, 1931, made the situation of the German exporters desperate and caused heavy industry to formulate an antidepression program which it could hardly hope to carry through without some Nazi help. Acting in the name of all German employer organizations, the Reich Federation of German Industry demanded that public expenses be cut down, that salaries be lowered according to the international market situation, that the social-insurance expenditure, including the subsidies to the unemployed, be slashed, and that the mail and freight tariffs be reduced. During the following weeks heavy industry made an all-out attack against the weak Brüning cabinet. The nationalist meeting in Bad Harzburg in October, in which Hugenberg and Hitler participated, became an assembly center of the industrial leaders, with men like Dr. Hjalmar Schacht, the Hamburg shipbuilder Blohm, the steel merchant Ravené, the United Steel head Ernst Poensgen, and a trusted agent of the steel people, Schlenker, in attendance. The debates centered largely around the currency question. After a long inner fight, heavy industry, in view of its interest in purchasing raw materials cheaply and in saving the Reich's inner purchasing power, refrained from advocating a German currency depreciation, which Dr. Schacht appears to have advocated. But in other respects Schacht was successful. Since the end of 1930 a public supporter of Hitler, the former president of the German Reichsbank and weathervane of German economic policy opened Hitler's way to the big banks. To show his recognition, Hitler cut the last tie that connected him with Gottfried Feder, the economic quack who in bygone days had impressed him greatly, but whose agitation against the "interest slavery" did not fit into the spirit of those days. Schacht saw to it that Feder was given a successor as Hitler's adviser in economics in a man better meeting the wishes of the industrialists: it was Dr. Walther Funk, an economic journalist who later became minister of economics and whom the Nuremberg court sent to prison for life.

Funk's appointment, effected with the help of Gregor Strasser, symbolized the rising interest that leaders of heavy industry took in the party. The mining industry subsidized Funk's orientation bulletin, the *Wirtschaftspolitischer Dienst,* with several thousand reichsmarks a month. In the performance of his new duties, Funk worked in close connection with Schacht, Dr. von Stauss, of the Deutsche Bank und Diskontogesellschaft, Hermann Göring, and Göring's helpers and associates in this field, Directors Hilgard, of the Alliance Insurance Corporation and Curt Schmitt of the Munich Reinsurance Corporation as well as Dr. Lubert, of the Verkehrswesen Ltd. and of the big building firm Lenz and Co., all of whom he introduced to Hitler. Schmitt later became Hitler's minister of economics.

Hitler was too good a politician, however, not to see the dangers which his ties with big business created both for his movement and himself. To be sure, he was not opposed to the making of profits by capitalist producers, as long as their ways did not cross his own. He felt, however, that his intended dictatorship called for the destruction of all elements of the existing society that could hamper his rule, comprising both union labor and all producers who refused to cooperate with him. The thought that his becoming a hireling of Hugenberg made him dependent on a type of businessman unwilling to accept his rule and the planned economy it involved drove him almost to physical despair. It is reported that during the Harzburg meeting in October 1931, when he was forced by the penury of his movement to cooperate with Hugenberg in a public demonstration, he showed signs of hysterical fury and behaved like an irresponsible madman. Before long, he took steps to break out of this ambiguous situation. "During a conversation which I had with the Führer in December, 1931," Wilhelm Keppler relates, "the Führer said: 'Try to get a few economic leaders—they need not to be Party members—who will be at our disposal when we come to power.' " This was the start of the so-called Circle of Friends, the entering wedge of the Nazis into the ranks of heavy industry as a whole. Keppler, a depression-stricken small businessman who had become Hitler's agent in economic matters, states that the Führer mentioned no other names aside from Dr. Schacht and, presumably, Albert Vögler, the director general of the United Steel Works, leaving it up to him, Keppler, to solicit members during the trips he took. He adds that in doing so he, Keppler, used the services of his distant relative, Kranefuss, a small industrialist like himself who was Heinrich Himmler's personal adjutant and who later succeeded in ousting him from the leadership of this group.

At the end of 1931 the results of this activity became gradually visible. In a New Year's article for 1932 Friedrich Reinhardt, director of the Commerz-und Privatbank, and one of the first nine members of the Keppler circle, launched a campaign for German economic self-sufficiency, a policy which spelled doom for the German consumers, merchants, and exporters but which was welcome to the producers of steel and coal and called for rearmament and imperialism, to make up for the sacrifices it involved. In the same days the press reported that Hitler had gained the support of Ludwig Grauert, the secretary general of the important Federation of German Employers, Group Northwest (Ruhr), who determined the attitude of heavy industry in wage questions. Grauert's attitude caused Schlenker, the executive secretary of the northwest German steel industry and of the so-called "Long Name Federation" (Federation for Safeguarding the Business Interests of Rhineland and Westphalia), to follow suit.

The big steel producers, during those days, clashed sharply with the steel-processing industry, since they no longer felt able to pay it the customary reimbursements for the price difference between the international and the inland prices for steel, in the case of exported steel goods. As the German steel prices were 214 percent above the international level, this change in policy was a deadly blow to exporters. To maintain the domestic price level, heavy industry, facing sudden bankruptcy, started looking for public orders.

This general situation was the background for an event which Otto Dietrich later called decisive in the history of the movement: it was Hitler's speech in the Industry Club in Düsseldorf on January 27, 1932. Initiator of this meeting was Fritz Thyssen, next to Kirdorf the most prominent of Hitler's supporters in the ranks of the industrialists. A son of a stern and hard-working father who had founded one of the three largest privately owned industrial empires in the Ruhr, Fritz Thyssen, suppressed, unsteady, and errant, was the problem child of the Reich Federation of heavy industry and the target of ire of his workers, who hated the feudal manners of this overbearing and pleasure-loving magnate. Several decades younger than Kirdorf, who always remained a Bismarck admirer, Thyssen admired the last kaiser. He hoped that Hitler would help the industrialists to reestablish the Wilhelmian regime. This being so, Thyssen took a certain pride in presenting Hitler to the greatest assembly of industrialists the later Führer had ever met. In his speech, Hitler as usual expressed his dissatisfaction with the Treaty of Versailles and with the democratic system and declared it to be his general aim to rearm Germany and to take affirmative action in order to achieve German objectives in foreign affairs. He stated that "Germany's power position . . . is . . . the condition for the improvement of the economic situation" and that "there can be no economic life unless behind this economic life there stands the determined political will of the nation absolutely ready to strike, and to strike hard." Otto Dietrich says that in this speech Hitler succeeded in breaking through the reserve of the western German captains of industry, and Thyssen expresses the view that the "speech made a deep impression on the assembled industrialists, and in consequence of this a number of large contributions flowed from the resources of heavy industry," a statement which seems somewhat exaggerated.

The day following the speech at the Industry Club, Ernst Poensgen and Albert Vögler met Hitler, Göring, and Röhm at Thyssen's castle, Landsberg. The content of their conversation is unknown. Poensgen states, however, that Göring asked the industrialists whether they would allow Ludwig Grauert, Hitler's newly won supporter, and head of the employers Organization Northwest, to become minister of labor in a Hitler cabinet.

In the person of Albert Vögler, Kirdorf's associate in the chairmanship of the Gelsenkirchen board, chairman of the Federation of German Steel Miners, and director general of by far the biggest German steel combine, the United Steel Works (Vereinigte Stahlwerke), Hitler met, not for the first time, the man who next to Kirdorf was the most representative figure of the German steel industry of those days and whose experience even a Thyssen could not match. An ardent nationalist and imperialist who in the First World War had headed the drive for the incorporation into the Reich of the French iron-ore basin of Briey and Longwy and who later financed Dr. Stadtler, Vögler supported the Nazis in the apparent hope of saving his combine from disaster by a policy of lowering wages, soliciting government orders, and sponsoring general rearmament. As already said, he was one of the two persons whom Hitler mentioned by name when urging Keppler late in 1931 to organize the Circle of Friends, the other man being Dr. Schacht, the close friend of Dr. von Stauss, of the Deutsche Bank und Diskontogesellschaft. What Hitler presumably did not yet know was the fact that Vögler's industrial combine, the United Steel Works, was threatened by a disaster similar to the one which in the summer of that year had overpowered the German banks and had forced the Reich to intervene and take over some of their functions.

Victims to a large extent of their own rationalization and price policy which created unemployment and prevented recovery, the Vöglers and Stausses expected to obtain salvation by endorsing a dictatorship that would spend for rearmament. In doing so, they inevitably provoked the ire and the bitter criticism of scores of other businessmen and producers who were not "in" with the big concerns and resented the latters' Nazism. This type of criticism later furnished one of the bases for the many misstatements and exaggerations by the defense in Nuremberg when it tried to prove that big business as a whole hated Hitler. In the weeks of January and February 1932 when Poensgen, Vögler, and the three top Nazis deliberated, Vögler, as will be shown presently, secretly notified the Reich bureaucracy, that the big steel combine he headed was facing disaster, unless supported by public means. His statements were made jointly with a man who from being a comparatively unknown little industrialist had reached, in those days, a position of great influence in German heavy industry: Friedrich Flick whom the Nuremberg tribunal later sentenced to seven years in prison for having committed crimes against humanity. Like Vögler, Flick too, considered cooperation with the Nazis to be one of the many ways that might lead him out of the disaster that was threatening him and all his allies. Through the initiative of Walther Funk he in February 1932 had a first interview with Hitler. None of these steps, however, had immediate success. Hitler, as was his habit, submerged his visitor in a torrent of words which prevented Flick from saying what he wanted. Besides Hitler, during those days, was hardly able to make definite promises which would have saved the steel magnates from disaster.

Having decided to run against old President von Hindenburg in the presidential elections, Hitler was not much less of a gambler than was a man like Flick. During the electoral campaign, he saw with dismay that the bulk of German industry still supported the German People's party, the comparatively moderate group once headed by the late Stresemann, which joined the parties of the Weimar Coalition in advocating von Hindenburg's candidacy. To Hitler's anger, the opponents of his rule and advocates of cooperation with union labor still controlled the commanding positions of the German Republic and German industry. This basic situation did not change even after Reich President von Hindenburg, reelected on April 10, 1932, in a hard fight at the polls against the self-styled Führer, turned his back on his voters, the Weimar parties and others, dismissed the Reich chancellor, Dr. Brüning, and with the consent of Reichswehr and Nazis appointed a Junker-controlled cabinet, under Franz von Papen. While most of the measures envisaged by the new cabinet, such as the restriction of democratic liberties, the absorption of the jobless by public works and the suppression of the Weimar regime in Prussia corresponded to Nazi ideas, Hitler saw with mounting fury that the credit for this policy was going to men who were out to destroy him.

The entire year 1932 is marked by a series of efforts to carry out his program without giving him personal power and to use his party as a policeman in the interest of others. Champions in this game were first Reich Chancellor von Papen and his Junker cabinet and, after von Papen's resignation in November, the Reichswehr leader General Kurt von Schleicher. Since none of these men dared openly to violate the constitution and, instead of governing without a parliament, resorted to the means of Reichstag dissolutions, the day of parliamentary reckoning was going to come sooner or later. But Hitler's unsuccessful running for Reich president, in the spring of that year, and the two consecutive Reichstag dissolutions that followed, loaded down his party with heavy debts, in the amount of ca. 12 million gold marks, and made it highly improbable that, in the decisive moment, he would still be a political factor to reckon with. Recognizing the intentions of the von Papen cabinet to wear him down and to make Junkers and heavy industry the sole masters of the Reich, Hitler during that entire eventful year was like a madman racing against time. . . .

The interest the United Steel group took in his cause enabled Hitler to overcome the party crisis of the fall of 1932, when the Nazis almost succumbed to the von Papen policy of exhausting them by a series of expensive election campaigns. The party crisis even increased the aid the Nazis received from the steel group, since it coincided with a development that made them indispensable to the steel men. Down to November most producers, including even many of those who hoped for Nazi support, endorsed the cabinet of von Papen who represented both Junkers and industrialists, and who tried to use the Nazis merely as a Frankenstein, in order to terrify the leftists in the Reichstag. Fortunately for the Nazis, the chancellor, since the fall of 1932, no longer had the support of the Reichswehr minister, General von Schleicher, whose intrigues early in the spring, had brought his cabinet into power. In November, von Papen resigned and von Schleicher took over the chancellorship. Unlike von Papen, the general was more concerned with finding a mass basis for the increase of the army than with maintaining shaky class privileges. With grave anxiety Junkers and heavy industry witnessed the efforts made by von Schleicher to come to an understanding with union labor and with the left wing of the Nazis, and to draft an antidepression program which in every respect contradicted their wishes. While both von Papen and von Schleicher were agreed that the depression should be fought by public spending and an armament program, the general, distrustful of the military ambitions of leading Nazis, would have been happy if granted the backing of the Socialists in the Reichstag. This outcome would have deprived both Junkers and industry of the profits they hoped to reap from militarization, not to mention the danger many of them incurred by a Reichstag investigation of the *Osthilfe* matter or by a socialization of heavy industry based upon the Reich's ownership of the Gelsenkirchen shares. Thus Hitler, in the very last moment, when his party, weakened by three big election campaigns within eight months, was facing both bankruptcy and a catastrophic loss of votes, obtained the long-expected chance of presenting himself as the savior of society. He even was saved from financial distress by the very same circles that he was expected to save politically.

Still, heavy industry was far from giving the Nazis its unanimous and unqualified support. The independent producers, while deeply concerned over the von Schleicher trend, feared the economic dictatorship of the men around United Steel much too strongly to fall in with their political wishes. Walther Funk's trip through the Ruhr late in 1932 to collect money for the party, became a dismal failure the only major contribution being an amount of 20 to 30,000 RM given to him by Steinbrinck for Flick. Hardly more lucky than Funk in his efforts to help the Nazis was Otto Prince zu Salm-Horstmar, one of the old wirepullers of German economic imperialism who in the middle of October urged Gustav Krupp to sign an appeal—as it appears in favor of Nazi admission to the government—which had been decided on the day before by a small committee. After the November elections in which the Nazi vote sank to 33.1 percent of the total votes as compared to 37.4 percent in the elections of July 31, Curt von Schroeder, banker of the United Steel group, Albert Vögler, United Steel director, and Dr. Hjalmar Schacht approached the leading industrial circles with the request to sign a petition in which President von Hindenburg was urged to make Hitler chancellor. The response they found outside the circle of the United Steel group was not encouraging. Paul Reusch and Fritz Springorum of the Hoesch steel group informed Vögler that they agreed with the petition but did not desire to add their signatures. The same answer was given by the directors Kiep and Cuno, of the Hamburg-American Steamship Line. Dr. Schacht's report to Hitler on the progress of the campaign was couched in most careful terms. "Permit me to congratulate you on the firm stand you took," he wrote immediately after the elections. "I have no doubt that the present development of things can only lead to your becoming chancellor. It seems as if our attempt to collect a number of signatures from business circles for this purpose was not altogether in vain, although I believe that heavy industry will hardly participate, for it rightfully bears its name 'heavy industry' on account of its indecisiveness."

The Goebbels diaries of those weeks show most clearly how both the morale and the financial situation of the party, under these conditions, sank to an unheard-of low, and how the party was threatened with a split. Fortunately for Hitler, the moderate wing of big business which backed von Papen was hardly less interested in preventing a complete downfall of the party than were the Nazi enthusiasts around the United Steel Works. Threatened with the von Schleicher solution which involved a likely blow to both Junkers and big business as a whole, the von Papen group, centered in the Herrenklub circle, was prepared to listen to compromise proposals made by its Nazified colleagues. This is the background for the famous meeting between von Papen and Hitler of January 4, 1933, in the house of the Cologne banker, Curt von Schroeder, the business associate and confidant of Vögler, Kirdorf, Thyssen, and Flick. "The general aim of the industrialists at that time," von Schroeder later told allied interrogators who questioned him about his arranging this meeting, "was to see a strong leader come to power in Germany who could form a government which would long remain in power. When on the 6th of November 1932, the NSDAP suffered its first set-back and had thus passed its peak-point, the support of German heavy industry became a matter of particular urgency."

About his personal interest in bringing about a political turn which would help to make United Steel a going concern and prevent the socialization of the German steel industry, von Schroeder in his various testimonies did not talk. The general picture, however, is obvious enough. Immediately after the Hitler–von Papen meeting, which before the end of the month resulted in von Hindenburg's appointing Hitler as Reich chancellor, with von Papen as vice-chancellor, a consortium of industrialists, headed by Vögler and Springorum and including many members of the Circle of Friends, gave von Schroeder's bank, J. H. Stein, 1 million RM for distribution among the SS. The consortium also saw to it that the Nazi party's most urgent election debts were paid. Thyssen, to be sure, remained uninformed about the Cologne meeting but he had good reason to be happy about its outcome. To open his pro-Nazi activity Hermann Göring at that time called him up and told him that the Communists planned his assassination. For German industry as a whole, the meeting of Cologne had far-reaching consequences which even outweighed the settling of the Gelsenkirchen matter as such.

Hitler's final rise to power became equivalent in the industrial field, to a victory of the steel producers and coal miners—Thyssen, Vögler, the Tengelmanns, Springorum, Knepper, Buskuehl—and of their allies in the insurance business and in the chemical industry such as Keilermann, von Schnitzler, and Gattineau over the representatives of the big independent family enterprises, such as Krupp, Peter Kloeckner, Paul Reusch, of the Haniel-controlled Gute Hoffnungshütte, Hugo

Stinnes, Jr., and Carl Friedrich von Siemens, the head of the famous Siemens electrical firm. It would appear that the old industrial families of the Ruhr feared Hitler's budding totalitarianism much more strongly than did the directors of the anonymous companies who live on big salaries, instead of on individual profits. . . .

Summing up, one might say that the big concerns which supported Hitler's rise to power consisted mainly of those groups which—more or less thanks to their own doing—had been hardest hit by the depression, and thus hoped for the coming of a "savior." Among these groups the big banks, some of which had collapsed in 1931, were conspicuous, since all of them faced the threat of socialization. In the Circle of Friends and other Nazi agencies, this group was represented by men like Friedrich Reinhardt, Emil Meyer, Emil von Stauss and, as their agent, Hjalmar Schacht. The other group, leading in industry, consisted of the United Steel Works circle which has been dealt with here at length. The rest of the big industrial concerns, while welcoming Hitler as an ally against labor, would have preferred to see him being used as a mere tool in the hands of a cabinet controlled by industry and Junkers. Even such ardent Hitler supporters as Thyssen would doubtless have been happier if Hitler, in the long run, had helped them to reerect the monarchy instead of playing kaiser himself. When this proved not to be feasible, however, they supported Hitler as the lesser of two evils, eager to make the best of his coming to power, both politically and economically. In this respect, all documentary sources concur, though many gaps remain to be filled, since the Nuremberg trial records which are our best available source of material were assembled for juridical rather than for historical needs.

While Hitler was strongly assisted by the industrialists' funds, one cannot say that industry "made" his movement. A movement of such enormous size as his, which in 1932 controlled 230 seats in the Reichstag, is not made by any individual or group. It might be more correct to state that heavy industry by its very existence and social nature caused the movement, or, at least, helped to cause it and once it was given birth tried to use it for the industrialists' purposes. Mechanization and economic concentration, maintenance of monopoly prices and monopoly agreements, with the resulting pressure on small competitors, were the fertile ground on which mass fascism grew. In the period of Locarno and the following years this development was still counterbalanced by boom and employment. But in the depression years after 1929 it became suddenly apparent that the German middle class, in the postwar inflation, had lost the remnants of its economic independence. In Germany, the nation of military Prussia, the declining middle class was too strongly inspired by military and aristocratic ideologies to turn Socialist or New Deal or to attack the existing society, with its unsound and obsolete agrarian structure, and its expansion-minded concerns. On the other hand, neither was it conservative. Deeply mistrusting the men in control of the command positions of German economy, it turned desperado and strengthened the power of a leader half a vagabond and half a policeman, half a slave and half a ruler, who, in the manner of a condottiere, offered the ruling classes "protection" against criminal punishment and labor troubles and, by a mixture of threats and blackmail, made himself master over both wealthy and poor.

Henry Ashby Turner, Jr.
THE LEGEND OF CAPITALIST SUPPORT

Did German big business support Adolf Hitler's climb to power? A quarter of a century after the demise of the Third Reich, this remains one of the major unresolved questions about its inception. For Marxists, or at least those who adhere to the Moscow line, the answer to this question has never been a problem. From the outset, they have viewed Nazism as a manifestation of "monopoly capitalism" and the Nazis as tools of big business. Among non-Marxists there has been no such unanimity. Some have in large measure agreed with the Marxist interpretation; others have rejected it. Most have adopted a cautious middle position, asserting that some capitalists aided the Nazis but avoiding any precise analysis of the extent or effectiveness of that aid. This wide range of views is in part clearly the product of

From Henry Ashby Turner, Jr., "Big Business and the Rise of Hitler," *The American Historical Review* 75 (October 1969): 56–70, by permission of the author. Footnotes omitted. A German translation is available in the author's *Faschismus und Kapitalismus in Deutschland* (Göttingen, 1972).

ideological differences. But another factor has been the scanty, sometimes ambiguous, and frequently dubious nature of the evidence on
which all previous studies of the subject rest. Few aspects of the
history of National Socialism have, in fact, been so inadequately re-
searched. Now that new documentation is available, the time has
come for another look at the problem.

None of the new evidence contradicts the widespread impression
that German big businessmen were unenthusiastic about the Weimar
Republic. Most were not, as is often assumed, unreconstructed monarchists; they displayed, on the whole, a surprising indifference to
governmental forms. What offended them about the new state was its
adoption of costly welfare measures, its introduction of compulsory
arbitration in disputes between labor and management, and, most
particularly, the influence it accorded to the prolabor Social Democratic party, which was most pronounced in the government of the
largest federal state, Prussia. Despite abundant objective evidence
that the republic, at least during its years of prosperity, provided
generally favorable conditions for business enterprise, Germany's
business leaders continued to eye it with misgiving. Their attitude
had much in common with that of the army: they, too, refused to
commit themselves to the new state, regarding it as a potentially
transitory phenomenon, while viewing themselves as the guardians
of something of more permanent value to the nation—in their case,
die Wirtschaft, the industrial sector of the economy.

In spite of its reserved attitude toward the new German state, big
business was nevertheless politicized by the changes resulting from
the Revolution of 1918. Whereas in the empire its leaders had been
able to influence governmental policy without wholesale commitment
to partisan politics, in the republic they found it necessary to assume
a more active political role. In far greater numbers than in the empire,
they joined the ranks of the *bürgerlich,* or nonsocialist, parties and
sought places in the parliaments for themselves or their spokesmen.
For most big businessmen, politics was more a matter of interests
than of ideology. When they took the trouble to describe their political outlook, the words that reoccurred with greatest frequency were
"national" and "liberal." The term "liberal" has always been prob-
lematical in German usage, but in business circles of this period it
was more so than usual, as was revealed by one businessman who,

writing to an acquaintance, explained: "As you well know, I have always been liberal, in the sense of Kant and Frederick the Great."

Although big business entered the politics of the republic, it never found a political home there. From the beginning, its spokesmen were scattered among the four principal nonsocialist parties, the Democratic party, the Catholic Center party, the German People's party, and the German National People's party. This dispersal divided and thus weakened the business leaders politically. Within each party they had to compete with numerous other pressure groups whose interests rarely coincided with their own and who could usually deliver far more votes. Sometimes the spokesmen of big business succeeded in gaining the backing of their parties, but more often they were defeated or forced to settle for less than they regarded as acceptable. Contrary to the belief of the Marxists, economic power did not translate readily into political power in the Weimar Republic. And nowhere was this recognized more acutely than in big business circles.

The political impotence of money was strikingly demonstrated by the fate of a project that enjoyed wide support from big business during the last years of the republic. Having grown impatient with the multiplicity of parties with which they had to deal, a number of influential businessmen proposed the formation of a single, united nonsocialist party, a *bürgerliche Einheitspartei,* as it was generally labeled. The plan called for such an organization to absorb the squabbling older parties, sweep away their superfluous and anachronistic ideological differences, and erect an impregnable barrier to Marxism. It was confidently expected, moreover, that in such a united party the interests of *die Wirtschaft* would at last receive their due. Much enthusiasm developed for this plan in the ranks of big business during the period 1930–1932. But although considerable pressure was exerted on the politicians, including the withholding of financial contributions during election campaigns, nothing came of the project. Despite a barrage of importunities, threats, and punitive measures, the existing parties tenaciously defended their independence and the politicians their party posts. Again, the limits to the political utility of economic power had been revealed. The result was further disillusionment in big business circles, not only with the parties but with the democratic, parliamentary system as a whole—a disillusionment that deepened as a succession of unstable cabinets struggled unsuccessfully to cope with the Great Depression.

Crucial to the subject of this inquiry is the question of whether the unmistakably mounting discontent of big business led it to support Hitler and his movement during the last phases of the republic. The answer is, on the whole, no. The qualification is necessary because, as is well known, certain big businessmen, such as Fritz Thyssen, heir to one of the great steel enterprises of the Ruhr, did give money to the Nazis. If, however, one examines the political record of big business, it quickly becomes evident that these pro-Nazis are conspicuous precisely because they were exceptions. The failure to recognize this basic fact has led to great exaggeration of their importance, as has the reliance on untrustworthy sources, such as *I Paid Hitler,* a book published over the name of Thyssen, but not actually written by him.

A number of legends about industrial support for the Nazis have been perpetuated by previous literature and, largely by virtue of repetition, have come to be accepted as fact. According to one of these legends, large sums of money flowed to the Nazis through the hands of Alfred Hugenberg, the reactionary press lord who became head of the right-wing German National People's party in 1928. This allegation probably derives from Hugenberg's role in the campaign against the Young Plan in 1929. As one of the organizations supporting that campaign, the Nazi party did receive a share of the funds that Hugenberg helped to raise at the time. There is not a trace of documentary evidence, however, that any of Hugenberg's resources were thereafter diverted to the Nazis. Indeed, this seems highly unlikely: as the leader of a party that was itself beset by financial problems, Hugenberg had little motive to share any funds he received from big business, least of all with a party that was taking votes away from his own. The amount of big business money at Hugenberg's disposal has, in any event, been grossly exaggerated. Contrary to the widespread belief that he was one of the foremost spokesmen of big business throughout the republican period, most of the industrial backers of his party had opposed his election as its chairman in 1928, rejecting him as too inflexible, too provocative, and too highhanded for their tastes. In the summer of 1930 a large segment of his party's industrial wing took issue with his opposition to Heinrich Brüning's cabinet and seceded to join the new Conservative People's party. Even among those who did not take that step, there was a strong movement to replace Hugenberg with a more moderate man. As a result, Hugenberg, who had enjoyed wide support from big business during the first decade of the republic, was forced, during its last years, to rely increasingly upon the backing of agricultural interests.

Another persistent legend concerns Emil Kirdorf, long universally regarded as a kind of industrial *alter Kämpfer.* Kirdorf, an octogenarian survivor of the beginning phase of German heavy industry in the 1870s, was the first really noteworthy business figure to join the Nazi party, entering in 1927. But despite the tributes lavished upon him by Hitler and the party press during the Third Reich, he was far from a loyal Nazi. In 1928, only a little over a year after joining the party, Kirdorf resigned in anger, a fact that the Nazis long succeeded in concealing from historians. Eventually, it is true, he rejoined the party, but only in 1934, when on personal orders from Hitler Kirdorf's records were rewritten to make his membership seem uninterrupted. But during the crucial years 1929–1933 Kirdorf was a supporter of the German National People's party, not the Nazi party. Nor is there any evidence that Kirdorf contributed appreciable sums to the Nazis during the struggle for power. Since he had retired from all active business posts even before joining the party for the first time in 1927, he had no access to corporate or associational funds. Anything he gave had to come from his own pocket, and he was not known as a man who spent his money either gladly or lavishly. Kirdorf's reputation as a patron of National Socialism rests not on documented facts but on a myth created in large measure by the Nazis themselves following his reentry into the party, when they appropriated the aged industrialist as a symbol of respectability.

The reason for Kirdorf's resignation from the party is indicative of the attitude of most big businessmen toward National Socialism in the years before Hitler achieved power. Kirdorf did not withdraw because the Nazis were antidemocratic, aggressively chauvinistic, or anti-Semitic (even though he, like most business leaders, was himself not an anti-Semite). What drove him out of the party was the social and economic radicalism of the left-wing Nazis. Like millions of other Germans of middle-class background, including big businessmen, Kirdorf was attracted to Nazism by its assertive nationalism and its implacable hostility toward Marxism, but like most big businessmen, he was at the same time repelled by the fear that the National Socialists might eventually live up to their name by turning out to be socialists of some kind. Hitler, who began earnestly to court the business community in 1926, went to great pains to allay this fear. In 1927, at the request of Kirdorf, he wrote a pamphlet that was secretly printed and then distributed in business circles by the old industrialist. In the pamphlet, as in his speech before the Düsseldorf Industrie-Klub in January 1932, Hitler sought to indicate that there was no need to fear socialism from his party. It is safe to assume that he said much the same thing in his numerous other meetings with representatives of big business. His efforts, however, were repeatedly compromised, as in the case of Kirdorf, by the radical noises emanating from the left wing of the Nazi party.

As a consequence, most of the political money of big business went, throughout the last years of the republic, to the conservative opponents of the Nazis. In the presidential campaign of 1932 most of the business community backed Paul von Hindenburg against Hitler, despite the Nazi leader's blatant appeal for support in his Industrie-Klub speech. In the two Reichstag elections of 1932, big business was overwhelmingly behind the bloc of parties that supported the cabinet of Franz von Papen, the first government since the Revolution of 1918 to arouse enthusiasm in business circles. If money could have purchased political power, the republic would have been succeeded by Papen's *Neuer Staat,* not by Hitler's *Drittes Reich.* But the effort to transform marks into votes proved a crushing failure.

There were, to be sure, exceptions to this pattern. Certain big businessmen did give money to the Nazis, particularly after the 1930 Reichstag election showed them to be a major political factor. Some of these contributions can best be described, however, as political insurance premiums. This was clearly the case, for example, with Friedrich Flick, a parvenu intruder into the ranks of the Ruhr industrialists, who by the early 1930s had managed to secure a dominant position in the country's largest steel-producing firm, the United Steel Works (Vereinigte Stahlwerke). Flick's speculative transactions and his questionable dealings with the Brüning cabinet left him vulnerable to attacks from the press and apprehensive about the attitude of future cabinets toward his enterprises. His solution was to spread his political money across the political spectrum, from the liberal and Catholic parties to the Nazi party. Flick may be a deplorable example of the politically amoral capitalist, but he was by no means an enthusiastic supporter of National Socialism prior to 1933. Nor is there any indication that he was especially generous toward the Nazis. According to the records he produced at his war crimes trial in Nuremberg, the Nazis received little more than token contributions in comparison to the sums that went to their opponents.

The political activities of the I. G. Farben chemical trust were characterized by much the same pattern as those of Flick. From its formation in 1925, the company maintained contact with all the nonsocialist parties and made financial contributions to them. According to the postwar accounts of one official of the trust, the Nazis were added to the list in 1932. That same official estimated the total contributions for one of the Reichstag election campaigns of 1932 (it is not clear whether he was referring to the July or November elections) at approximately 200,000 to 300,000 marks. Of this, he reported, no more than 10 to 15 percent had gone to the Nazis. I. G. Farben, like Flick, had special reason to be concerned about maintaining the good will of the political parties. In its case, this concern arose from heavy investments in elaborate processes designed to yield high-grade synthetic gasoline. Since the costs of production were initially high, the company could hope to break into the domestic market only if a protective tariff were imposed on oil imports. Such a tariff had been put into effect by the Brüning cabinet and maintained by the Papen regime, but in view of Germany's obviously chronic political instability, the tariff question remained a source of considerable anxiety to the leadership of the firm. When attacks on Farben appeared in the Nazi press in 1932, concern developed about the attitude of what was by then the country's strongest political party. Two minor officials were, accordingly, sent to Munich in the autumn of 1932 to sound out Hitler on the project. Much has been made of this episode by some writers, who have inferred that it produced a deal that brought Farben behind the National Socialist movement at a crucial time. From all available evidence, however, the firm's representatives came away with only vague assurances from Hitler that he would halt the attacks in the party press. The Nazis apparently received at most the small share of the relatively modest political funds described above, although even this may, in view of the ambiguity of the evidence, have been granted earlier, at the time of the summer election campaign, and thus quite independently of the Munich meeting with Hitler. There is, in any case, no evidence that the chemical combine wanted a Nazi triumph or threw its financial support decisively to National Socialism. All indications are, in fact, that the leaders of Farben, acutely aware of their firm's dependence on exports, were apprehensive at the prospect of a take-over of the government by a party that preached economic autarky.

As in the cases of Flick and I. G. Farben, most of the big business money that found its way to the Nazis was not given simply, or even primarily, with the aim of bringing them to power. Whereas Flick and Farben were seeking to buy political insurance against the eventuality of a Nazi capture of the government, others were attempting to alter the nature of the Nazi movement. This they hoped to accomplish by giving money to "sensible" or "moderate" Nazis, thereby strengthening that element and weakening the economically and socially radical tendencies that had always been the chief obstacles to cooperation between big business and National Socialism. There was, however, no agreement as to who the "sensible" Nazis were. Thyssen, one of the few who really wanted a Nazi triumph, was nevertheless concerned about radicalism in the party. He sought to counteract it by subsidizing the man he regarded as the bulwark of moderation, Hermann Göring, who used at least a considerable portion of Thyssen's money to indulge his taste for lavish living. Hermann Bücher, head of the large electrical equipment concern, Allgemeine Elektrizitäts-Gesellschaft, tried to combat Nazi radicalism by giving financial aid to Joseph Goebbels' rival in Berlin, storm troop leader Walter Stennes, in his short-lived revolt. Surprisingly, the directors of the principal organization of the coal industry, the Bergbau-Verein, saw their "moderate" Nazi in Gregor Strasser—usually classified as a leader of the left wing—and for a time channeled funds to him. Still others gave money to Walther Funk, the former editor of a conservative financial newspaper, who bore at least the title of economic adviser to Hitler and who was regarded in some business quarters as a "liberal" Nazi and a potential moderating influence.

Not all attempts to alter the Nazis' economic and social attitudes involved financial contributions. Kirdorf, for example, maintained cordial personal relations with Hitler even after resigning from the party in 1928 and sought to exert influence on the Führer by making clear his objections to the left-wing Nazis and to the radical planks in the party program. Much the same attempt was made by the *Keppler-Kreis,* the group of businessmen assembled in the spring of 1932 at Hitler's request by one of his advisers, Wilhelm Keppler. Later, during the Third Reich, after this group was appropriated by Heinrich Himmler and transformed into his *Freundeskreis,* it became a source of enormous contributions for the SS. But prior to the acquisition of power by the Nazis, it was merely an advisory body, seeking, without success, to bring about a commitment of the party to conservative economic policies; it did not serve as a channel for business contributions.

The question of whether the Nazis were aided appreciably by the big business money that did reach them from those who were seeking either to buy protection or to alter the nature of the party cannot at present be definitively answered: ignorance about Nazi finances is a major handicap that deserves far more attention than it has received. But it is known, from Goebbels's diary and other sources, that the Nazis were plagued by acute money problems until the very moment of Hitler's appointment as chancellor. It thus seems clear that the sums received were not sufficient to solve the party's financial problems. The significant point, in any case, is that the funds reaching the Nazis from big business were but a small fraction of those that went to their opponents and rivals. On balance, big business money went overwhelmingly against the Nazis.

In spite of all this, it is nevertheless true that most business leaders were favorably inclined toward the new cabinet installed on January 30, 1933, with Hitler as chancellor. It has been alleged that this was only the expression of attitudes already discernible at least as early as November, when, following the poor showing of the Papen bloc at the polls, some businessmen had, at the instigation of the *Keppler-Kreis,* petitioned Hindenburg to appoint Hitler chancellor. But the attitude of those who signed the petition was not typical of the outlook of big business in November 1932; nor did the list of signatories include any major business figures, aside from Thyssen, who had for some time made no secret of his support for the Nazis. Another signatory, Hjalmar Schacht, is often assigned to the ranks of big business, but as of 1932 he is more properly classified as a political adventurer.

The change of outlook occurred for most businessmen in December 1932; its primary cause was Kurt von Schleicher. It is difficult to exaggerate their distrust and fear of the man who became chancellor on December 3. They were hostile to him in part for his role in bringing down Papen, the one chancellor they had admired and trusted. But even more important was Schleicher's apparent indifference to orthodox economic principles and traditional class alignments. Shortly after becoming chancellor he caused the gravest apprehension in business circles by announcing that he was neither a capitalist nor a socialist. He also flirted openly with the trade unions, raising the specter of an alliance of the military and the working class against the propertied elements of society. As a result, Germany's big businessmen feared that Schleicher might turn out to be a socialist in military garb. It was more from a desire to be rid of him than from enthusiasm for what was to replace him that they applauded the events of January 1933.

Contrary to what has often been asserted, big business played no part in the intrigues of that month. Much has been made of the role of Baron Kurt von Schroeder, the banker at whose home in Cologne Hitler and Papen met on January 4 to conspire against Schleicher. Schroeder was, however, not acting as an agent of big business. His importance lay in the fortuitous fact that he was acquainted with both Papen and Keppler, Hitler's adviser, and could thus serve as a convenient intermediary between two sides anxious to join forces. Nor is there any evidence that the meeting at his house began a flow of business money to the Nazis, as has repeatedly been alleged. Money was, in any event, not what mattered in January 1933. What counted was influence with Hindenburg, and big business had little or none of that. From the president's Junker standpoint, even the most powerful bankers and industrialists were little better than shopkeepers.

Most of the leaders of big business were, to the very end, under a basic misapprehension about the nature of the new cabinet taking shape in January 1933. Their information came mainly from Papen and his circle, and they were led to believe that what was coming was a revival of the Papen cabinet, with its base widened through the inclusion of the Nazis. Even when it was learned that Papen would be vice-chancellor under Hitler, big business continued to assume that he would be the real leader of the new government. In the eyes of the business community, January 30, 1933, seemed at first to mark the fall of the hated Schleicher and the return of the trusted Papen, not the advent of a Nazi dictatorship

By the time the leaders of big business were disabused of this illusion, they were ready to make their peace with Hitler. One factor in this turn of events was the ability of the new chancellor, as the legally installed head of government, to appeal to their respect for constituted authority. But even more important, once he was in office Hitler demonstrated that he was, as he had always reassured them, not a socialist. He therefore had no difficulty in extracting large sums from big business, starting with the campaign for the Reichstag election of March 1933. These contributions unquestionably aided Hitler significantly. But they aided him in the consolidation of his power, not in its acquisition. He had achieved that without the support of most of big business, indeed in spite of its massive assistance to his opponents and rivals.

These observations are in no sense intended as an exoneration of German big business. Its political record in the period that ended with the establishment of the Third Reich is hardly praiseworthy. In numerous ways its leaders contributed indirectly to the rise of Nazism: through their failure to support the democratic republic; through their blind hostility to the Social Democrats and the labor unions; through their aid to reactionary forces, most conspicuously the Papen regime; and through the respectability they bestowed upon Hitler by receiving him into their midst on a number of occasions. Some contributed more directly, by giving money to the Nazi party, or at least to certain Nazis. None of this, however, should be allowed to obscure the central fact that the great majority of Germany's big businessmen had neither wanted a Nazi triumph nor contributed materially to it.

The last statement, it should be emphasized, does not necessarily apply to the German business community as a whole. There are, in fact, indications that Hitler received considerable support from small- and middle-sized business. This is not surprising, for it was there that the real and potential entrepreneurial victims of the Great Depression were to be found. The giant businesses of the country knew from past experience that their importance to the national economy was so great that no government could afford to let them go bankrupt; in fact, the cabinets of the republic repeatedly came to the aid of ailing big business concerns rather than face the sharp increase in unemployment that their collapse would entail. Smaller, less visible firms could expect no such protection from the abrasive mechanisms of cyclical contraction; for their owners and managers, economic extinction was a real possibility, with the consequence that they were often genuinely desperate men. But the fact nevertheless remains that these small- and middle-sized businessmen can by no stretch of the imagination be included in the ranks of German big business, or, to use Marxist terminology, "the monopoly capitalists." Therefore, unless one is willing to accept the simplistic *cui bono* approach, according to which the eventual economic beneficiaries of Hitler's acquisition of power must necessarily have supported him beforehand, or the sophistic distinction between subjective and objective roles in history that is so popular in Marxist circles, it must be concluded that during its rise to power National Socialism was, in socioeconomic terms, primarily a movement not of winners in the capitalist struggle for survival but of losers and those who feared becoming losers.

It can, of course, be argued that even if the big businessmen did not support Hitler, National Socialism was nevertheless a product of capitalism. Certainly the deprivation and anxiety occasioned by the downward turn of the capitalist economic cycle after 1929 heightened the susceptibility of many Germans to the panaceas offered by the Nazis. The country's capitalist economic system also fostered and exacerbated the class animosities that the Nazis exploited and promised to eliminate. It spawned as well the other long-term economic and social problems to which Nazism was in large measure a response, although a response that offered mainly quack remedies and flights from reality rather than real solutions. National Socialism was thus undeniably a child of the capitalist order. Still, care must be taken not to attach undue significance to that fact. Only a few capitalist societies have produced phenomena comparable to Nazism; on the other hand, the latter shares its capitalist parentage with every other political movement that has emerged from modern Europe, including liberal democracy and communism.

Gordon A. Craig
MANIPULATION BY THE MILITARY

In the critical years of the Weimar Republic, as in previous periods of German history, the army played a decisive part in determining the political destiny of the nation. The most dangerous enemies of the republic realized that they could not hope to overthrow it unless they secured at least the sympathetic neutrality of the army; and Hitler for one was guided by that knowledge in all phases of his policy before 1933. Hitler set out deliberately to play upon the dissatisfaction which existed within the army, and while his promises of a restored and expanded military establishment gradually enticed the bulk of the junior officers to his support, his charges that the republican regime lacked national spirit and failed adequately to defend the interests of the state found a sympathetic response in the hearts of the officer corps in general. Thus the fateful political change of January 30, 1933, was supported, at least tacitly, by the army. . . .

The last unhappy phase in the history of the Weimar Republic was one, therefore, in which the army was more continuously and intimately involved in domestic politics than it had been under either Seeckt or Groener. This was made abundantly clear in the negotiations which led to the formation of the Papen government. It was Schleicher who urged Hindenburg to appoint Franz von Papen as Brüning's successor, who first broached the matter to Papen himself, who nominated most of his ministerial colleagues, and who conducted the negotiations which were designed to win Hitler's forbearance as the new cabinet began its work. And in all this, as Papen himself has written, "Schleicher left . . . no doubt that he was acting as spokesman for the army, the only stable organization remaining in the State."

The first fruits of Schleicher's grand design were hardly impressive. Papen's appointment as chancellor was received with considerable stupefaction by a country which, with reason, had never been able to take the gentleman jockey, and wartime military attaché in the United States, very seriously; and wits were quick to point out that the only qualifications for a ministerial portfolio in the new

From Gordon A. Craig, *The Politics of the Prussian Army, 1640–1945* (Oxford, 1955). Reprinted by permission of the Clarendon Press.

government seemed to be a background in the Gardekürassier Reg-
iment or the title Freiherr (Baron). The initial criticism deepened as
the consequences of Schleicher's negotiations with Hitler became
apparent. In return for an equivocal promise to support the new government, Hitler had been assured that new elections for the Reichstag
would be held and that the decree abolishing the SA would be re-
pealed. The Reichstag was consequently dissolved on June 4 and the
SA *Verbot* rescinded on the fifteenth. Hitler immediately turned his full
attention to the task of scoring new gains in the forthcoming elections, and he loosed his liberated storm troopers against his opponents. A new wave of violence swept over the country, reaching its
peak in riots at Altona on July 17 when fifteen persons were killed
and fifty injured.

These events, which weakened whatever meagre popular support
the new government possessed, did not disturb Schleicher or cause
him to deviate from his course. He agreed with his fellow cabinet
ministers—for he had undertaken to serve as Reichswehr minister in
Papen's government—that it would be expedient to reimpose the
ban on political demonstrations and parades, even if this was likely
to strain Hitler's "tolerance" to the breaking point. But at the same
time, he insisted that the time had come to strike out at the Social
Democrats, and in a way designed simultaneously to placate Hitler
and to advance the government's plan of centralizing political authority in the country. The main stronghold of Social Democratic
power since 1929 had been the Prussian government; and Prussia
was currently governed by a Socialist-Center coalition government,
the Braun-Severing government, although this no longer represented
a majority in the Landtag and was ruling ad interim. Schleicher proposed the deposition of the Prussian ministers and their replacement
by a Reich commissioner; and, to justify such high-handed action, he
secured from friendly sources within the Prussian Ministry of the Interior what purported to be evidence that the Prussian department of
police was under Communist influence, that it had been lax in dealing
with Communist demonstrations and that, consequently, it was responsible for the disorders at Altona and elsewhere.

Papen was in full agreement with the proposed plan. After se-
curing the approval of the president and ordering General Gerd von
Rundstedt, commanding Wehrkreis III, to alert his troops for immediate action, the chancellor and the Reichswehr minister on July 20

informed the flabbergasted Prussian ministers that they were to be replaced by a Reich commissioner in the person of Papen. The angry officials protested loudly but in vain, and, on the same day, were physically ejected from their offices. Neither on the twentieth nor on succeeding days did anything resembling active resistance materialize, for neither the Reichsbanner nor the trade unions were, in the opinion of their leaders, strong enough to oppose the government's stroke, and the police could not be counted on to test their strength against that of the local garrisons.

For Papen and Schleicher, however, this well-executed coup was an empty victory. Neither it, nor Papen's success in freeing Germany from reparations at the Lausanne conference, nor even his carefully calculated withdrawal from the disarmament conference on July 23 served to increase the reputation or the popularity of the government; and this was made unmistakably clear in the national elections of July 31. When the votes were counted and the Reichstag seats apportioned, it was patent that the Cabinet of Barons had been rejected by an overwhelming majority of the people. The only two parties upon whom Papen could rely with any assurance—the Nationalists and the Volkspartei—won only 44 seats between them. On the other hand, the Nazis—whose thunder Schleicher and Papen had hoped to steal by their coup in Prussia—doubled their representation, winning 230 seats and becoming the largest party in the Reichstag. There was now no hope that Hitler would tolerate Papen further. The Nazi chief burned for power and, when it was refused him in the now famous interview with Hindenburg on August 13, he wasted no time in going on the offensive. When Papen met the Reichstag for the first time on September 12, he was forced to dissolve it immediately, for the Nazis and the Communists combined to defeat him overwhelmingly in a vote of confidence. This necessitated new elections and, when they were held, in the first week of November, Papen fared little better than he had in July. Ninety percent of the votes cast were still against the government.

In mid-October Joseph Goebbels had written in his diary: "The Reichswehr has already fallen away from the Cabinet. Upon what will it base itself now?" The remark was perceptive, if premature. It was only after the November elections that army support was withdrawn from Papen, and this, of course, was Schleicher's doing. The general had, without doubt, become increasingly displeased with Papen in the weeks since the July coup, for the chancellor had not only developed an irritating habit of making up his own mind on important issues, but was also in a fair way to supplanting Schleicher in the affections of the president. But it was the November election results which raised more basic differences. The most salient feature of the elections was the sharp setback suffered by the Nazis—a loss of 2 million votes and thirty-four Reichstag seats. To Schleicher this proved that the time had come to put into effect the second part of his program, the operation designed to split the National Socialist party. He was aware that Gregor Strasser, the leader of that party's powerful political organization, was deeply discouraged by the election returns, and believed that they foreshadowed a precipitous decline in party fortunes. Schleicher thought that Strasser would be willing to join a new government and that he would be supported by important elements of the party, including Röhm. To make this new combination possible, however, Papen would have to step down, for neither Strasser nor Röhm would be prepared to serve under him.

Papen, on the other hand, had developed a love for office which was—despite all the disclaimers which he makes in his memoirs—to persist until 1945. He had no intention of stepping down. He would, he insisted, make a last effort to secure, by negotiation with the parties, a workable parliamentary majority. If this failed, as it almost certainly would, he would summon Hitler and demand that he either demonstrate that he could obtain such a majority or that he enter the cabinet as vice-chancellor. If Hitler refused, then all attempts to observe constitutional propriety must be abandoned. The Reichstag—and if necessary the opposition parties, and the trade unions—should be dissolved and the cabinet should rule quite openly by presidential decree backed by the authority of the army.

With the president's backing, the first steps of the Papen program were taken. The parties were canvassed and emphatically rejected the suggestion that they support the cabinet. For five days, between November 19 and 24, Hindenburg, his secretary Meissner, and Papen conducted acrimonious negotiations with Hitler, only to receive in the end his flat refusal to accept anything but a grant of full power. After that there was nothing left for Papen but the third alternative—the open violation of the constitution; and in an interview with Hindenburg and Schleicher on December 1, he proposed this.

The fact that the president, despite his sincere desire to remain true to his constitutional oath, gave his approval to Papen's plan, shows how completely he had fallen under the spell of the *Herrenreiter*. Hindenburg, indeed, proved wholly impervious to all of the rather disingenuous arguments which Schleicher now made in favor of legality, and he was frankly sceptical of the general's claim that he could destroy the Nazis without departing from the letter of the constitution. He preferred, he said, to go on with Papen. In consequence, Schleicher was compelled to resort to the same kind of forcing play which had served to get rid of Groener and Brüning. He brought the influence of the army to bear against the chancellor.

At a meeting of the full cabinet on December 2 Schleicher came out flatly against the Papen proposals. . . .

The chancellor repaired to Hindenburg who listened in silence to the news. Then the president said: "My dear Papen, you will not think much of me if I change my mind. But I am too old and have been through too much to accept the responsibility for a civil war. Our only hope is to let Schleicher try his luck."

Thus Schleicher himself—rather reluctantly, since he knew that his political talent was best exercised behind the scenes—became chancellor in the first week of December. A few days later, Goebbels wrote cheerfully in his diary: "A Jew has written a book called 'The Rise of Schleicher,' of which a huge edition is being published. A great pity, since when it appears in the shop windows von Schleicher will have disappeared from the political stage." Once again the little doctor's gift of prophecy was working well. Schleicher's chancellorship, which marked the highest point of army influence in the history of the republic, was brief and inglorious. It was notable, however, in one respect. Despite its brevity, it was long enough for Schleicher and the generals who supported him to execute a remarkable volteface. In early December they were determined that Hitler must not come to power and confident that they could prevent this. By late January they were determined that he *must* come to power and frightened lest something should occur to postpone his doing so.

The failure of Schleicher's chancellorship was made inevitable within a week of his assumption of office. He had staked everything on his ability to detach Gregor Strasser from Hitler's side, and his confidence in his influence over Strasser was, in fact, justified. He erred, however, in assuming that Strasser's defection would break up the National Socialist party; and, basically, his mistake arose

from his over-estimation of Strasser's capacities and his underesti-
mation of Hitler's political genius in moments of crisis.

On December 3 Schleicher invited Strasser to join his cabinet as
vice-chancellor and minister-president of Prussia. For the next five
days there were heated discussions in the inner circles of the Nazi
party, with Strasser urging that the offer must be accepted in order
to avoid new elections which might be disastrous for the party, and
Göring and Goebbels staunchly opposing this course as being the
rankest kind of defeatism. After momentary hesitation, Hitler vetoed
the Strasser policy and, on December 7, accused the chief of the
party's political organization of seeking to replace him as leader.
Strasser hotly denied the charge and, on the following day, resigned
from the party. But there his resistance stopped. Far from seeking to
carry all or part of the party with him, as Schleicher had expected, he
washed his hands of the whole business and took his family off for a
vacation in Italy.

Hitler, on the other hand, in an explosion of that demoniac rage
which always cowed his party comrades when they were exposed to
it, threatened to commit suicide if the party fell to pieces and then
proceeded to smash the political organization which Strasser had
ruled so long, to set up a new central party commission under Rudolf
Hess, and to bully the deputies and gauleiters into new pledges of un-
conditional loyalty. By mid-December the party was unquestionably
united behind the leader; and that fact spelled failure for the scheme
which Schleicher had elaborated in the cabinet meeting of December 2.

The chancellor was forced then to do what Papen had done before
him—to make the dismal round of the parties, seeking support which
would give him a workable majority when the Reichstag reconvened.
But here his past record for deviousness told against him in his negotiations with the middle and Left parties, while the promises he
made in order to allay their suspicions alienated the parties of the
Right. Remembering the coup in Prussia, the directorate of the Social Democratic party not only rejected Schleicher's initial overtures,
and advised the trade union leadership to do the same, but was
openly scornful when the chancellor promised fundamental reforms to
relieve unemployment and a scheme of land settlement to alleviate
the distress of the peasantry. The only tangible effect, indeed, of the
last mentioned plan was to destroy what support Schleicher had in

conservative circles, for, on January 12, the *Landbund* delivered a broadside against the government, accusing it—as it had once accused Brüning—of desiring to impose agrarian bolshevism on the eastern districts of the Reich. The persistence with which Schleicher clung to his agrarian policy—and his threat to publish details of the *Osthilfe* scandals of 1927–1928 if the resistance of the *Landbund* did not cease—not only influenced the decision of the Nationalist party to withdraw its support from the government—a step announced on January 20—but sensibly weakened Schleicher's popularity in the army, whose officer corps, after all, was still recruited from the very families which would suffer most from the execution of his projects.

Schleicher ended up then with even less party backing than his predecessor. And, this being so, he was forced to go to the president and make precisely the same request that his predecessor had made on December 1. On January 23 he told the president that the Reichstag must be dissolved and that Germany must be ruled, under Article 48 of the constitution, by what amounted to military dictatorship. Hindenburg was a very old and infirm man who suffered frequent lapses of memory, but he had no difficulty in remembering the arguments which Schleicher had used against this very solution only two months before.

> On December 2 [he said] you declared that such a measure would lead to civil war. The Army and the police, in your opinion, were not strong enough to deal with internal unrest on a large scale. Since then the situation has been worsening for seven weeks. The Nazis consider themselves in a stronger position, and the left wing is more radical in its intentions than ever. If civil war was likely then, it is even more so now, and the Army will be still less capable of coping with it. In these circumstances I cannot possibly accede to your request for dissolution of the Reichstag and carte blanche to deal with the situation.

The president ordered Schleicher to go on with his search for a majority, and the chancellor went through the motions of doing so. But Schleicher was well aware that his fall was only a matter of days away, and he felt that the time would be better spent in influencing the choice of a successor. This was, after all, a matter which vitally concerned the army, and Schleicher still claimed to speak for that body.

Practically speaking, there were only two possible successors: Hitler and Papen. Hitler, whose fortunes had seemed to be on the downgrade in January, had been strengthened by the establishment of relations with a group of Rhenish-Westphalian industrialists and bankers who assumed responsibility for the debts of his party and were openly calling for his elevation to power. The ebb tide of party fortunes seemed to have turned, and in local elections the Nazis had registered heavy successes within the past weeks. Hitler's appointment to the chancellorship would have seemed a certainty if it had not been for Hindenburg's past record of opposition to him and the president's deep affection for Papen. There was no doubt that Papen wanted office again; and, in view of Hindenburg's feelings, he had an excellent chance of getting it.

Of the two solutions Schleicher preferred the first. His reasons for this were not entirely rational and certainly by no means free of personal prejudice. But he seems to have calculated—as so many others did—that if Hitler assumed the responsibilities of office he would become more moderate in his views and would be susceptible to management by other agencies, notably by the army. If, on the other hand, Papen became chancellor, Hitler might well raise the standard of revolt, and the army would be placed in the awkward position of having to defend Papen. The general never doubted that the army would have fought cheerfully against Hitler for a Schleicher cabinet; but he refused to believe that it would do the same for Papen, or that it should be forced to do so.

In the last days of January 1933 Schleicher was desperately anxious lest a new Papen government be formed. On January 27 he asked Hammerstein to use the occasion of General von dem Bussche's customary report to the president on personnel affairs in the officer corps to sound Hindenburg out on his intentions. Hammerstein did so and was severely snubbed for his pains, being told that he would be better advised to spend his time thinking of ways of improving maneuvers rather than in meddling in political matters. However, the president added, "I have no intention whatever of making that Austrian corporal either minister of defence or chancellor of the Reich." This alarmed Schleicher even farther. On the following day, when he went to the president to tell him that the cabinet was resolved to resign unless the powers requested on the twenty-third were granted, he tried to argue that the formation of a new Papen government would be disastrous for Germany. The only response he received was a set speech accepting his resignation.

Until the formation of a new government, of course, Schleicher was still chancellor and minister of defense and, with his friend Hammerstein, had direct command over the army. But on January 29 Schleicher learned that General Werner von Blomberg, commanding Wehrkreis I and currently a member of the German delegation to the disarmament conference, had been ordered by the president to return to Berlin and to report to him personally rather than to the Bendlerstrasse (War Ministry), as custom required. This seemed to denote an intention on Hindenburg's part of removing the army from the control of its present commanders by appointing Blomberg as minister of defense, after he had promised army support to Papen. In short, if Schleicher and Hammerstein were to block Papen, they were, they thought, going to have to move fast.

The true measure of their desperation in these last days is shown by the fact that the idea of arresting the president and his entourage was frankly discussed by Schleicher's intimates. More important, at least two plain intimations of this possibility were made to Hitler. On the afternoon of January 29 Hammerstein—the man who Groener had believed would oppose a Nazi seizure of power "with brutality"— was dispatched by Schleicher to ask Hitler about the state of his current negotiations with Papen and to tell him that, if he thought that Papen was planning to form a government which would exclude him, the generals would be willing "to influence the position." That same night Werner von Alvensleben, one of Schleicher's close associates, went—again at the general's request—to Goebbels's house where a group of Nazi chieftains was anxiously awaiting final confirmation of Hitler's appointment as chancellor and of the president's willingness to dissolve the Reichstag. Alvensleben took the occasion to say to Hitler: "If the Palace crowd are only playing with you, the Reichswehr Minister and the Chief of the *Heeresleitung* will have to turn out the Potsdam garrison and clean out the whole pig-sty from the Wilhelmstrasse."

These were astonishing demarches, so astonishing, indeed, that Hitler does not seem to have known what construction to place upon them and secretly took precautions to guard against an army putsch, which might be directed against himself. The Führer's suspicion, while understandable, was unjustified. At this crucial moment in German history, the army command had swung to his side. The only putsch which Schleicher and Hammerstein now contemplated was one which would make certain his appointment. Such action was not, it is true, necessary; and Hitler became chancellor on January 30 without the intervention of the Potsdam garrisons. But surely the will was as important here as the deed would have been; and Hitler himself later admitted that "if . . . the Army had not stood on our side, then we should not be standing here today.". . .

Gerhard Ritter
MILITARISM AND NAZISM

The question regarding the relationship between the military and politics in Germany is one which can be answered by examining the nature of German "militarism." There is no other topic which stirs public opinion in Germany as much as this one. And why not? After all, Adolf Hitler's state was nothing but an attempt to militarize the entire German nation. During his time, soldierly conduct, preparedness, eagerness to serve, and a martial mind were considered the highest of all political and social virtues. Then came the destruction of Germany by Allied air raids and the collapse in 1945 followed by three terrible years of want and hunger. A veritable deluge of Allied antimilitaristic propaganda flooded Germany. The public prosecutors of the Nuremberg trials accused the entire German general staff of being a criminal organization for destroying world peace. This general indictment was refused, but numerous high-ranking military leaders had to go to presumptive arrest and most generals had to endure a long period of war captivity which they considered humiliating. On top of this the German public was aroused to great excitement by what became known of the so-called Landsberg trials.

These very energetic efforts by the Allies to "reeducate" the militaristically educated German nation towards a fundamental paci-

From Gerhard Ritter, "The Military and Politics in Germany," *Journal of Central European Affairs* 17 (October 1957). Reprinted by permission of S. H. Thomson and Gerhard Ritter.

fism have not remained without far-reaching consequences. That which had, since the War of Liberation against Napoleon I, 150 years ago, become the greatest pride of every patriot, namely, to defend the Fatherland with weapon in hand, had suddenly acquired a stigma. The martial mind and readiness to serve state and nation were suspected of being forms of rowdyism. Military discipline was pilloried and ridiculed as "blind obedience" and slandered as lack of individual courage. The lack of freedom-mindedness was called a basic vice of the German people. Considerable sections of the German people, especially of the younger generation and the working classes, were eager to accept these new teachings. Their effectiveness was increased by a religious pacifism being preached in the churches, especially those of the Protestant faiths. They gained many adherents. Doubtless the one factor that is working most strongly against the German people's readiness to serve is the fact that at the end of the war, after untold miseries and sacrifices, the German soldier was not released to go home immediately after the end of fighting, but was at first kept in labor camps abroad, in many cases—especially in Russia—for long years, where he was sentenced to forced labor, just like a war criminal, apparently for having done his duty as a soldier. The horrors of the Russian prisoner-of-war camps are the strongest possible propaganda against war and against being a soldier. There is no way of telling how all these experiences will hamper the attempt suddenly to build up a new German army. For the time being I am under the disquieting impression that those who today voluntarily resolve to put on a uniform again and to take upon themselves the hard duties of a soldier find that the German people meet them with so little sympathy and with so much distrust and dislike—even open hatred—that especially persons of the greatest moral value are being deterred.

The question about the nature of the so-called German "militarism" has always had an importance for German internal politics that can hardly be overestimated. It is imperative to see without bias the positive achievements of the German profession of arms as well as its dangers and shortcomings, and to distinguish clearly between being a soldier and "militarism," which are not at all identical. It is equally urgent to correct certain wrong ideas which for a long time have enjoyed popularity abroad about the German military and its influence on German politics and society. I can imagine that especially for an American it will be hard to understand correctly this aspect of German life, since all the historical conditions of Germany differ widely from those across the ocean. There can hardly be a greater contrast of international political conditions than there is between the United States and Germany. Up to World War I the United States lived very remote from the struggles for power being fought on the old European continent. From the military point of view it was practically unassailable from without owing to its separation from other countries by water. It was known that Thomas Jefferson had believed and hoped the United States would always pursue a policy of peace without employing military might. Thus, in America the army has, up to the beginning of this century, played an active role only in rare and exceptional cases, and fostering a martial spirit was not necessary in the young American nation. How totally different, however, was the situation of Germany, and above all of Prussia, in the middle of Europe! Without continuous effort and without strong military armament Prussia and Germany would never have been able to gain and maintain independence and freedom. Being without protection by natural boundaries in the east and west, it always faced the danger of being conquered from without and becoming the battleground of the great continental powers. That explains why in Germany the army, the profession of arms, occupied a much more central position in life than in England and the United States. . . .

Looking back on the past 100 years we notice that the War of Liberation of 1813–1815, as well as the wars of 1866 and 1870–1871, brought about great and lasting success relatively quickly, achieving it without extremely heavy sacrifices. It is natural that to us Germans war appeared in a somewhat idealistic light, a physical, spiritual, and moral test of the people. Its destruction of culture was considered secondary. The universal conscription (without proxy), since 1867 extended over all of Germany, gradually funneling the entire growing generation through the army, resulted in a rapidly increasing influence of military thinking on wide strata of the population. It became the ambition of the educated youth, as reserve officers, to adapt themselves to the social customs of the active officer corps in which the nobility was still predominant. The younger generation carried a great deal of these customs over into civilian life, and soon national occasions were unthinkable without military parades. The

FIGURE 6. Everyone Loves a Parade. This scene, taken in Nuremberg, was repeated a thousand times over in Germany's small towns and cities in the 1930s. *(Library of Congress)*

notions "smart" or "soft," originating from military drill on the drill field, were also used to judge political conditions, especially when criticizing the official foreign policy of the Reich. The ideal of "standing smartly," of "resolute behavior," and of "plucky tone" did a great deal to confuse the political ideas of the German citizenry. Wherever "standing smartly" and "resolute behavior" showed through the daily life and in the behavior of the individual German, they naturally made the German disliked abroad and gave him the reputation of being a hard-to-bear "militarist." In fact, if "militarism" is to signify that military thinking and military behavior play too great a part in a nation's life, it cannot be denied that throughout the last decades of the Bismarck state there was a German militarism and that, in its effect upon politics, it was not harmless.

It is a totally different question whether the official course of German foreign policy also was ruled by too great a military preparedness or even by direct influences from the army. It is not easy to answer in a few words. . . .

Taken together the generals' attitude during the Third Reich showed very clearly that these soldiers had also learned from the experiences of the First World War and were aware that Germany's powers would never be sufficient to fight a Second World War—not even should an ultramodern armament secure her initial superiority over her neighbors. The concept that the German generals of 1939 were just like the militaristic "Supreme Army Command" of 1914–1918, which was the case especially in England, had truly fateful results during the Second World War, one of them being the completely wrong judgment of the military opposition to Hitler.

The rapid rise to power of the National-Socialist Party after 1931 cannot be explained by any political activity of the military. To be sure many officers sympathized with Hitler because he promised them a quick and strong rearmament. But there also were decided enemies of his proletarian, noisy, people's movement, especially among the highest leaders. In January of 1933, the commander in chief, Baronet von Hammerstein, formally protested to the Reich president against the selection of Hitler as Schleicher's successor, saying it would be "intolerable" for the Reichswehr. There is no doubt that the Weimar Republic was not "steamrollered" by army "militarists," but rather by the militarists of a nationalistic people's movement. And yet it will be impossible immediately and without discrimination to denounce as militarists all of these civilian followers of Hitler. The great majority of those hailing the dangerous demagogue did not expect from him a new war but something quite different: a bridging of the previously described deep gap that divided the nation—the gap between Left and Right, between the followers of nationalist fight slogans and the socialist advocates of welfare and reconciliation—a new unity in a community of the people, the "National Socialists," forming an arch over all the parties. Out of the inner regeneration of the German people thus to take place there was to result, all by itself and without a new war, a tremendous increase of German power and of German prestige in the world. All that would soon be achieved by breaking the "shackles of Versailles." Thus Hitler preached, and that was the hope of the mass of people who voted for him.

In fact, as is only too well known, no expectation has ever been more cruelly disappointed. For our topic the figure of Hitler is interesting above all since it shows more clearly than the others how little the outer organization of state leadership means in comparison to the spirit which imbues the leading men. Organizational means can never solve the problem at hand. Never has the army been more dependent upon the political state leadership than was the case under Hitler. Never has the organizational unity of the leadership of the armed forces, as well as the predominance of the political leader over the soldier, been as perfectly assured as under him. Had he been a genuine statesman, there never would have been so splendid a chance as there was under his leadership, really to overcome the dangers of militarism and to employ so massive a fighting force to safeguard European peace, and for a healthy and lasting order on our continent. Instead, in the event the General Staff vainly tried before as well as during the war to bring an element of moderation into politics (reversing a well-known quotation of Clausewitz) basing their position on military-technical arguments! Thus the natural relationship between the political leaders and the military was in fact completely reversed. . . .

Everything that came later, the total mobilization and militarization of our people by Hitler, did not originate with the generals, just as the Second World War did not, but rather from a political people's movement. To be sure, Hitler was able to find support in the martial instincts and the basic preparedness of the German people. However, he misused them badly against the particular protests of the generals. If I may dare suggest a practical solution from all these historical experiences it will be that building a new German army need not necessarily push our political leadership on a militaristic track and make it dependent on the militaristic direction of any generals. Even the Weimar Republic on the whole successfully kept the army its obedient tool; neither Kapp's coup of 1920 nor Schleicher's policy of 1932 may be interpreted as actions of the army. And yet the army, led by von Seeckt and other former imperial officers, was facing the republican government with more than cool reserve—basically even with an extremely strong inner aversion. . . .

IV THE SOCIAL IMPACT OF NAZISM

Once Hitler became chancellor and his party grasped the levers of political authority, they were able to begin the elaborate process of "coordination" (Gleichschaltung)—little more than a euphemism for the establishment of a dictatorship, whether by brutal means or by more gentle persuasion. Whatever the tactics, the objectives were much the same: to break down what Tocqueville called the "intermediary bodies" between the state and the people, to neutralize actual or potential pockets of resistance, and thereby to transform the composition of society so as to ensure a maximum of compliance. The extent to which the Nazis succeeded in this effort, evaluated in the excerpts that follow, is certain to occupy historians for many years to come.

Robert H. Lowie warns that any attempt to gauge the German response to Nazism must take full account of the intrinsic complexity of German society, both in itself and as part of the entire Western European culture area. Different people and groups reacted for diverse reasons; and the existing varieties of region, class, and social status cannot be ignored in any comprehensive sociological account. Without offering an apologia, Lowie identifies and dismisses some of the easy clichés which the serious analyst of German society must forego.

William Sheridan Allen takes a microhistorical look at the immediate effects of Nazism on a single German town, to which he lends the fictitious name of Thalburg. He also introduces a new social type, the Nazi mayor, given the pseudonym Kurt Aergeyz. As in Lowie's macrohistorical perspective, Allen's picture reveals the complexity of social organization and, on the local just as on the national level, the intense rivalry among various social and political factions. Allen describes the progressive terrorization and atomization of individuals after 1933 and the resulting loss of a sense of community. This might suggest not that Nazism arrived as a mass movement but that, once entrenched, it succeeded in creating one.

Gerard Braunthal traces the dissolution of the German labor movement in the face of the Nazi incursion. He uncovers the reasons for the trade unions' failure to resist effectively and shows how they were soon nullified by the new regime. When confronted with a bald choice between immobility and civil war, they capitulated. The consequences were soon visible: the dismemberment of the unions, and the inception of a homogeneous and compliant Nazi Labor Front in which all German workers were required to participate.

Guenter Lewy considers the fate of another bellwether institution of German society, the Roman Catholic Church. Unlike the labor movement, against which the Nazis moved swiftly and directly, the Church was treated with more discretion. Yet the ultimate effect of this indirect coordination was similar: the legitimacy of Hitler's regime was never seriously challenged on religious grounds. Lewy's discussion has a polemical bite, stressing as it does the possibilities for resistance after 1933 and arguing that the massive destruction of the war and the concentration camps might have been averted to some degree by more outspoken clerical opposition.

David Schoenbaum surveys the social mutations of the Nazi years, concluding that they were more apparent than real. The lower strata of society and the traditional elites were disoriented, but not displaced. Workers continued to labor, peasants to farm, bureaucrats to administer, preachers to sermonize, generals to command, businessmen to profit. The social map was nonetheless redrawn, Schoenbaum explains, and every individual had to discover his bearings anew. Moral confusion, rather than social transformation, was the chief characteristic of the Third Reich.

There is a paradox in these interpretations. In retrospect Nazism appears to have been all movement, pure flux, without firm principles or finite objectives. And yet the only fixed point in German society after 1933 was the leadership of the Nazi party apparatus, around which everything revolved. When this was destroyed by force of arms in 1945, the entire structure collapsed and Nazism disappeared. Only the wreckage remained.

Robert H. Lowie
THE COMPLEXITY OF GERMAN SOCIETY

The question of how Germans reacted to the anti-Jewish program of the National Socialist party merges into the wider problem of how they reacted to the Nazi program in its totality and how they reacted and are likely to react to the democratic principles which the Western Allies regard as essential for international safety.

The first thing to note is that relevant attitudes of Germans were not stationary during the years of Nazi rise and ascendancy; indeed, the chronological factor is all-important. Let us then try to picture an average German confronted with the situation between 1918 and 1933. The disastrous First World War had brought spiritual and material distress. Patriots writhed under the stipulations of the peace treaty, which assailed Germany as the sole nation guilty of starting the war, deprived her of her colonies, reduced her European territory, and imposed heavy reparations. The victors flouted the new republican government, making it constantly lose face before its own people, to many of whom the concept of a free commonwealth was strange and repulsive. In consequence, the Weimar regime weakened until at times it ceased to govern large sections at all. It was unable to enforce federal legislation in Bavaria. It was unable to prevent the assassination of its officials. It was unable to thwart the murderous brawls of contending factions. The boasted order that had reigned in the empire was irretrievably gone. Economically, an unprecedented inflation wiped out fortunes and beggared all whose income was derived from pensions or fixed salaries. In the fall of 1923 Driesch paid 16 billion marks for a streetcar ticket; in 1924 I paid 1.25 million crowns a week at my boardinghouse in Vienna and tipped the maid 150,000 [crowns]. Stabilization of the monetary unit did, indeed, bring relief, but only temporarily; and when the world crisis reached the Reich, it brought havoc once more in its wake. One chancellor after another tried to do away with unemployment and high prices, but failed. In 1929 the number of jobless Germans was 2,895,000; at the end of 1930 the figure had risen to 3.25 million. Hitler made extrava-

From Robert H. Lowie, *Toward Understanding Germany* (Chicago: University of Chicago Press, 1954). Copyright © 1954 by The University of Chicago. All rights reserved. Reprinted by permission of the publisher.

gant promises, but the people were in a mood to catch at any straw that might lift them from their Slough of Despond. Even so, it should not be forgotten that in November 1932 only 33.1 percent of the voters supported Hitler, and even in the last "free" election under his regime he had won over only 43.9 percent.

It may be asked, nevertheless, why so large a minority could possibly lend ear to an uneducated rabble-rouser whose book had flaunted the most extreme and in part repulsive doctrines. Germans answer that though many bought *Mein Kampf,* few read it or much of it; and those who did assumed, plausibly enough, that its most radical utterances were never meant to be followed up by action. Again, those who perused the allegedly immutable program of the party found little there to recoil from on moderately liberal principles, apart from the racialist paragraphs, and even these were not couched in offensive language. The platform opposed the spoils system. It demanded a greater Germany, but the Allies themselves had proclaimed the principle of self-determination and of the national state, though they had repudiated it as regards Austria. The platform postulated the state's duty "to promote the industry and livelihood of citizens," all of whom were to enjoy equal rights and obligations. War profiteering was to be squashed by ruthless confiscation. There was promise of ampler old age pensions and of a far-reaching land reform. Gifted children of poor parents were to be educated at the expense of the state, which was further pledged to raise the standard of health by banning child labor and by furthering physical training. To be sure, the program also contained ominous suggestions of a controlled press; and, of course, we now know that the subsequent masters of Germany's destiny were really interested, above all, in gaining and preserving despotic control of the country. But the impoverished, jobless, politically naive man in the street, longing for delivery from present evils, did not know it. He was neither a skeptical analyst nor a prophet: he wanted precisely one thing—relief from an unbearable present.

It is important to note that this relief, whatever its means, actually came. A Swiss colleague who attended the University of Berlin in 1933 told me that he was struck by the rapidity of a change for the better. The dismal sight of woebegone men and women begging for alms suddenly vanished completely. As a former Nazi states: "People were once more laughing and singing in Germany; they were hoping and had once more a sense of secure existence. The meanest laborer knew that he would never again be jobless, never without provision and help."

The same writer, who remarks that young people conceived the new movement as directly the reverse of what Hitler made of it, goes on to say: "What convinced us at the time of National Socialism was the fact that it made new, better men out of people we knew. There was the lazy-bones who suddenly sacrificed his leisure time and holidays without receiving compensation. There was the beaten-up, hospitalized SA who in his delirium yearned for his next performance of duty; there were miserly peasants who furnished potatoes, fat, and hams for the SA auxiliary kitchens. There were the youngsters who, with radiant eyes, rendered a thousand services and often were in despair because they were not yet old enough to 'march' along with us." Similarly, the historian Meinecke, who was not a Nazi, declares that National Socialism had an immense number of harmless, uncritical, decent, and even idealistic fellow-travelers.

For men of all classes outside the ranks of intransigent cosmopolitans, the sudden rise of Germany in the international theater was a matter of the utmost moment. The Allies had harassed and intimidated the republican government, had insisted on the admission of German guilt, to the humiliation of all German patriots, including the majority of Social Democrats. But when Hitler began to talk, the Allies changed their tune; the bullies of the 1920s turned into the cravens of the 1930s. According to Pechel, a sufferer from Nazi vengeance, nothing gave the resistance movement a greater setback than the concessions now made to the dictator when they had been denied to a moderate republican government. The contention is plausible, for apparently no national group is immune to the charm of power when wielded by its own head. The English glory in the days of Elizabeth I and Cromwell, considering the atrocities of their reigns little more than venial peccadilloes; and Napoleon still lies in state in the Invalides. Hence the gain Hitler secured for his country in point of international prestige inevitably won over the hearts of innumerable compatriots at the beginning of his leadership. Later, when the true nature of his designs had become clear, effective open counteraction was no longer possible. On this subject our ex-Nazi 693044 says: "Since 1945 people have more than amply preached to us that even before the war we ought to have chased

Hitler to the devil. We ought to have seen that he was fomenting war, that he was planning crimes. This chasing to the devil is a thoroughly excellent idea, only no one has revealed the recipe how that is to be done in an authoritarian state." The same man reveals the mentality of his type in further confessions: "If now someone were to ask me, 'Do you repent for having been a National Socialist?' I must answer, 'No! I repent that my faith was misused on behalf of an evil cause, I repent every unexpiable crime committed in my and my comrades' name, I repent that the faith and unheard-of self-sacrifice and devotion of German workers was betrayed by Hitler—but I do not repent having loved my people above everything, that I rendered every sacrifice, that I believed and hoped.' In a French author I read a formula that consoled me: 'It is finer and better ardently to serve a great error than pettily to drudge for a petty truth.' "

The motives that drove the masses into the Nazi ranks have been dispassionately summarized along similar lines by a strong anti-Nazi of the old conservative type. It was the promise of work and bread, the feeling of solidarity the people at large were yearning for, Silens contends, that proved the great drawing card. Germans were *not* craving a world war, had no desire to conquer the world, to persecute and exterminate human groups. They acclaimed Hitler for apparently assuring peace and employment, not as the leader of an offensive war, of clandestine crimes and atrocities. Many initially regarded the ranting against Jews as mere campaign claptrap. Very few party members read Rosenberg's *Mythos des 20. Jahrhunderts,* the official exposition of the Nazi world view. Silens even conjectures that though millions bought *Mein Kampf,* few read it through; and educated readers did not take seriously what seemed incredible or nonsensical in it. . . .

We cannot repeat too often that no finding about the Germans is scientifically valid until we know the distribution of the phenomena in space and time. No trait, no attitude, is *the* German trait or attitude unless it is pan-German and pan-diachronically so; and it is not distinctively German unless it is found only among Germans. By this test, the Bavarian is farther from the Hamburger than the Hamburger from the Briton; the Viennese proletarian has more affinity with a Danish worker than with a Styrian peasant. There is not only regional and class differentiation among Germans, but the differences are such as to align some Germans with aliens rather than with fellow-

Germans. The concept of a German culture sphere with which we have been tentatively operating thus turns out to be an ill-defined, if not indefinable, entity.

If anything, the differences within the same people at different periods is even more instructive—witness the history of national literatures. Elizabethan England was healthily unrestrained; the Puritans, in reaction, closed theaters, flogged actors, and put the press "under the guardianship of austere licensers"; Restoration authors, reacting in turn, dropped all pretense to decency (Macaulay). It would be absurd to suppose that "the English" by mutation completely and repeatedly changed their innate character in three successive generations. What happened was obviously that certain literary leaders impressed their individuality on their contemporaries and that leaders of a different mentality succeeded in stamping *theirs* on the following generation. Sane exuberance, priggish zealotry, and abandoned profligacy are human phenomena likely to be found everywhere; which of them becomes typical at a certain stage of a country's literature depends on historical circumstances.

In retrospect, it is from this point of view that the remarkable alterations in German orientation from 1750 until the present find partial explanation. Not all Englishmen were priggish zealots under the Puritans, not all of them were reckless libertines under Charles II; both types coexisted throughout, each merely "going underground" when the other gained temporary ascendancy. In Germany there was corresponding alternation of polar trends: particularism and centralism became alternately dominant and recessive, as did cosmopolitanism and nationalism. That either eliminated the other for good is an illusion.

Of course, not all the differences that have divided Germany from other Western countries can be regarded in this way. The effects of industrialism do not seem to be cyclic but rather appear as a sequence of irreversible phenomena. The fundamental fact here seems to be simply that Germany, becoming industrialized later than England, showed the social consequences of industrialism later, say as regards family life. Again, the comparative approach corrects first impressions. The status of German women, legally and practically, has not been inferior to that of Spanish, Italian, or French women. Further, it has altered with changing conditions, which have brought it more in line with Anglo-Saxon standards. Even the ideology of Nazism was able to arrest the development only for a brief period before the Second World War.

Germans, then, cannot easily be treated as a unit marked off from the rest of Western civilization. Their alleged patriarchalism, their love of military glory, their fondness for abstract principles, can all be paralleled in French culture. The political incompetence deplored by the Germans themselves can hardly be an immutable trait in the light of Alemannic history.

It is when particular social strata are set beside their equivalents elsewhere that convincing contrasts appear. The yearning for titles in the upper classes has certainly—with a partial exception in Switzerland and the Hanseatic cities—been obtrusive throughout the last two centuries. As pointed out, the failure to evolve the "gentleman" concept is enviously admitted by Germans themselves. With this lack may be correlated that intemperateness in controversy, that substitution of uninhibited violence for sober judgment, that "methodical vehemence" (Röpke) which so frequently mars the utterances of educated Germans. Every nation has its scum, but one does not expect a Schopenhauer to revile a Hegel in the language of a guttersnipe, nor the venomous obscenities of the Viennese students inspired by Schönerer. As Röpke says, his countrymen tend to extremism, exaggerating bad as well as good ideas, carrying them out to their very last consequences.

Such intensity has its positive aspect in German thoroughness, whether in research or in the household, in the love for work as an end in itself. In one of its noblest forms it appears as the proletarian's craving for intellectual and aesthetic culture.

The contention, then, is not that Germans are exactly like other peoples, but rather that Western Europe as a whole presents a continuum—one culture area with admittedly innumerable local variations. This impression is deepened when we take into account the demonstrable changes in dominant outlook during the last two centuries in every country involved. Again the history of national literatures furnishes a clue to understanding. French letters and formal restraint are commonly taken as synonymous, but France had her Rabelais and Victor Hugo as well as her Racine. Let us get away from stereotypes. When the cultures of Britain, France, Italy, and Spain are once studied from the comparative point of view, we shall have a sounder factual basis for dividing the Western European area into cultural subdivisions than the inexpensive one of national or even linguistic boundaries.

William Sheridan Allen
THE NAZIFICATION OF A TOWN

What, then, is to be learned from Thalburg's experience in the years 1930 to 1935, the years of the Nazi seizure of power?

In the first place, it is clear that an essential arena in the Nazi electoral surge and the seizure of power was on the local level. Thalburg's Nazis created their own image by their own initiative, vigor, and propaganda. They knew exactly what needed to be done to effect the transfer of power to themselves in the spring of 1933, and they did it apparently without more than generalized directives from above. Exactly how much was initiated locally and how much was promoted by the example of other Nazi groups in other towns or by the district and national Nazi leadership remains to be determined. It would be extremely interesting to know exactly what means were used by the NSDAP to instill the sense of purposefulness and initiative into its local groups, which were then used by the movement as a whole. It would be useful to know how coordination was combined with flexibility in this authoritarian instrument. The material available for this study of Thalburg did not supply answers to these questions. It has, however, made clear that there would have been no Nazi revolution in Thalburg, at least not of the totality that has been described here, without an active and effective local organization. Hitler, Goebbels, and the other Nazi leaders provided the political decisions, ideology, national propaganda, and, later, the control over the government which made the revolution possible. But it was in the hundreds of localities like Thalburg all over Germany that the revolution was made actual. They formed the foundation of the Third Reich.

As for the reasons behind the particular experience in Thalburg, the most important factor in the victory of Nazism was the active division of the town along class lines. Though there was cohesion in Thalburg before the Nazis began their campaigns leading to the seizure of power, the cohesion existed within the middle class or within the working class and did not extend to the town as a whole. The victory of Nazism can be explained to a large extent by the desire on the part of Thalburg's middle class to suppress the lower class and especially its political representatives, the Social Democratic party.

This is why Thalburgers rejoiced in the gains of the Nazis, and this is why they applauded the institution of the dictatorship. The antipathy of the middle class was not directed toward individual members of the SPD, but only toward the organization itself; not toward the working class as such, but only toward its political and social aspirations; not, finally, toward the reality of the SPD, but mainly toward a myth which they nurtured about the SPD. For a variety of reasons, Thalburg's middle class was so intent on dealing a blow to the Social Democrats that it could not see that the instrument it chose would one day be turned against itself.

Exactly why Thalburgers were so bitterly opposed to the Socialists cannot be answered on the basis of a study of this town alone; the answer lies in the history and social structure of imperial and Weimar Germany, and possibly can be given only by a social psychologist. Nevertheless it seems clear that the nature of the SPD had something to do with the burghers' attitudes. Thalburg's Socialists maintained slogans and methods which had little correspondence with reality. They maintained the facade of a revolutionary party when they were no longer prepared to lead a revolution. They never seriously attempted to mend fences with the middle class and frequently offended bourgeois sensibilities by their shortsightedness and shallow aggressiveness.

Yet it would be wholly incorrect to place all the blame upon Thalburg's Social Democracy. The middle class responded to the existence of the SPD in ways which were almost paranoid. Its members insisted upon viewing the SPD as a "Marxist" party at a time when this was no longer so. They were determined to turn the clock back to a period when the organized working class was forcibly kept from exerting influence. They felt threatened by the very existence of this organization. This view of the SPD was not in accord with reality, since by any objective standard the goal of the SPD in Thalburg was to maintain the kind of town that Thalburg's middle class itself wanted.

Perhaps the behavior of the good burghers of Thalburg becomes more understandable when one realizes the extent to which they were committed to nationalism. The excess of patriotic feeling in the town during the pre-Hitler period was the great moral wedge for Nazism. In many ways the actions and beliefs of Thalburgers during the last years of the Weimar era were the same as if World War I had never ended. It was in this sort of atmosphere that the SPD might seem treasonable and the Nazi reasonable.

A similar effect was wrought by the depression. While Thalburg's middle class was not decisively affected by the economic crisis, the burghers were made desperate through fear and through an obsession with the effects of the depression, especially the sight of the unemployed. As for the effect of the depression upon the lower classes, it was equally large. There is no doubt that the progressive despair of the jobless, as reflected in the longer and longer periods of unemployment, weakened the forces of democracy in the town. It may be that this sapped the SPD's will to fight and led it into ritualistic responses to Nazism. It was hard for Socialists to bend all their efforts to combating Nazism when this involved defending a system which could produce this sort of economic misery. Had the SPD seriously undertaken to introduce democratic socialism in response to the depression, it seems likely they would have found new sources of strength among their own followers, and very likely might have won the votes of the many Thalburgers who cast ballots for the NSDAP simply because the Nazis promised to end the depression.

The depression weakened Thalburg's Socialists in other ways, too. The use of economic pressure at the sugar factory and at the railroad deprived the SPD of much of its prestige and power. If it could not even defend its own people when the chips were down, how could it defend democracy, and how could it bring about the socialist society? The success of the action at the railroad yards no doubt opened up several possibilities for the Nazis. It was there that they learned how economically vulnerable the workers were; it was there that they learned essentially that the SPD would not fight.

But the main effect of the depression was to radicalize the town. In the face of the mounting economic crisis, Thalburgers were willing to tolerate approaches that would have left them indignant or indifferent under other circumstances. Thus the disgusting and debilitating party acrimony and violence mushroomed in the years before the dictatorship. The extent of the violence in Thalburg was an expression of the radical situation, but it also added to it by making violence normal and acceptable. With the growing nationalism and increasing impatience over the depression, violence and political tension were significant factors in preparing the town for the Nazi takeover.

All these factors were exploited with considerable astuteness by Nazi propaganda. In the face of the senseless round of political squabbling and fecklessness, the Nazis presented the appearance of a unified, purposeful, and vigorous alternative. Their propaganda played upon all the needs and fears of the town and directed itself to almost every potential group of adherents. By their own efforts the Nazis captured the allegiance of the confused and troubled middle class.

This set the stage for the actual seizure of power, but the revolution itself was also conducted in such a way as to insure success. The fact that this was, in the words of Konrad Heiden, a *"coup d'état* by installments"* kept the Reichsbanner from responding decisively at any one point. By the time the SPD had been broken, the terror system had been inaugurated, largely through social reinforcement.

The single biggest factor in this process was the destruction of society in Thalburg. What social cohesion there was in the town existed in the club life, and this was destroyed in the early months of Nazi rule. With their social organizations gone and with terror a reality, Thalburgers were isolated from one another. This was true of the middle class but even more true of the workers, since by the destruction of the SPD and the unions the whole complex of social ties created by this superclub was effaced. By reducing the people of Thalburg to unconnected social atoms, the Nazis could move the resulting mass in whatever direction they wished. The process was probably easier in Thalburg than in most other places, since the town contained so many government employees. By virtue of their dependence on the government the civil servants were in an exposed position and had no choice but to work with the Nazis if they valued their livelihood. Especially Thalburg's teachers—who formed the social and cultural elite of the town—found themselves drawn into support of the NSDAP almost immediately. As other Thalburgers flocked to the Nazi bandwagon in the spring of 1933, and as terror and distrust became apparent, there was practically no possibility of resistance to Hitler.

Beyond this, the Nazis took considerable action to strengthen support, especially in the early months. There were the constant parades and meetings which gave the impression of irresistible enthusiasm and approval. There was the vigor in the economic area which more than anything else seemed to justify the dictatorship. But in addition to Nazi efforts on their own behalf, there were other factors that favored them. Many signs indicate that the depression was slowly curing itself by 1933. Moreover, there was the public works money allocated under the previous regime, but available just as the Nazis came to power. And one should probably also take into account the fact that the essential work of establishing the dictatorship came during the spring—a time when enthusiasm seems appropriate and revolution not wholly unnatural.

Thus many factors combined to make Nazism a possibility for Thalburg. At the same time the town itself influenced the nature of Nazism as it manifested itself locally. It seems probable, for example, that the general lack of violence during the first months of the Third Reich was due to the nature of Thalburg as a small town. Much as the Nazis hated all that the Socialists stood for, both sides knew each other too well for cold and systematic violence to occur. The SA might be willing to pummel their neighbors in a street fight, but they seemed to shrink from attacking the Socialists when they were defenseless. This is not to say that no violence took place, but it does help explain the fact that no one was killed and no one sent to a concentration camp from Thalburg during the early years of the Nazi regime. On the one occasion when Kurt Aergeyz seemed determined to turn the Stormtroopers loose on Karl Hengst and his little tobacco store, it was not members of the Thalburg SA who were to do the dirty work; truckloads of Stormtroopers from another town were imported for the occasion. The subsequent relationship of

Hengst and Aergeyz substantiates this again; it was hard for even the worst fanatic to be utterly ruthless against someone who had grown up in the same block with him.

The smallness of Thalburg, the fact that many families had known each other for generations undoubtedly modified the nature of the mature dictatorship. The Nazis could come and go but the "Club for the Defense of Old Thalburg Privileges"—composed of old city dwellers of every hue in the political spectrum—continued to meet and work together to make sure they would receive their annual ration of free beer, their eighteen marks' worth of wood from the town forest. There were other things that seemed to stay the same after Hitler came to power. While the Nazis claimed uniqueness for their charity efforts, it can be shown that Thalburgers gave just as much to their various separate charity organizations before 1933. While the Nazis felt they were doing something new by bringing the army to Thalburg, it should be remembered that the love of the military was something that Thalburg had been noted for long before Kurt Aergeyz ever thought about it.

In fact, in many ways Aergeyz and his Nazi administration were simply the embodiment of the small-town chauvinism that Thalburg displayed in the pre-Nazi period. When it came to a choice between Nazi ideals and promoting Thalburg as a tourist center, Aergeyz had no hesitation. If important visitors came to Thalburg, he made sure they were lodged in the Hotel Georg-Friedrich, because it was the best hotel in town, even if its owner was a leading Nationalist party member and a master of the forbidden freemasons. On the other hand, there were Thalburgers who saw nothing new in Nazism, except possibly the chance to put into effect policies they had hoped for over a long period. To several leading members of the Thalburg shooting societies, for example, the introduction of the Hitler regime meant simply that they could now have their 300-meter target range. To several of the town's businessmen, Nazism simply meant that now was the time to promote the concept that Thalburgers ought to do their shopping at home.

Finally, it is possible to construe the actions of Kurt Aergeyz after he came to power as expressive of the class divisions of Thalburg. Nothing is more difficult to discover than the truth about personal motivation, but many of the actions taken by Aergeyz and his closest friends suggest that they were a product of social resentment.

Aergeyz was of the lower middle class and this undoubtedly made its mark upon him in a town where government and society were dominated by an elite which freely expressed its cool sense of superiority over the petite bourgeoisie as well as over the workers. When the Nazis came to power in Thalburg they destroyed the SPD and its suborganizations and hounded Socialist leaders, but this is explicable because of the intransigent political opposition between Nazism and Social Democracy. What Aergeyz wanted of the Socialists was that they be rendered impotent, not degraded (except insofar as this would produce a sense of political futility). Thus he was capable of producing one of his rare smiles when a common worker defied him; when he attempted to harass Karl Hengst's brother, Hengst was able to stop this by telling Aergeyz: "Look, if you want someone to pick on, try me—but leave my family alone." This Aergeyz respected; what he hated were the upper classes of the town. In this he was seconded by his clique. As Otto Made once said of Walther Timmerlah: "An honest Communist is more to my liking than such a *Scheiss-Akademiker.*"

As a result, Aergeyz did things to the town's elite which he never did to outright political opponents. The methods used in the long and sordid process of ousting Mayor Johns were as unnecessary as they were disgusting. The attempt to degrade Dieter Thomas falls in the same category. Aergeyz's treatment of the shooting societies and the Retail Merchants' Association went beyond customary "coordination"; they were a measure of his contempt. The same approach characterized all of his relationships with the town's upper crust, Wilhelm Spatel of the GHC being the most conspicuous example. The final expression of this attitude was in Aergeyz's struggle against the church, which was more bitterly pursued in Thalburg than in most other places in Germany. By attacking the citadel of the town's respectability with such extreme means and degrading methods, Kurt Aergeyz was possibly attempting to triumph over the environment in which he had grown up and which had condemned him previously to the condescension of his social betters.

This is not to say that the Nazi dictatorship affected only a few in Thalburg. Ultimately almost every Thalburger came to understand the Third Reich. Most Thalburgers learned what a dictatorship meant when they sensed the general breakdown of trust and social communication. All became aware of it when Hitler's policies brought war to them. Despite the superpatriotism in the pre-Nazi years, there was no cheering in the streets when the Thalburg battalion marched out of town in 1939. The war brought hunger with it, especially after 1945, and the sons of many Thalburgers learned to temper their love of militarism on the cold steppes of Russia.

But no one foresaw these consequences in the days when Thalburg's middle class was voting overwhelmingly for the introduction of the Third Reich. And that, perhaps, is the most significant lesson of all to be gained from Thalburg's experiences during and prior to the Nazi seizure of power. Hardly anyone in Thalburg in those days grasped what was happening. There was no real comprehension of what the town would experience if Hitler came to power, no real understanding of what Nazism was.

The Social Democrats failed to comprehend the nature of the Nazi appeal. So did the Jews and Lutherans, both of whom were to suffer bitterly under the Nazi whip, and even the convinced members of the NSDAP itself, such as Walther Timmerlah. Each group saw one or the other side of Nazism, but none saw it in its full hideousness. Only later did this become apparent, and even then not to everyone. The problem of Nazism was primarily a problem of perception. In this respect Thalburg's difficulties and Thalburg's fate are likely to be shared by other men in other towns under similar circumstances. The remedy will not easily be found.

Gerard Braunthal
THE GERMAN LABOR MOVEMENT

A democratic nation, especially if faced with powerful extremist forces of the political Left and Right, ought to have a free and dynamic trade union movement to help safeguard the liberties of its citizens. For the sake of survival alone, labor not only should make its members aware of the political problems of the day, but also should participate

From Gerard Braunthal, "The German Free [Socialist] Trade Unions during the Rise of Nazism," *Journal of Central European Affairs* 15 (January 1956). Reprinted by permission of S. H. Thomson and Gerard Braunthal.

in those national and international affairs which affect its broader interests. If the movement in an hour of political crisis withdraws from this participation, there is grave danger that it will be unable to resist the onslaughts of totalitarianism. This is precisely what happened in Germany in 1933. Therefore, it seems appropriate to make a case study of the attitudes and policies of the German free trade unions during the crucial period of transition from the Weimar Republic to fascism.

Three independent and competing organizations represented organized labor in Germany at the end of the nineteenth century. These were based on ideological and political differences. The Socialist unions adhered to the concept of Marxist revisionism, the Christian unions to Catholic social action and the Hirsch-Duncker unions to Manchester liberalism. Of the three, the Socialist unions were by far the largest and politically the most active. Consequently, this article will be concerned only with these unions. By the end of the Weimar period, they had become constituent members of three national federations working in close cooperation:

1. the German Federation of Trade Unions, ADGB (Allgemeiner Deutscher Gewerkschaftsbund), composed of national industrial and craft unions, with a membership of nearly 5 million;
2. the Free Federation of Salaried Employees, AFA (Allgemeiner freier Angestelltenbund), with almost 500,000 members;
3. the German Federation of Civil Servants, ADBB (Allgemeiner Deutscher Beamtenbund), numbering approximately 170,000 members.

The three federations, representing about 25 percent of the total labor force, were closely allied with the Social Democratic party (SPD or party) and rather consistently espoused its aims. Unlike American organized labor at that time, the German unions were committed to political parties and directly involved in the affairs of the nation. German labor upheld the democratic regime on many occasions, and most notably at the time of the right wing Kapp putsch in 1920 when a prompt general strike call contributed to the failure of the uprising. It must be emphasized that for the most part both the members and leaders of the "free" unions were Socialists and staunch opponents of the Communists and Fascists.

Yet, when democracy was threatened in the latter period of the

Weimar Republic, the movement had lost its élan and was close to paralysis. With the depression organized labor confronted crucial problems: unemployment had risen steeply, and the economic survival of the nation was at stake. Was it not, however, important also that labor realize the danger of pursuing a politically sterile and negative course of action in the face of imminent danger to the organization as well as to the nation?

In order to understand the attitudes which actually prevailed and the decisions which were made, the role played by the Socialist unions during the authoritarian regimes of von Papen, von Schleicher, and Hitler must be reviewed.

*   *   *

On July 20, 1932, Chancellor Franz von Papen dramatically ousted the legitimate Prussian coalition government headed by Otto Braun, Social Democrat. The conservative chancellor held no brief for Socialists and trade unionists. On the pretext that law and order were not being preserved in Prussia, long a stronghold of the Socialists, Papen had himself appointed commissioner for Prussia by presidential decree. Then, on the broad authority given him, he dismissed the eight Prussian cabinet ministers, who forthwith appealed to the Supreme Court, on the grounds that an outright dismissal of ministers by federal decree was unconstitutional. But it was too late. The court decision, generally in their favor, was not rendered until October 25, when it could no longer be of significance. This coup d'état undoubtedly was one of the chief factors in bringing about the rise of fascism, and was the first of numerous illegal acts performed by irresponsible German governments.

How did the Socialist trade unions react to Papen's dramatic move? On the part of the rank and file, the response was an immediate work stoppage in a few plants, followed by a pause for instructions. Berlin workers in the sprawling Siemens and I. G. Farben plants assembled to hear their leaders speak. Small formations of the Iron Front, a semimilitary, Socialist-led defense organization, gathered in various sectors of Berlin to wait for directions. But no call for a general protest strike or even a token demonstration came from their chiefs.

The ADGB Board and Executive met immediately on the afternoon of the twentieth and decided not to take any action. Their reasons were similar to those voiced by SPD leaders on the following day: unemployment and increasing defeatism among the workers rendered immediate action impracticable, but cautious preparations for a possible future general strike should be made. A spokesman for the Railroad Workers Union claimed that his men had no wish to strike as many unemployed workers were ready to step into their jobs. Also, reportedly, it was argued at the meeting that Papen had acted within the limits of his constitutional powers and that consequently the unions must reject any strike call.

The SPD called on its Executive Committee and Board members to attend an emergency meeting in Berlin on July 21. At this conference it was decided to bring all organizations to a state of readiness, but to refrain from immediate action. Three main considerations led to these decisions: the hope that the July 30 election, then ten days off, would turn the tide against fascism by increasing the vote for the Left; the desire at all costs to avoid a civil war, with the Reichswehr fighting the workers; and the belief that Papen was still attempting to prevent Hitler's assumption of power. The SPD moreover rejected the proposal of the Communist party for a general strike, declaring that, in view of the collaboration between Communists and Nazis in a plebiscite against the Prussian government the previous year, it preferred to act on its own.

Once immediate action was ruled out, Otto Wels, party chairman, systematically sounded out trade union, party, and Iron Front leaders on the feasibility of future resistance. Fearing bloodshed, they responded negatively. The chairman of the Frankfurt trade union council, Otto Misbach, in a typical reply to the query, categorically refused to engage in any "experiments" which were doomed to failure. The spokesman of the Metal Workers Union and Reichsbanner (Socialist militia) Council in Frankfurt, Mulanski, declared that the Reichsbanner did not even have sufficient equipment at its disposal to transport workers to a possible scene of action.

The Iron Front[1] Executive members also held a caucus at which most party and union spokesmen stressed their fear that an immediate general strike would lead to civil war. They decisively rejected a proposal by Karl Höltermann, head of the Reichsbanner, and Sieg-

[1] In 1931, the Reichsbanner, a Social Democratic defense organization, and other groups jointly set up the paramilitary Iron Front to combat the enemies of democracy.

fried Aufhäuser, AFA president, that, at the very least, a demonstration strike be held.

Though the no-strike decision reached at the three meetings was revealed without delay, it was followed by supplementary declarations. On July 20 and 21, the Berlin locals of the national unions issued two appeals warning workers of provocateurs who, in the name of the Iron Front and without authorization, were agitating for a general strike. The appeals asked the workers to follow only the legitimate union leadership. Another official declaration asserted that, despite the excitement of the workers, exemplary discipline must be maintained, especially since no solution could be reached in Prussia until the Supreme Court had rendered its decision. These releases once more clearly demonstrated that labor was not ready to risk a civil war, but preferred to await developments. The first setback to the party and union occurred on July 31, when the National Socialists registered further gains in the nationwide election, thus becoming an increasing menace to the fragile structure of the Weimar Republic.

In retrospect, whether the no-strike decision was the correct one remains a matter of debate. Had the trade unions decided on a general strike or token demonstration, the party would have backed them up. Conversely, the party could not possibly have initiated a strike with the unions opposing it. Which organization made the original decision remains a moot question, although all indications are that the unions were primarily responsible.

Certain differences in political outlook within the party and within the union which were never overcome in the Weimar period stood out clearly in the 1932 crisis. As the danger of fascism grew, the ideological split between the minority who wanted more militant action and the majority who feared any hasty action was intensified within each organization.

Whatever one may have thought of the feasibility of calling a general strike, the decision of the union and the party not to act weakened any hope of further resistance to fascism. Symptomatic of the passive mood of the two organizations was their refusal even to consider a demonstration strike to rally the masses. Thus the only major forces available at that critical hour which could perhaps have saved the deteriorating situation failed to make the attempt.

*   *   *

General Kurt von Schleicher, Reichswehr leader and war minister in the cabinet of von Papen, succeeded his chief as chancellor on December 3, 1932. Before forming the cabinet, Schleicher, who lacked an organized party following of his own, considered different combinations of the various political and trade union groups.

One plan called for the creation of a labor government led by German generals. Apparently, Schleicher believed that such a coalition would prevent the rise of Hitler. But, of course, no such collaboration was possible then since the two groups had no basis for agreement. The general reportedly also toyed with a rightist combination of the Reichswehr, allied with Papen, Göring, and Hitler, but the Nazi chiefs refused to enter into any cabinet in which Schleicher would be chancellor. In another move, the general held conversations with the "moderate" group of Nazis headed by Gregor Strasser and with the trade union leaders, in an attempt to reconcile the major social forces. He intended to split the Nazi movement by offering Strasser the twin posts of vice-chancellor and Prussian prime minister, but the negotiations crumbled when Strasser's prestige and mass support in the Nazi party declined.

In his parleys with organized labor, Schleicher seemed to have short-range and long-range goals in mind. He often expressed the hope in private conversations that all trade union organizations would sever their links with the political parties, unite in one labor front, and counteract the Nazi menace by exercising more power in the state. He also envisioned the eventual organization of the economy into guilds, and the institution of a corporative government based largely upon the trade unions.

With some of these goals in mind, Schleicher paid compliments to ADGB President Theodor Leipart at a Berlin assembly of works council representatives in October 1932. On November 28, five days before he assumed the chancellorship, Schleicher invited union representatives to a personal conference. Their acceptance, however, aroused particular controversy in some party and labor circles where it was feared that the union would make a deal with the general.

Gustav Noske, former SPD war minister, describes in his memoirs an episode which supposedly occurred immediately after Schleicher's request for such a conference came to the notice of the SPD Executive members. "At once Leipart was asked to come to Party headquarters. . . . There Breitscheid told him that the Party rejected any collaboration with reactionary Schleicher, and expected the same attitude from him (Leipart). Leipart, who described this conversation to me, yielded to the Party pressure." The conversation nevertheless took place. Leipart and Wilhelm Eggert, union heads, participated and, as reported by the official union and party organs, stressed the need to initiate an employment policy and render void Papen's unpopular wage-slashing decree of September 5. Schleicher asked Leipart to submit these demands to him on the following day in written form. According to another source, the general made a favorable impression on Leipart and Eggert at the meeting when he told them that Papen had donated too much money to Prussian Junker estates, and that Papen's wage cuts were too drastic. The two labor leaders thereupon dropped their demands for socialization of key enterprises, but demanded a large public works program as a condition for supporting Schleicher.

After several days of negotiations with the various parties and trade union organizations, Schleicher finally formed his cabinet on December 3, retaining, with only two exceptions, the same conservative ministers who had served under Papen. The SPD and other parties, for conflicting reasons, did not support the new government, which thus rested on precarious foundations.

                          *   *   *

Papen's backstage intrigues and pressures forced Schleicher to resign on January 28, 1933. Two days later, President Hindenburg administered the oath of office to the new chancellor, Adolf Hitler, who, ironically enough, promised to uphold the constitution. January 30 proved to be a fateful day in German history. It marked the definite end of the Weimar period and the beginning of the fascist era.

Would the unions undertake any last-minute move to rescue the nation, or yield to the fascist assumption of power? We know that they chose the latter path, and failed again to use their most potent weapon, the general strike. There were many diverse excuses given for this lack of action: it was pointed out that the chancellor had assumed his office legitimately, and that the odds were against the workers, since any uprising would be crushed by the Reichswehr. It was argued later that the unions could not yet discern the totalitarian character of the fascist movement, that they believed Hitler would not remain long in power, and that they could hope to save themselves from extinction by ending the collaboration with the party.

There was apathy among all ranks of labor, caused partly by the failure of the leaders to present any positive plan for counteracting the Nazi policies. The union might have advanced an effective anti-depression program of deficit financing, as was practiced by the United States' New Deal and the Swedish labor governments in the thirties. It might have rallied the workers to a political program of broad scope; it might have demanded, for instance, that the major democratic parties bury their differences and unite against the Right. But by now it was too late. A general strike would undoubtedly have led to civil war, and the union leaders were not willing to risk it. . . .

In its declarations, the union characteristically asked the workers to remain calm and to follow the slogan of the hour: "Organization, not demonstration." It still entertained hope for the future and asserted that even the new government would not be able to crush the workers and their unions. In line with the policy during the Schleicher administration, the union announced that it intended, despite its opposition to the government, to present the demands of the workers to the nation's leaders.

The ADGB Board, on January 31, issued a carefully worded statement, in which it was implied that, if necessary, a compromise in order to conform with government policies might be accepted. The board argued that while the desire of the workers to take action against the new administration was understandable, such a step would merely harm their interests. Governments are transitory, it was emphasized, and reactionary ones do not necessarily destroy the labor movement. While this release was issued in order to preserve the organization, it nevertheless left no doubt about the passive mood of the ADGB staff officials and their mistaken appraisal of the new regime.

During the month of February, it is true, there was hope that the unions would stand firm. They protested Nazi chief Göring's order to the police, SA and SS (Nazi semi-military units) to unite against the Left, but were ignored. Furthermore, some union speakers urged SPD and KPD (Communist party) workers to bridge their differences and unite. In Berlin, Clothing Workers and Lithographers unions asked the ADGB to seek an agreement between the SPD and the KPD, but the ADGB took no action, for it had already decided a year earlier that it would not put its weight behind a unity campaign until the KPD stopped attacking the Socialist unions and the SPD.

Despite the formal union appeal to its members to vote for the SPD in the March 5 nationwide election, the next two months, March and April, gave rise to indications that the union, in order to preserve itself, was beginning to adopt a neutral political attitude. In a letter to the right-wing SPD leader Wilhelm Keil, dated March 3, Leipart categorically asserted that he intended to remain in the political limelight no longer, and hoped that organized labor would now benefit from his earlier modest role in the activities of the party.

After the March 5 Nazi election victory, gained as a result of a wave of terror against all opposition parties, the AFA Executive (Federation of Salaried Employees) drew up a resolution which stated in part:

> *It cannot be the task of the trade unions to take a stand on the political consequences of this election. However, [they] . . . are cognizant of their duty to continue to work for the fulfillment of their social and economic task in this historic, significant moment for the country and its people.*

Ten days later, the ADGB Executive issued a document of great importance, which was similar in content to the AFA resolution. The ADGB declared that a trade union must be independent of political parties as well as of employers. Its social tasks must be fulfilled no matter what government is in power, but it should not attempt to interfere directly in politics.

Following these official declarations, most local labor weeklies urged their readers not to voice political opinions but to devote their time entirely to economic problems. In a similar vein, the ADGB journal declared that the union was more than ever occupied with its immediate tasks, and that the reduced political role of the workers must be balanced by strengthening the organization.

These policy declarations did not have the desired effect. Hopes of saving the movement crumbled when the Nazis increased their relentless persecution of the unions, thereby causing much hardship. The many-pronged attack was carried out against the property of the unions, their leaders and press, and the newly elected officials of the works councils.

The attacks on union property constituted flagrant violations of democratic procedure. On March 8, the ADGB training school in

Bernau was occupied by SA men. The ADGB Executive immediately protested to Vice-Chancellor Papen and Prussian Commissioner Göring, who had the building cleared and returned to the union. Renewed Nazi attacks on union property prompted further protests. On March 10, the ADGB appealed to the president to stop the infringements of the law, the acts of terror against union members, and the destruction of property. The appeal was in vain. More headquarters were occupied or closed by the police, labor leaders were arrested, and it was decreed in many German states that no union official could hold a party office or agitate against the government.

In another type of crackdown, the Nazis periodically confiscated and suppressed labor newspapers. This caused the newspapers to exercise great caution in their comments on Hitler's speeches to the Reichstag and on other Nazi pronouncements.

The government brazenly dismissed from office ADGB candidates successful in the works council elections. Once again, the union appealed to the administration, but received no satisfaction. It was belatedly realizing that its efforts were becoming increasingly futile.

There was no unanimity in labor ranks regarding the policy that should be pursued as a result of the illegal Nazi acts. In a book of doubtful reliability, Hermann Seelbach, head of the ADGB training school of minor union functionaries, and secretly a Nazi party member, reveals that among his students there was as little agreement as at the top level. A large group favored yielding to the Nazis (an attitude prompted by Seelbach himself), a second smaller group counseled a "let us wait and see" attitude, and only a small group advocated illegal anti-Nazi action. The groups engaged in constant discussions on the future role of the unions, but the decision was not in their hands; it rested with the union Executive. Yet, at Executive meetings the debates merely centered on methods of countering individual Nazi attacks. Broader issues and policies were rarely touched upon, according to Seelbach, chiefly due to the lack of knowledge of government plans.

Apparently the majority of union leaders, partly under the influence of Seelbach and other minor chieftains, who later revealed themselves as NSDAP members, did favor a compromise with the Nazis. Accordingly, at the demand of the ADGB, Professor E. R. Huber, an associate of Hitler's advisor Carl Schmitt, drafted a document on the future legal position of the organization. It recommended the recognition of the unions in the state and, simultaneously, their transformation into public legal bodies by a coordination (*Zuordnung*) with the Third Reich.

The unions also attempted to clarify their precarious position by engaging in discussions with Nazi representatives. Since Minister of Labor Seldte and other conservative cabinet members no longer held any influence over Hitler, the unions were forced to negotiate directly with the National Socialist Shop Organization (NSBO). A conference was thereupon held on April 5 between leading ADGB and NSBO staff officials. NSBO chief Bruckner took the initiative. He outlined the Nazi program, and revealed that the government intended to form a unitary labor organization, headed by an appointed leader, and would regulate wages and prices. Bruckner asked for the resignation of the ADGB president. Labor officials Leipart, Grassmann, Eggert, and Leuschner retorted that the unions had fought a valiant struggle in the past to obtain their goals, and could not agree to the arbitrary appointment of a new leader. Leipart refused to resign from his post, still under the illusion that he could save the unions from extinction.

On March 28, a week before this conference, the AFA Executive gave indications of yielding to the government by evolving reorganization plans. On April 6, however, the ADBB Executive (Federation of Civil Servants) agreed to disband its organization before any further administration measures would crush the labor movement. The ADGB continued its precarious existence, even though its leaders, once active in the SPD or in the international labor movement, were resigning.

The methodical pressure on organized labor increased. The government decreed that May first, a holiday traditionally celebrated by the forces of the Left, would be a "National Labor Day." Apparently, this was a calculated Nazi maneuver to win the allegiance of the workers to the fascist state. Simultaneously, plans were made to crush the free labor movement the day after the celebration. NSDAP chief Joseph Goebbels records that on April 17 he discussed with Hitler plans for May Day and the seizure and occupation of trade union buildings on May 2. Goebbels foresaw the possibility of a few days of struggle.

On April 15, the ADGB Executive asserted that it welcomed the government's May Day decision. The declaration left up to the members the question of whether to participate in the official demonstrations. After pressure reportedly was exerted by other trade union organizations, the ADGB Board issued a declaration on April 19 requesting the members to participate "for the honor of creative labor, for the complete incorporation of the working masses into the state." The manifesto represented a clear-cut capitulation to the fascist government, and was followed by the Nazi-sponsored May Day demonstrations.

A few columns appeared in the official union journal which compromised even with the Nazi ideology. In its final issue, an article welcomed the May Day and the "socialist" principles embodied in National Socialism. The article read in part:

> We certainly need not strike our colors in order to recognize that the victory of National Socialism, though won in the struggle against a party which we used to consider as the embodiment of the idea of socialism (SPD), is our victory as well; because, today, the socialist task is put to the whole nation.

Even this last desperate effort to save the union failed completely. For the Nazis, a compromise with the trade unions was out of the question. The democratic labor movement, a potential opposition in a totalitarian state, had to be destroyed. Accordingly, the day after "National Labor Day," union leaders Leipart, Grassmann, Wissell, and numerous others were arrested by the Nazis, and on May 13 all union property was confiscated. The Christian and liberal trade union organizations also were subsequently suppressed. A new Nazi Labor Front was created which remained in power until Germany's defeat in World War II.

A fundamental question must be posed. Why did eminent labor leaders, holding socialist convictions in the twenties, attempt to compromise with the Nazis during the initial months of the Hitler era? Several factors may have had a bearing on the course of action chosen by these men. The depression demoralized the labor movement both physically and psychologically. The faith in socialism of some leaders gradually receded and was being replaced by a stress on nationalism, which could have led to an ideological capitulation to the Nazis. Moreover, the leaders expected the Nazis to spare their movement, painfully nurtured through bitter struggles, from the totalitarian web. But they failed to foresee the ruthlessness of the new policy, its drive toward total elimination of the democratic institutions, and its opposition to any nonfascist ideologies. The labor officials were not the only ones, however, to have lacked this vision. The burden of guilt must be placed on most leaders of the democratic groups, since few had the courage to oppose actively the National Socialists at the critical hour.

It was not always so. During most of the Weimar era, the union, in cooperation with the Social Democratic party, was able to wield considerable power within the state machinery. It served as a potent weapon for the protection of the republic against internal and external onslaughts. Only when the fragile democratic structure began to decay from within, did the union, as a major national institution, gradually lose its power to act. When the crisis came, neither the democratic regime nor the free labor movement had the strength of will to cooperate any more in halting the plunge into the abyss. In this failure to act lay the tragedy of Germany.

Guenter Lewy
THE ROMAN CATHOLIC CHURCH

After the unsuccessful assassination attempt upon Hitler in Munich on November 8, 1939, Cardinal Bertram, in the name of the German episcopate, and Cardinal Faulhaber for the Bavarian bishops sent telegrams of congratulations to Hitler. The Catholic press all over Germany, in response to instructions of the *Reichspressekammer,* spoke of the miraculous working of providence that had protected the Führer. And on November 12 in the Cathedral of Munich a Te Deum was sung "in order to thank the Divine Providence in the name of the archdiocese for the Führer's fortunate escape from the criminal attempt made upon his life." It is noteworthy that back in February 1919 Faulhaber had refused to order the ringing of bells and the

From *The Catholic Church and Nazi Germany,* by Guenter Lewy. Copyright © 1964 by Guenter Lewy. Used with permission of McGraw-Hill Book Company and George Weidenfeld and Nicolson Ltd. Footnotes omitted.

showing of flags of mourning after Kurt Eisner, the Socialist prime minister of Bavaria, had been assassinated by a Catholic nobleman.

In his justly celebrated sermons of July and August 1941 Bishop Galen courageously condemned the power of the Gestapo which subjected perfectly loyal citizens to arbitrary arrest and kept them in concentration camps without an ordinary court trial. But none of these misdeeds were seen by Galen as a justification for opposing the Hitler regime as such. He went out of his way to make clear that he was opposed to any forceful resistance to the state, or to any weakening of the German war effort:

> *We Christians make no revolution. We will continue to do our duty in obedience to God, out of love for people and fatherland. Our soldiers will fight and die for Germany, but not for those who . . . disgrace the German name before God and man. We will continue to fight against the external enemy; against the enemy in our midst who tortures and beats us, we cannot fight with arms and there remains only one weapon: strong tenacious, obstinate perseverance.*

When later that year the anti-Nazi underground, or perhaps the Gestapo seeking to ruin the bishop, circulated a bogus sermon in which Galen was quoted as calling for the elimination of the godless regime of injustice that oppressed Germany, the bishop of Münster disowned this sermon and let it be known that it stood "in glaring contradiction" to his own views and attitudes. It is reported by all of Galen's associates that the "Lion of Münster" was indeed resolutely opposed to any and all attempts to depose the Nazi regime by force or to cause a German defeat.

It might be argued that the German episcopate not only acted prudently in dissociating the Church from any violent tactics, but that the bishops were also bound by traditional Catholic teaching which, in recent centuries at least, had frequently condemned revolutions and tyrannicide. . . . It is appropriate to indicate here that Catholic theologians were, and still are, by no means in agreement on the morality of resisting tyranny.

In a number of instances in recent history the Church has sanctioned armed rebellion. The Mexican hierarchy in 1927 approved of and blessed the revolt of the *Cristeros,* bands of peasants so called because of their rallying cry, *"Viva Cristo Rey,"* and frequently led by Catholic priests. Pope Pius XI, in his encyclical *Firmissimam Con-*

stantiam of March 28, 1937, on conditions in Mexico, distinguished between just and unjust insurrections and left the door open for defensive violence against constituted powers that "arise against justice and truth even to destroying the very foundations of authority . . . [and] make use of public power to bring it to ruin." After the majority of the Spanish hierarchy had sided with the rebellion of General Franco and had called for a crusade against communism and for Christianity and justice, Pius XI gave his blessing to "those who have assumed the difficult and dangerous task of defending and restoring the rights and honor of God and of religion." And after Franco, generously helped by Hitler and Mussolini, had succeeded in defeating the Loyalists, Pius XII sent the Spanish Catholics his expressions of "immense joy" and "fatherly congratulations for the gift of peace and victory with which God has deigned to crown the Christian heroism of your faith and charity, proved through such great and generous sufferings." Clearly some rebellions were acceptable and could receive the blessing of the Church.

If the German bishops had wanted to sanction active resistance to Hitler, there were thus many precedents for such a stand. The fact that they consistently opposed such resistance will therefore have to be explained on grounds other than the inhibiting effects of Christian theology. In the first few years of Hitler's reign the bishops probably had hopes that the Nazi state would relinquish its anti-Catholic policies if the Catholics only showed sufficient willingness to cooperate and support the Third Reich. Later, when this hope was disappointed, the episcopate had committed the Church to a course of loyal obedience which it would have been very difficult to reverse. Most of the bishops moreover were conservatives and out of sympathy with any policy likely to lead to an open clash between church and state. Once the war had broken out they considered it their patriotic duty to support the German war effort.

The apparent hopelessness of any successful resistance to Hitler's machinery of terror may also have played a role But the net effect of the episcopate's exhortations to obedience and their warnings against any seditious activity was, of course, to discourage *any* spirit of opposition and to burden the conscience of those, such as the men of the military resistance group, who felt impelled to resist the Nazi regime. A popular uprising, no doubt, had little chance of success, but the military dissidents were in a stronger position and their cause was by no means a lost one from the start. Bishops are not expected to be plotters and leaders of insurrections, but they could alternatively have explained to their followers what, according to Catholic teaching, are the rights of the individual against an unjust political regime, and then left it to each believer how to act upon this moral guidance. At the very least, the episcopate could have elected to adopt a policy of discreet silence on the entire subject of disobedience and rebellion. . . .

There can be little doubt that the bishops grossly underestimated the strength of their position, especially during the war period. The reports of the provincial administrators and of the Gestapo, *Hitler's Table Talk* and the diaries of his henchmen give abundant testimony to the Church's popularity and to the political risks the Nazis saw in proceeding against the episcopate. In the few important instances when the strength of popular feeling led the bishops to take a resolute stand, the regime was forced to back down. The cessation of the euthanasia program has . . . been mentioned in this connection and there were a number of other such occurrences.

The joint pastoral letter of the Bavarian bishops protesting the highly unpopular dismissal of all nuns teaching in the public schools, scheduled to be read on June 21, 1936, had been forbidden by the Bavarian Political Police. On June 20 orders had been issued to take into custody all priests who dared to read the pastoral letter in violation of the ban. But when Vicar General Buchwieser of Munich (in charge of the archdiocese in the temporary absence of Cardinal Faulhaber) instructed the clergy to read the pronouncement despite this order, the government yielded. The same evening the Bavarian minister of the interior countermanded the earlier order by instructions merely to record the names of priests who read the pastoral letter. Afterwards a number of provincial administrators reported that in the event of arrests the population would not have accepted these measures without resistance, and that disturbances would probably have resulted. "The priest," the *Regierungspräsident* of Upper Bavaria wrote, "is still a person enjoying the greatest respect and that is true especially in rural districts. Even the currency and immorality trials have been unable to change this fact to any substantial degree. When the priest yet appears as a martyr for his convictions, he is defended even by people who normally have little to do with the Church."

Two other examples of the efficacy of public protests are provided by the abortive attempts to remove the crucifixes from public buildings that took place in the predominantly Catholic states of Oldenburg and Bavaria in 1936 and 1941 respectively. On November 4, 1936, the minister of religion and education in Oldenburg had ordered the removal of all religious symbols such as crucifixes from public buildings by December 15. The order caused tremendous agitation. Local officials everywhere were put under pressure to threaten to resign their posts unless the order was revoked; special prayers were ordered by Bishop Galen. Delegations from all corners of the state converged upon the town of Oldenburg, the seat of the state government, to protest the ordinance. On November 25 the Gauleiter and Reichsstatthalter of Oldenburg addressed a mass meeting where he was heckled throughout his address. At the end he declared that a wise government must know when a mistake has been made and that the order of November 4 stood revoked. Bishop Galen ordered special services of thanks to be held, and in a pastoral letter expressed the hope that this courageous conduct of the people of Oldenburg would be followed by other Christians everywhere.

The same strength of religious feelings was revealed five years later in Bavaria. An order of April 23, 1941, by the gauleiter and minister of education and religious affairs, Adolf Wagner, had prohibited the opening of the school day by a prayer, and suggested the gradual removal of all crucifixes. Whenever an attempt was made to enforce this ruling, unrest and resistance were obvious. Parents refused to send their children to school, and in many places demonstrations took place that led to the restoration of the crucifixes. In one small town 500 aroused men and women overpowered the mayor and recovered the crucifixes he had hidden. In another place where the local priest had been arrested for preaching a sermon strongly critical of the removal of the crucifixes, 50 women informed the mayor that unless the priest were released, they would cease to work and deliver produce and would surrender the medals earned for having given birth to a large number of children. On July 26 Faulhaber, in the name of the Bavarian bishops, added his voice to this storm of largely spontaneous protest. "The German soldier," he wrote Wagner, "is honored publicly by being called a crusader against Bolshevism. This title of honor would not be deserved, if at the same time at home war is declared on the cross." A month later the Bavarian government yielded. On August 28 the ordinance in question was revoked.

To be sure, not all protests led to such results. After the arrest in June 1937 of the Jesuit Rupert Mayer, a highly popular preacher in Munich, Cardinal Faulhaber delivered a sermon in which he most vigorously condemned the action of the authorities, but Father Mayer was not released until December, only to be arrested again about a week later. Despite Mayer's great popularity in Munich, he remained in custody or under house arrest for most of the war period. It should also be said that none of these cases of successful opposition involved essential parts of the Nazi program. One would not, therefore, be justified in deducing from these episodes that a similar outburst of popular sentiment would have dissuaded Hitler from his plan to exterminate the Jews of Europe.

Nevertheless, it seems clear that public opinion was a force to be reckoned with, even amidst the terror of the Gestapo. On November 1, 1941, Ulrich von Hassell, the former German ambassador in Rome and one of the continuing conspirators against Hitler, recorded in his diary: "Just as Bishop Galen has exercised not only a powerful and direct moral influence throughout Germany, but also certain indirect influence, it has been demonstrated that an energetic protest often does have an effect." . . .

Unfortunately we have only spotty information on the hierarchy's attitudes to the plans and actions of the military resistance group. At least two members of the episcopate seem to have been told by Carl Goerdeler, the spirited though somewhat careless civilian leader of the generals' plot, about the plans for revolt. They were Cardinal Faulhaber and Bishop Preysing. Count Claus von Stauffenberg, the man who planted the bomb on July 20, 1944, also visited Preysing. In neither case do we know how much concrete information was actually given the two churchmen. According to one report Bishop Preysing, in the event of a successful uprising, was to have become a papal legate with special powers in order to supersede Nuncio Orsenigo, who was considered compromised by his pro-fascist and pro-Nazi views. Joseph Müller, the contact between the plotting generals and the Vatican, tells of having approached Preysing at the pope's request in 1942 and 1943, and to have obtained his consent. The idea of Preysing's appointment supposedly came from Monsignor Kaas. However, no corroboration is available, and Walter Adolph, a close associate of the late bishop of Berlin, casts doubt upon its accuracy.

In December 1943 a Catholic chaplain, the Jesuit Hermann Wehrle, was asked by a young officer of Stauffenberg's staff, Major Leonrod, whether his knowledge of the plan to kill Hitler placed him in the state of sin. Wehrle consulted the article on tyrannicide in the *Lexikon für Theologie und Kirche* and then told Leonrod that the killing of a legitimate ruler by a private individual was forbidden, but that knowledge alone was not sinful. He advised Leonrod not to participate in the plot. The question had been posed under the seal of secrecy, but when the episode came to light in the trial of the plotters after the July 20 affair, Wehrle was indicted and condemned to death for complicity. In a sermon preached in 1946 Cardinal Faulhaber praised the chaplain as a fighter against Nazi tyranny.

After the failure of the plot, Faulhaber was questioned by the Gestapo about his talk with Goerdeler and is said to have expressed the most vigorous condemnation of the assassination attempt and to have affirmed his loyalty to Hitler. Two close colleagues of the cardinal agree that Faulhaber was probably opposed to this act of tyrannicide. He was an aristocrat in his thinking, they recall, and against "political murder." No information is available about the reaction of the other bishops.

In contrast to November 1939, this time no telegrams of congratulations seem to have been sent to Hitler, and a report of the propaganda office of Münster complained, "It is typical for the attitude of the clergy that no priest, including the bishops, has found a word of indignation for the treasonable assassination attempt or expressed thanks for . . . the preservation of the Führer." A Gestapo agent in Cologne reported that some clergymen decried the plot and had expressed feelings of shame "that something like this could happen among us. Some found it strange that the bishops had not commented at all." One pro-Nazi priest told the agent that the majority of the clergy regretted the failure of the assassination attempt. But all this is highly fragmentary evidence that does not allow us to make generalizations about the response of the Church. Mother Gallin in her study of the German resistance movement concludes that the bishops "offered no encouragement or support to any plans for a revolution by which the Nazis would have been removed from power. Revolution was specifically rejected and denounced by them on several occasions." This conclusion can certainly be accepted.

A number of eminent Catholics were members of resistance groups. Augustinus Rösch, the provincial of the Society of Jesus in Bavaria, and the Jesuit Alfred Delp belonged to the Kreisau Circle, a group of men led by Count Helmuth von Moltke. This group had met since the summer of 1940 to discuss the political, economic, and spiritual foundations of the new Germany that would arise after the downfall of the Third Reich. Father Rösch narrowly escaped with his life after July 20, 1944. The brilliant, thirty-eight-year-old Delp, a convert to Catholicism and a former editor of the Jesuit monthly *Stimmen der Zeit,* was hanged on February 2, 1945; his ashes were scattered to the winds. Both men apparently knew nothing of the plan to assassinate Hitler and, had they known, would probably not have approved of it. The Goerdeler-Beck group responsible for the plot included several well-known Catholics, among them the former labor leaders Bernhard Letterhaus and Jakob Kaiser. Stauffenberg himself was a Catholic, though he did not regularly practice his religion.

A large number of Catholic priests were either executed or died in prisons and concentration camps. Many of them had run afoul of ordinances such as those that forbade listening to foreign broadcasts, or were severely punished for other trivial offenses. But some were martyrs to their convictions. Dr. Max Josef Metzger, a life-long pacifist and founder of the Una Sancta movement, was sentenced to death and executed on April 17, 1944, for having had "seditious" contacts with the bishop of Upsala in Sweden. Father Alfons Maria Wachsmann of Berlin was condemned for having undermined the morale of the armed forces. The same charge took the lives of Josef Losch, a parish priest in Bavaria, and of three clergymen in Lübeck. [There was] the martyrdom of Provost Lichtenberg and Franz Reinisch, . . . and there were still others who sealed their testimony to human dignity with their blood. And yet, it is sad to record, these courageous few were no more representative of the

Church than Goerdeler was of the German bureaucracy, or General Beck of the military.

If by resistance to Nazi rule we mean not criticism of certain specific measures, but opposition to the regime as such, then the Church as an institution did not resist. A good number of individual Catholics of extraordinary courage and moral integrity, on the other hand, who disregarded the constant exhortations to loyal obedience in the pronouncements of their spiritual superiors, belong on the honor roll of the resistance. Men like Letterhaus and Delp were part of that "other Germany," which has done so much to safeguard and restore the honor of the German name, because they were prepared to flout the official line of their Church and listen instead to the voice of their consciences. The Church fought for her confessional schools, her press and organizations, her monasteries; she clashed with the government on some issues of moral teaching, such as sterilization and euthanasia. But at no time did the Church challenge the legitimacy of the Nazi regime or give her explicit or implicit approval to the various attempts to bring about its downfall. While thousands of anti-Nazis were beaten into pulp in the concentration camps, the Church talked of supporting the moral renewal brought about by the Hitler government. This line of cooperation was never abandoned.

It has been said that the bishops exercised restraint in their protests in order not to aggravate the tribulations of the lower clergy, who had to bear the brunt of the Church's persecution. It is true that the regime frequently punished those who read a certain pastoral letter but shied away from laying hands on the bishop who had composed it. Bishop Galen is said to have become far less outspoken after 1943, when three priests in Lübeck were executed, one of the accusations having been that they had distributed copies of Galen's sermons to soldiers. We also know that bishops like Galen and Preysing felt hindered by their more conciliatory colleagues, with whom they frequently disagreed in matters of tactics, but to whom they deferred in order not to jeopardize the shaky unity of the episcopate. Some bishops, like Ehrenfried of Würzburg, were convinced monarchists; others, like Faulhaber, were aristocrats, anchored in the politics of an imperial Germany that had long passed away. Most of them were ardent patriots and entrapped in a legalistic approach that had some relevance to the Wilhelmian *Rechtsstaat,* but was sadly unsuited to the realities of life in Hitler's dictatorship. In this basically conservative group, men like Galen and Preysing, advocating a more resistant stand, could not prevail.

It is doubtful anyway whether the masses of the faithful would have been prepared to follow a more radical leadership. Most of the Catholics, like human beings everywhere, were not heroes and merely wanted to live in peace. These were the simple people, regular churchgoers, who might be willing to send an unsigned postcard to the authorities like this one found in the files of the Bavarian government: "We regard the campaign against Jewish Bolshevism as a crusade. With the name of the Savior on their lips thousands of soldiers now sacrifice their lives. We protest against the removal of the crucifixes from the schools. The school prayer should also continue." With such "resisters" nothing much could be done to check the crimes of the Nazi regime.

A small minority, sometimes organized in informal groups led by priests, rejected the official irenical line of the Church. Many of these Catholics had belonged to the Catholic youth movement. Some had a loose connection with the Catholic periodical *Hochland,* and with the Catholic writer Theodor Haecker; others may have been influenced by the sonnets of the Catholic poet Reinhold Schneider that circulated clandestinely all over Germany during the war years. Most of these men and women did not plot revolts, but they did maintain their spiritual integrity. The nationalistic pronouncements of the episcopate bewildered and distressed them; every critical note in a pastoral letter or sermon was eagerly welcomed. The personal courage of a Galen inspired and fortified them; the silence of the Church in the face of the most revolting crimes created a crisis of confidence in their spiritual superiors which, for some, still exists today.

For these Catholics the bishops' struggle to save the Catholic organizations and to defend other rights guaranteed by the Concordat meant relatively little; the progress of the liturgical movement seeking the more active and intelligent participation of the faithful in the holy mysteries and prayers of the Church was more important to them than the fate of the Church's functional machinery. For these few the Church was free as long as she fearlessly adhered to her gospel of human dignity and love; and she became enslaved, no matter how many millions continued to attend services, when the Church chose a course of compromise with evil.

Had German Catholicism from the start adhered to a policy of resolute opposition to the Nazi regime, world history might well have taken a different course. Even if this struggle had ultimately failed to defeat Hitler and prevent all of his many crimes, it would in this view have raised the moral prestige of the Church immeasurably. The human cost of such resistance would undeniably have been great, but these sacrifices would have been made for the greatest of all causes. With the home front unreliable, Hitler might not have dared going to war and literally millions of lives would have been saved.

David Schoenbaum
THE ELEGY OF A SOCIETY

The Third Reich proved that a house divided against itself *can* stand, provided, at least, that the occupants have no alternative place to go and that the landlord pays attention to the wallpaper, if not to the walls.

The German house was no less divided in 1939 or 1945 than it was in 1933 when Hitler took possession of it. The Gemeinschaft invoked by Nazi ideology struck genuinely resonant notes in the hearts of a population desperate for authority and sick unto death of conflict. But real Gemeinschaft was no closer to realization in practice at the end of Nazi rule than it was at the beginning. With all good will, German society was finally united only in a negative community of fear, sacrifice, and ruin. The elimination of class conflict, the Third Reich's major social boast from 1935 on, was at best a half truth. Beneath the cover of Nazi ideology, the historic social groups con-

From *Hitler's Social Revolution: Class and Status in Nazi Germany*, by David Schoenbaum, pp. 275–288. Copyright © 1966 by David Schoenbaum. Reprinted by permission of Doubleday & Company, Inc. and George Weidenfeld and Nicolson, Ltd. Footnotes omitted.

tinued their conflicts like men wrestling under a blanket. Beneath the surface of apparent economic recovery, none of the basic problems of German society had been solved; a more equitable relationship had not been found between capital and labor, between big business and small business, or between industry and agriculture. The problems had at best been postponed, in the case of agriculture even exacerbated.

The division of the Nazi house was built into the party program. National Socialism was to turn the clocks back, to make the German-speaking world safe for small business, small farmers, and small-towners. The goal was not only political but social revisionism, revision of the tyranny of big industry, big cities, big unions, big banks; and at the same time a revision of Versailles. But the simultaneous revision of Versailles and of the twentieth—not to say the nineteenth—century, *in* the twentieth century, was an attempt to square the circle. Revision of Versailles, in Nazi dimensions, involved at the very least the threat of force. But the threat of force in an industrial age presupposes industry, and there is, as Nazi society conclusively proved, no industry without an industrial society.

The result was an inevitable rapprochement, at first with the industrialists, the generals, the diplomats, and the civil servants, whom the Nazi movement was expected to destroy; not, as should be obvious, because they were admired, but because they were necessary. Then came the inevitable rapprochement with labor, without which there is no industrial society, a rapprochement born of industrial recovery and full employment and sustained with both concessions and ideology. The effective common denominators were the values traditionally called "national"—the efficient administration of the state, the expansion of the economy, the growth of the military establishment, and beyond these, the extension of German markets and frontiers. But the effective lever was the legitimacy and the threat of a mass movement that Hitler had, and that the industrialists, generals, diplomats, and civil servants did not have, and knew they did not have.

Papen's intrigues, Hindenburg's senility, and the hubris of the nationalist Right too contributed to Hitler's success. But the basic justification of Hitler's appointment was that authoritarian government under Papen, who had scorned mass support, and under Schleicher, who had failed to find it, had reached a dead end. If the decision to yield power to this particular mass movement was a fatal illusion, the decision to yield power to a mass movement at all was, in its way, a moment of truth. It was also only a step from here to the conclusive demoralization of the industrialists, the intimidation of the generals, and the capitulation of the civil service that followed. What had not happened in 1918 happened in 1933. Nazi élan had its complement in the shattered self-confidence of the old social elites. Like the figures in an animated cartoon, they had gone over a cliff in 1918, still running though nothing was beneath them. This time they recognized the abyss and fell. With them fell the institutions of German middle-class society—the parties, the universities, and the churches.

But while Hitler opened the door on a vacuum, it was one he could only partially fill. Filling it entirely presupposed the necessary administrative, economic, and military skills that his following basically lacked; it meant the collaboration of those who had themselves created the vacuum. To this they agreed, paving the road to hell with rationalizations of self-interest and national interest, positivist legality, hopes for the best, and hopes of avoiding the worst. What Hitler offered them was what they thought they wanted anyway. What he threatened them with was the achievement of these aims without their help. This characteristic dialectic of "national" ends and mass means was the basis of a new synthesis, the carrot-and-stick principle that was the de facto constitutional premise of the Third Reich.

But this too had paradoxical implications. Its success depended on the assumption that the movement was there as a deterrent and not an object of use. The practical consequence in this case was the schizophrenia typical of Nazi society. So far as could be seen, everything had changed and nothing had changed. Revolution was both imminent and indefinitely suspended. Industry enjoyed record profits, the generals appeared to be unchallenged, and Meissner, for example, who had once sat in Ebert's office and Hindenburg's, now sat in Hitler's. Yet industry made concessions not even demanded of it by a revolutionary SPD, the army capitulated to a civilian administration like no other army in German history, and the Reich was represented by a set of "new men" compared to whom the revolutionaries of 1792 appear in retrospect like representatives of the ancien régime—abroad by a one-time wine salesman, at home by a neurotic ex-corporal who had failed in the pursuit of everything but power.

What held things together was a combination of ideology and social dynamics on a foundation of charisma and terror. As time went on, even ideology became increasingly unnecessary, particularly for a younger generation of true believers. Behind the entire system was an apparently total lack of alternatives. The official social goals were neither revoked nor seriously pursued, but indefinitely suspended. Symptomatically, Drexler's pamphlet of 1919, like Rosenberg's and Feder's commentaries on the party program, was still being published in the late 1930s, long after the authors had subsided into one or another form of oblivion. What mattered was faith, and faith was rewarded. In the last analysis, anything could be rationalized with a reference not to Versailles but to 1932. Industrial production did go up, unemployment did go down, Austrians, Sudeten Germans, and Memellanders did come *heim ins Reich* (home to the Reich), foreign diplomats did capitulate, and foreign armies surrendered. Did it matter that the department stores survived and that big business grew bigger? The Communists, the Jews, and ultimately the war itself were the explanation and the apology. Utopia was suspended for the duration. But if Feder and Darré disappeared, their petit-bourgeois fantasies marched on, all evidence of social reality notwithstanding.

The SS and the Labor Front, the Third Reich's most successful institutional innovations, demonstrate the impact of social necessity on ideological orientation. From beginning to end, Himmler preached "racial" elitism, presided—as he saw it—over a new knightly order, dreamed of feudal domains, new gods, a state of nature. At the same time, his policy precluded anything of the sort. Institutional survival in an industrial society requires administrators, not knights; diplomas, not blue eyes. Himmler consequently recruited administrators and diplomas. The success of his organization itself depended on its abstention from the very ideology it represented and in which at least some of its members really believed. In turn, the SS's success derived from its accommodation to a society its members were sworn to destroy. Only this initial accommodation, the organizational basis of administrators and diplomas, permitted the subsequent recruitment of knights and blue eyes at all. The *Ordensideologie* (the ideology of a knightly order), to the extent it was ever realized, was necessarily realized in the social vacuum of the occupied Eastern territories, not in Germany.

By comparison, Ley's Ordensburgen, which nominally practiced *Ordensideologie* at home, which recruited not frustrated officers, civil servants, and doctors, but *"ganze Kerle"* ("all good fellows," by general agreement, another expression for yokels), vegetated in every sense, including the geographical, on the margins of Nazi society. So did the Hitler Youth with its uncomprehending complaints about the consistently bad results of its own consistently executed selection policy for the Adolf Hitler Schools. Both cases demonstrate the limits imposed even by the Third Reich on careers for the untalented.

If the SS was the bridge that carried the old social elites into the heart of the Third Reich, it was the Labor Front that carried the plebs. In the case of the Labor Front, success was not a result of administrative talent or particular organizational solidarity, but more or less automatic. The premise of mass support in a society resolved and compelled to be industrial made concessions from the regime inevitable. The full employment produced by total industrial mobilization then made concessions from employers inevitable too. In both cases, concessions derived from the decision to reverse Versailles, irrespective of, even despite the interests and intentions of the respective partners. The lesson might be that an industrial society cannot exist without a labor movement. If one does not exist, it has to be invented.

What is striking in both the case of the SS and the Labor Front is the reorientation of support without any equivalent change of ideology, a paradox based on the adaptability of its supporters as well as adaptability of the ideology. In the years before 1933, the SS had lived in the shadow of the SA. The NSBO, predecessor of the Labor Front, had existed in the shadow of the party and an electorate of irate shopkeepers, small businessmen, and small farmers and their Nazified pressure groups and front organizations. The ascent of the SS and the Labor Front after 1933 was matched by the decline of the SA and the party. This meant a fundamental shift in the sociological basis of Nazi support. But there was no consequent redefinition of Nazi goals. A movement carried to power by the outsiders of Weimar society was now carried beyond it by the earlier insiders—at least passively. Labor and *Bildungsbürgetum* (educated middle class) alike surrendered to the stronger battalions by joining them.

This process helps to account for the remarkable durability of Nazi society despite the centrifugal forces it created. In the context of both ideological mobilization and industrial recovery, every social group was integrated, almost overnight, into the new system. The immediate dissatisfactions were wiped out. The unemployed returned to work, the economic curve went up, the farm price index held firm. The new dissatisfactions, to the extent they were perceived at all, were rationalized and sublimated in a system whose very fluidity promised eventual solution to those with enough faith and hard enough elbows. Success promised more success, and war obviated the need for producing it. In the meanwhile, as a kind of advance payment on success, there were opportunities for the taking—by those with talent and those without it, those with education and those without it, those with money and those without it.

The conflicts that might have arisen from extended reflection on the limits of such successes and the reality of such opportunities were resolved by the genuine conceptual difficulties the new situation presented. In the Third Reich, relative approximation of class and status came to an end. Discontent presupposes its recognition. The disillusion induced by one's awareness of his own importance or unimportance presupposes that one is aware of it—or at least is made aware of it by one's neighbors. This was next to impossible in the wonderland of Hitler Germany where there were no longer reliable indications of what was up and what was down. How important was a minister, a diplomat, a party functionary, a Labor Front functionary, a Hitler Youth leader, a member of an Ordensburg? The question was unanswerable.

A few examples indicate the problems involved in trying to answer it. Since the publication of *Mein Kampf,* Hitler had regularly and consistently declared his unambiguous contempt for the businessmen, diplomats, civil servants, and university graduates of official German society. There was no reason to doubt his sincerity. Deviations were never total but always qualified. Each audience was distinguished from "the others," an honorable exception to a general rule. Even at his most conciliatory, as in the famous Industry Club speech in Düsseldorf in 1932, Hitler left no doubt of his real position, tactfully but unmistakably reminding his audience of its share in the disaster of 1918, and leaving no doubt that business in the Third Reich was never again to achieve primacy over politics.

In an expansive moment in 1940, according to Rosenberg, Hitler spoke "very negatively of the civil service," to which a liaison officer of the Foreign Ministry "smilingly" asked whether the Foreign Ministry might be an exception. "It is a remarkable thing," Hitler replied, "that in every operetta the diplomats are portrayed as stupid (*doof*). This is no coincidence. The father of several sons let the most efficient take over the estate or something equally sensible. The one who was not all there was sent into the diplomatic service."

But what did all this say about businessmen, about the civil servants or the diplomats, all of whom continued to exist as before? Was it a coincidence that even among the new diplomats there was a von Jagow and a von Killinger? What was the German on the street, whether pro-Nazi or anti-Nazi, to conclude about the status of diplomats or about diplomats as a class? What, considering the labyrinthine diplomatic practices of the Third Reich, was in fact the status of diplomats? What, in the main, were its diplomats as a class?

The same problems arose in the anarchic relations of party and state. For Frick, Guertner, Ribbentrop, promotion to ministerial rank meant a loss, not a gain, in influence. Compared with their old party offices, promotion to governor general of Poland for Frank, to Reichsminister for the Eastern Territories for Rosenberg, "did not signify the climax but the end of their National Socialist careers." On the other hand, to cite two contrary examples, this was not true for Goebbels or for Göring, appointed to ministerial rank in 1933, or for Himmler in 1944. What did this say about the status of ministers and party officials? Hitler's ministers like Papen's tended to be university graduates, doctors, high civil servants. What did this say about Hitler's government compared with Papen's as a matter of class?

The answers depended on the observer. For the conservative observer, the old guard was the guarantor of continuity, of the historical state that demanded his confidence and his patriotism. For the radical observer, Hitler himself was the guarantor of change, of the new state that demanded his confidence and his patriotism. For even if the old guard was still on top, Hitler himself, the corporal and "building worker," was at the very summit. In an economy primed in the meantime with armaments appropriations and building contracts, a society burgeoning with new offices and new opportunities, further reflection could be avoided where objective analysis was in any case impossible. In an extreme case—again the SS—members had the opportunity of humiliating doctors, professors, and judges while being led by doctors, professors, and judges.

In the resultant collision of ideological and industrial revolution, traditional class structure broke down, and with it the traditional structure of political action. If no social group did well in the Third Reich, no social group did badly—or so badly that its discontent was not compensated by the contentment of another group. Labor's defeat was business's triumph, agriculture's frustrations labor's relief, small business's misfortunes the consumer's reward, the consumer's aggravation agriculture's compensation. *Kraft durch Freude* was supplemented by *Kraft durch Schadenfreude*. At the same time, at any given moment, some businessmen did well enough, some farmers did well enough, some workers did well enough, to distinguish their interests, their stake in the new regime, from that of their sociological fellows. The classless reality of the Third Reich was mirrored by its opponents, the historically unique coalition of aristocrats, civil servants, clergymen of both Christian churches, and trade unionists who joined forces in 1944 in a final desperate attempt to bring it down.

The net result was not so much a dual state of Nazi politics and capitalist economics as a dual society in which the status of both groups and individuals moved independently of their old objective underpinnings. There was no new class, still less a new elite. There was at best a new set of classes, a set of mutually competitive elites. It was a world that defied the laws of social gravity without replacing them. The average citizen, passive or participant, lived in a world of traditional relationships, forces, and status, and a Nazi world where the addition of a uniform or a lapel pin could immediately invalidate them. The conflicts of "real" world and "Nazi" world were then reproduced in every kind of combination and permutation. The Wehrmacht rejected the SA; the SA despised the SS; SA and SS deeply resented the party; SA, SS, and party resented the power of the incumbent civil service. Everyone seems to have joined in common contempt for the "golden pheasants" of Ley's

Ordensburgen. The reports of SS sergeants beating up the graduates of Napolas, of the muffled conflict between generations within the ranks of the party bureaucracy, indicate lines of division not only between but within institutions. Mutual recognition was the product not of consensus but of quasi-diplomatic negotiations between quasi sovereignties like the Labor Front and the industrialists at Leipzig in 1935, between the Hitler Youth and the Labor Front, the Hitler Youth and the party or SS, or between any of them, as in the case of the Four Year Plan, and the relevant branches of the civil service.

The synthesis was a world of frustration and exaltation. But above all it was a world of general perplexity in which, even before the war, "Nazi" and "German" merged indistinctly but inseparably, and the *Volksgemeinschaft* of official ideology acquired a bizarre reality. In a society accustomed to identify political conflict with class conflict, conflict—in the sense that it had hitherto resulted in organization and action—seemed to have disappeared altogether. Instead, it reproduced itself in forms so diverse that their only common denominator seems in retrospect to have been the near universality with which they were misunderstood. In a world where the purge of June 30, 1934, for example, meant not the end but the transitional phase of a revolution and where an informed and intelligent foreigner could maintain plausibly in 1937, shortly before the second—if bloodless—purge, that the conservative forces were now regaining control of German society, the contemporary, observer and participant alike, was without a map. Reluctant to return to the original entrance, he not surprisingly plunged ever deeper into a forest he found ever harder to describe. It is revealing that the most profound analysis of the Third Reich in the context of the social history of the preceding century, Thomas Mann's *Doktor Faustus,* was a novel, written by a man who never set foot in the Third Reich at all.

The social consequences of this ultimate disorientation were correspondingly paradoxical. A consistent extension of German history, the Third Reich consistently perpetuated the historic discrepancy between objective social reality and its interpretation. Objective social reality, the measurable statistical consequences of National Socialism, was the very opposite of what Hitler had presumably promised and what the majority of his followers had expected him to fulfill. In 1939 the cities were larger, not smaller; the concentration of capital greater than before; the rural population reduced, not increased;

women not at the fireside but in the office and the factory; the inequality of income and property distribution more, not less, conspicuous; industry's share of the gross national product up and agriculture's down, while industrial labor had it relatively good and small business increasingly bad. The East Elbian estates continued to be run by the gentry, the civil service by doctors, and the army by generals whose names began with "von." Not surprisingly, the history of the Third Reich is a story of frustration, cynicism, and resignation, the history of an apparently betrayed revolution whose one-time supporters, Otto Strasser, Rauschning, Feder, and Rosenberg, one after the other, denounced it as vehemently as its opponents.

Interpreted social reality, on the other hand, reflected a society united like no other in recent German history, a society of opportunities for young and old, classes and masses, a society that was New Deal and good old days at the same time. Like no world since 1914, it was a world of career civil servants and authoritarian paternalism, a world of national purpose and achievement where the army was once again "the school of the nation." It was no less a world where officers and men ate the same meals and conversed "as men to men."

"Formerly when I went to the theatre with my wife," a prison camp guard told Hans Habe, "there was always trouble. We got a seat in the twentieth row. But Huber, our chief accountant, and his wife were in the tenth row. And afterward all hell broke loose. Why can the Hubers afford the tenth row and not ourselves? Nowadays, six nights a week, all the seats in the theatre cost the same. First come, first served. Sometimes the Hubers sit in the tenth row, and we sit in the twentieth. But my wife knows that's because the Hubers live nearer the theatre."

"For the first time in my life," a Marburg Gymnasium teacher told Milton Mayer after the war, "I was really the peer of men who, in the Kaiser time and in the Weimar time, had always belonged to classes lower or higher than my own, men whom one had always looked down on or up to, but never *at*. . . . National Socialism broke down that separation, that class distinction. Democracy—such democracy as we had had—didn't do it, and is not doing it now."

The interpreted social reality, in turn, had its own objective reality where a prince of Schaumburg-Lippe served as Goebbels's adjutant and a prince of Hesse answered Göring's telephone; where Prussian marshals saluted an Austrian corporal; where a bourgeois Berlin school girl, fleeing the stuffiness of her German Nationalist home in search of "working youth," sought it in a career in the Hitler Youth and the Labor Service; and an audience of Göttingen law students told a bemused von Salomon, "We don't want a state, we want a *Volksgemeinschaft.*"

It is axiomatic that very few of the participants in this world were seriously alienated from the "real" world, let alone clinically abnormal. Sadists, paranoids, ne'er-do-wells, represented the smallest of minorities, and a minority that tended to be eliminated, not concentrated, from 1933 on. Of the Nuremberg defendants, only two, Hess and Streicher, could be regarded as clinically abnormal, and both were men who had failed in Nazi society rather than succeeded. In both cases, real insanity had proved to be a professional obstacle, not an advantage. The rest, not mad but, in Riesman's phrase, "other-directed" men, were the real executors of the Third Reich, in Hannah Arendt's expression "banal" in their evil, the "normal" representatives of a pathological society.

The basic problem was not political or economic, but social, the problem of an arrested bourgeois-industrial society, convinced by its guilt feelings and its impotence of its own superfluousness, and prepared to destroy itself with the means of the very bourgeois-industrial society it aimed to destroy. The "conservative" motives of so many of the ostensible revolutionaries make the Third Reich a novelty among revolutions since 1789, but a revolution nonetheless, united by a community of enemies and supported by representatives of every social group. Destruction alone was a common goal after all others—*Beamtenstaat* and *Volksgemeinschaft,* "back to the land" and back to the boundaries of 1918, the salvation of private property and the achievement of "national socialism"—had eliminated one another in a process of mutual cancellation. In the end, with the achievement of each partial goal, the destruction of unions and aristocracy, of Jews, of the Rights of Man and of bourgeois society, destruction was all that was left.

"The insensate hate which presided over and directed this enterprise," writes Rousset, "derived from the specter of all the frustrations, of all the mean, deceived aspirations, of all the envy and despair engendered by the extraordinary decomposition of the German middle classes between the wars. To pretend to discover in these the atavisms of a race is to echo the mentality of the SS. With each economic catastrophe, with each financial blow, the structure of German society collapsed. Nothing remained but an extraordinary nudity composed of impotent rage and criminal malice, thirsting for vengeance."

In a simultaneous revolution of their situation and their awareness of it, the pillars of society—the Junkers, the industrialists, the *Bildungsbürgertum*—joined forces with their own enemies to pull down the roof that had hitherto sheltered them. Goebbels invoked the splendid egalitarianism of the bombs falling around him, the total social revolution of total war. His invocation was not only the appropriate elegy of the Third Reich but the elegy of a whole German society.

Suggestions for Additional Reading

Befitting the importance of the subject, the historical literature on Nazi Germany is so extensive that a separate volume would be required just to list all of the titles published within the last three decades. And no end of research and writing is in sight. A brief bibliography can, therefore, offer only a selective and provisional guide to the most useful studies now in print. These are confined here to books available in English which set the standard of current scholarship or represent vintage works of enduring value. Nearly all of them contain extensive bibliographies of their own, which can lead the reader further into documentary materials, memoirs, earlier analyses, and specialized accounts in various languages. Corresponding to the structure of this anthology, the selected titles have been divided into four sections. Within these limits this bibliography should provide a fairly comprehensive panorama of the best current scholarly investigations of the Nazi era.

I. The Nazi Movement and German History

As broad surveys of Germany's national experience since the early nineteenth century, three moderate and fair-minded volumes are outstanding both for reliability and literary grace: Koppel S. Pinson, *Modern Germany: Its History and Civilization,* 2d ed. (New York, 1966); Golo Mann, *The History of Germany since 1789* (London, 1968); and Hajo Holborn, *A History of Modern Germany, 1840–1945* (New York, 1969). Three readable books, which are much briefer and which are limited to an analysis of the twentieth century, are Hermann Mau and Helmut Krausnick, *German History, 1933–1945* (London, 1959); Hannah Vogt, *The Burden of Guilt: A Short History of Germany, 1914–1945* (New York, 1964); and David Childs, *Germany since 1918* (New York, 1971). Two recent syntheses, appearing in the Rise of Modern Europe series edited by William L. Langer, combine scope with erudition: Raymond J. Sontag, *A Broken World, 1919–1939* (New York, 1971), and Gordon Wright, *The Ordeal of Total War, 1939–1945* (New York, 1968). The studies by A. J. P. Taylor, *The Course of German History* (London, 1945) and *The Origins of the Second World War* (New York, 1962), can be recommended only with reservation as clever and idiosyncratic commentaries on the political and diplomatic development. For somewhat different reasons, caution is likewise necessary in reading William L. Shirer, *The Rise and Fall of the Third Reich* (New York, 1960), a book useful primarily as a narrative of political and military affairs. To these may be added the retrospective views of an octogenarian historian who lived through it all and who tried to comprehend what had happened to himself and to his nation: Friedrich Meinecke, *The German Catastrophe: Reflections and Recollections* (Cambridge, Mass., 1950).

The twin volumes of Arthur Rosenberg, *Imperial Germany: The Birth of the German Republic,* 3d ed. (New York, 1966) and *A History of the German Republic* (London, 1936), are still perceptive general statements by a leftist historian deeply disappointed by the revolution of 1918. The insurrectionary events of that period, from which the Nazi movement emerged as part of a general reaction, are analyzed in the more monographic works of F. L. Carsten, *Revolution in Central Europe, 1918–1919* (Berkeley, 1972); A. J. Ryder, *The German Revolution of 1919* (Cambridge, 1967); and Allan Mitchell, *Revolution in Bavaria, 1918–1919* (Princeton, 1965). The standard chronicles of the succeeding years are S. William Halperin, *Germany Tried Democracy, 1918–1933* (New York, 1946), and Erich Eyck, *A History of the Weimar Republic,* 2 vols. (Cambridge, Mass., 1962–64).

The intellectual undercurrents of German culture have been charted by Fritz Stern, *The Politics of Cultural Despair* (Berkeley, 1961), and George L. Mosse, *The Crisis of German Ideology* (New York, 1964). A collection of Stern's essays during the past two decades is also available under the title *The Failure of Illiberalism* (New York, 1972). Various segments of the political spectrum have been evaluated by Klemens von Klemperer, *Germany's New Conservatism* (Princeton, 1957); Herman Lebovics, *Social Conservatism and the Middle Classes in Germany, 1914–1933* (Princeton, 1969); and Istvan Deak, *Weimar Germany's Left-Wing Intellectuals* (Berkeley, 1968). An interesting attempt to see this subject whole is Peter Gay's *Weimar Culture: The Outsider as Insider* (New York, 1968); not free of factual and conceptual problems, Gay's essay is presumably the preface of a more authoritative volume to come. A fascinating study of a special topic is by Barbara Miller Lane, *Architecture and Politics in Germany, 1918–1945* (Cambridge, Mass., 1968).

From the immense literature which places Nazism in the context of the growth of European fascism in this century, it is possible to select four representative titles: the pioneering effort of Hannah Arendt, *The Origins of Totalitarianism* (New York, 1951); the provocative analysis of philosopher-historian Ernst Nolte, *Three Faces of Fascism* (New York, 1966); the sweeping account of F. L. Carsten, *The Rise of Fascism* (Berkeley, 1967), a major section of which presents some original research on German National Socialism; and the anthology of Stuart Joseph Woolf, ed., *European Fascism* (New York, 1968).

Three excellent anthologies have provided a barometric reading of changing research interests during the past decades: Hans Kohn, ed., *German History: Some New German Views* (Boston, 1954); Fritz Stern, ed., *The Path to Dictatorship* (New York, 1966); and Hajo Holborn, ed., *Republic to Reich: The Making of the Nazi Revolution* (New York, 1972). In addition, a superb collection of scholarly articles on various aspects of Nazism has been recently published by Henry A. Turner, Jr., ed., *Nazism and the Third Reich* (New York, 1972); Turner's brief appendix listing "aids to research" should be of particular value to graduate students.

II. The Personality of the Leader

The standard biography, deservedly so, is by Alan Bullock, *Hitler: A Study in Tyranny,* rev. ed. (New York, 1964). More succinct, to the point of affording only a bare outline, is Helmut Heiber, *Adolf Hitler: A Short Biography* (London, 1961). The early years are described by William A. Jenks, *Vienna and the Young Hitler* (New York, 1960) and, utilizing more recently available sources, by Bradley F. Smith, *Adolf Hitler: His Family, Childhood, and Youth* (Stanford, 1967). These are a necessary corrective to the self-dramatization of his adolescence in Hitler's *Mein Kampf,* available in several editions. The first dramatic episode of Hitler's political career is related with extraordinary detail by Harold J. Gordon, *Hitler and the Beer Hall Putsch* (Princeton, 1972). A rapid and lively essay which places this event in perspective is Anthony Nicholls, *Weimar and the Rise of Hitler* (London, 1968). The indispensability of the leader in establishing the structure and in maintaining the initial impetus of his movement is confirmed by Dietrich Orlow, *The History of the Nazi Party, 1919–1933* (Pittsburgh, 1969). On a broader scale this theme is also central to Martin Broszat, *German National Socialism, 1919–1945* (Santa Barbara, 1966), and to Joseph L. Nyomarkay, *Charisma and Factionalism in the Nazi Party* (Minneapolis, 1967).

The view that Hitler maintained a certain intellectual consistency from the beginning is argued by Eberhard Jäckel, *Hitler's Weltanschauung: A Blueprint for Power* (Middletown, Conn., 1972). But the ambiguity and complexity of Hitler's ideas, as revealed in his later conversations and monologues, are stressed by Percy Ernst Schramm, *Hitler: The Man and the Military Leader* (Chicago, 1971). Personal sketches of Hitler and other important Nazi leaders are presented by Joachim C. Fest, *The Face of the Third Reich* (New York, 1968). No student of the period should miss the mixture of history and memoir by a chastened member of Hitler's personal coterie, Albert Speer, *Inside the Third Reich* (New York, 1970). The Führer's biography is concluded by H. R. Trevor-Roper, *The Last Days of Hitler,* 3d ed. (New York, 1966) and, adding certain details from the Russian autopsy, Lev Bezymenski, *The Death of Adolf Hitler* (New York, 1968).

All of the foregoing titles may be described as the products of a conventional biographical technique; they relate the "life and times" of Nazism's chief figure. The results of this work have been summarized and incorporated into the framework of a single book which best represents the quintessence of research in the first quarter of a century since 1945: Karl Dietrich Bracher, *The German Dictatorship: The Origins, Structure, and Effects of National Socialism* (New York, 1970). Bracher's volume is a solid platform of scholarship upon which future accounts may be securely constructed.

Beyond this are the more speculative enterprises of psychobiography and psychohistory. Two pioneering efforts were the chapter on Hitler in Erik Erikson's *Childhood and Society,* rev. ed. (New York, 1964), and the secret OSS report, completed in 1943, by Walter C. Langer, *The Mind of Adolf Hitler* (New York, 1972). These are soon to be complemented by Robert G. L. Waite's forthcoming study, *The Psychopathic God: A Biography of Adolf Hitler.*

The relationship of Hitler's personality to the collective psychology of the German people has also been a subject of serious investigation since the publication of T. W. Adorno et al., *The Authoritarian Personality* (New York, 1950), and G. M. Gilbert, *The Psychology of Dictatorship* (New York, 1950). These pursue a theme first articulated by Erich Fromm, *Escape From Freedom* (New York, 1941). Among the books which have tended in this direction three may be mentioned: Zevedei Barbu, *Democracy and Dictatorship: Their Psychology and Patterns of Life* (New York, 1956); James H. McRandle, *The Track of the Wolf: Essays on National Socialism and its Leader, Adolf Hitler* (Evanston, Ill., 1965); and Hans Buchheim, *Totalitarian Rule* (Middletown, Conn., 1968). For a more recent example and further bibliography, the reader is referred to the long article by Peter Loewenberg in the *American Historical Review* (December 1971), an excerpt of which is included in the present anthology.

III. Politics, Industry, and the Army

The political role of Germany's big business and industrial elites has been insufficiently treated to date. Only adequate as an outline of the general economic development in the century since national unification is Gustav Stolper et al., *The German Economy: 1870 to the Present* (New York, 1967). Louis P. Lochner, *Tycoons and Tyrants* (Chicago, 1954) tends to be unduly defensive toward the German industrialists. Scholarly and more sober are Burton H. Klein, *Germany's Economic Preparation for War* (Cambridge, Mass., 1959), and Arthur Schweitzer, *Big Business in the Third Reich* (Bloomington, Ind., 1964). The best available study of German industry under the Nazi regime is that of Alan S. Milward, *The German Economy at War* (London, 1965); Milward has also published monographs on economic organization by the Nazis in several of the occupied territories.

The literature on the German military establishment is far more extensive. Earlier books by Anglo-American historians were often harshly critical of the officer corps: Telford Taylor, *Sword and Swastika: Generals and Nazis in the Third Reich* (New York, 1952); John W. Wheeler-Bennett, *The Nemesis of Power: The German Army in Politics, 1918–1945* (London, 1953); and Gordon A. Craig, *The Politics of the Prussian Army, 1640–1945* (New York, 1956). Three works have dealt with the connection between military personnel and the Nazi movement during the Weimar years: Robert G. L. Waite, *Vanguard of Nazism: The Free Corps Movement in Postwar Germany, 1918–1923* (Cambridge, Mass., 1952); Harold J. Gordon, *The Reichswehr and the German Republic, 1919–1926* (Princeton, 1957); and F L. Carsten, *Reichswehr and Politics, 1918–1933* (London, 1966). This story is completed for the crucial period from the Nazi seizure of power to the outbreak of war by Robert J. O'Neill, *The German Army and the Nazi Party, 1933–1939* (London, 1966), and E. M. Robertson, *Hitler's Pre-War Policy and Military Plans, 1933–1939* (New York, 1967). A basic survey of the entire subject is Karl Demeter, *The German Officer Corps in Society and State, 1650–1945* (New York, 1965). The interplay of military and diplomatic considerations is evaluated by Gerhard L. Weinberg, *The Foreign Policy of Hitler's Germany* (Chicago, 1970). A topic with relevance to both military and social history is treated by Gerald Reitlinger, *The S. S., Alibi of a Nation, 1922–1945* (London, 1956); George H. Stein, *The Waffen SS: Hitler's Elite Guard at War, 1939–1945* (Ithaca, N.Y., 1966); and Heinz Höhne, *The Order of the Death's Head: The Story of Hitler's SS* (New York, 1970).

IV. The Social Impact of Nazism

What were the effects of the Nazi period on class organization and social status in Germany? The first to attempt a serious answer to that question was Franz L. Neumann, *Behemoth: The Structure and Practice of National Socialism, 1933–1944* (New York, 1944). The two most successful efforts since then have been David Schoenbaum, *Hitler's Social Revolution: Class and Status in Nazi Germany, 1933–1939* (New York, 1966), and Ralf Dahrendorf, *Society and Democracy in Germany* (New York, 1967); while Schoenbaum tries to present a total view within a brief time-span, Dahrendorf regards Nazism as one phase of "the German problem" from the Bismarckian empire to the present. Richard Grunberger, *The Twelve-Year Reich: A Social History of Nazi Germany, 1933–1945* (New York, 1971) relies more on anecdote than analysis. A much more sympathetic portrayal of the German national character under the stress of dictatorship is offered by Robert H. Lowie, *Toward Understanding Germany* (Chicago, 1954).

Several books focus on the period of transition from republic to dictatorship, among them Eliot B. Wheaton, *Prelude to Calamity: The Nazi Revolution, 1933–1935* (London, 1968). This problem has been successfully explored as a local history with wider implications by William Sheridan Allen, *The Nazi Seizure of Power: The Experience of a Single German Town, 1930–1935* (Chicago, 1965). Yet the fact the Nazi party was thereafter incapable of imposing total control in every sector of German society is stressed by Edward N. Peterson, *The Limits of Hitler's Power* (Princeton, 1969). This should be compared with Hans Buchheim et al., *Anatomy of the SS State* (New York, 1968).

The behavior of social elites under Nazism is the implicit theme of most studies devoted to the German resistance. Two older accounts still of value are the English abridgment of a work by Gerhard Ritter, *The German Resistance* (New York, 1958), and the essay by Hans Rothfels, *German Opposition to Hitler* (Chicago, 1962); both are extremely well disposed toward their subject. Laudatory but useful biographical sketches of resistance leaders have been collected by Annedore Leber, ed., *Conscience in Revolt: Sixty-four Stories of Resistance in Germany, 1933–1945* (London, 1957). Somewhat more critical is Terence Prittie, *Germans against Hitler* (Boston, 1964). Two monographs examine critical moments of failure: Harold C. Deutsch, *The Conspiracy against Hitler in the Twilight War* (Minneapolis, 1968), and Constantine FitzGibbon, *20 July* (New York, 1956); the former treats the situation prior to the invasion of France and the latter is an exciting recapitulation of the assassination plot against Hitler in 1944.

There is a special literature on religious institutions and elites. The best are Gordon C. Zahn, *German Catholics and Hitler's Wars* (New York, 1962); Guenter Lewy, *The Catholic Church and Nazi Germany* (New York, 1964); and John S. Conway, *The Nazi Persecution of the Church* (New York, 1968). Of these Lewy is the most severe in judging the Church's generally ineffectual opposition to Nazism on religious grounds and, in particular, the silence of most clergymen on the deportation and extermination of the Jews. Explanations of that subject have been attempted by Gerald Reitlinger, *The Final Solution,* rev. ed. (New York, 1961); Eugen Kogon, *The Theory and Practice of Hell,* new ed. (New York, 1960); and most authoritatively by Raoul Hilberg, *The Destruction of the European Jews* (Chicago, 1961). The background is supplied by Peter G. J. Pulzer, *The Rise of Political Anti-Semitism in Germany and Austria* (New York, 1964). To be consulted by all means is the controversial statement by Hannah Arendt, *Eichmann in Jerusalem: A Report on the Banality of Evil* (New York, 1963).

Some related topics deserve more thorough investigation than they have received. The only full-scale treatment of the youth movement,

Walter Z. Laqueur, *Young Germany* (New York, 1962), is far from exhaustive. The techniques and effects of the regime's sustained campaign to mold public opinion have been studied in various aspects by Oran J. Hale, *Captive Press in the Third Reich* (Princeton, 1964); Z. A. B. Zeman, *Nazi Propaganda* (London, 1964); and Ernest K. Bramsted, *Goebbels and National Socialist Propaganda, 1925–1945* (East Lansing, Mich., 1965). The fate of some who succeeded in escaping has been illuminated, but not fully investigated, by Laura Fermi, *Illustrious Immigrants: The Intellectual Migration from Europe, 1930–1941* (Chicago, 1968), and in the essays edited by Donald H. Fleming and Bernard Bailyn, *The Intellectual Migration: Europe and America, 1930–1960* (Cambridge, Mass., 1969).

The aftermath of the war, the political division of Germany, and the recovery of the successor states are already subjects of an extensive literature. It may suffice here to mention only one, the best of them all, by Alfred Grosser, *Germany in Our Time* (New York, 1971).

2 3 4 5 6 7 8 9 10